The Metabolist Imagination

The Metabolist Imagination

Visions of the City in Postwar Japanese Architecture and Science Fiction

WILLIAM O. GARDNER

MINNESOTA

University of Minnesota Press
Minneapolis
London

The University of Minnesota Press gratefully acknowledges the Suntory Foundation for its support of this publication.

The University of Minnesota Press gratefully acknowledges the financial assistance provided for the publication of this book by the Connie Hungerford Fund of the Provost's Office of Swarthmore College.

Portions of chapter 1 and chapter 3 were previously published in "Narratives of Collapse and Generation: Komatsu Sakyō's Disaster Novels and the Metabolist Movement," in "Beyond Fukushima: Culture, Media, and Meaning from Catastrophe," special issue, *Japan Forum* 26, no. 3 (2014): 306–24. Portions of chapter 2 were previously published in "From Parody to Simulacrum: Japanese SF, Regionalism, and the Inauthentic in the Early Works of Komatsu Sakyō and Tsutsui Yasutaka," in "Three Asias: Japan, South Korea, China," special issue, *Paradoxa* 22 (2010): 65–76. An earlier version of chapter 4 was published as "The 1970 Osaka Expo and/as Science Fiction," in "Expo '70 and Japanese Art: Dissonant Voices," special issue, *Review of Japanese Culture and Society* 28 (December 2011): 26–43.

Published by the University of Minnesota Press
111 Third Avenue South, Suite 290
Minneapolis, MN 55401-2520
http://www.upress.umn.edu

Printed in the United States of America on acid-free paper

The University of Minnesota is an equal-opportunity educator and employer.

27 26 25 24 23 22 21 20 10 9 8 7 6 5 4 3 2 1

Library of Congress Cataloging-in-Publication Data
Names: Gardner, William O., author.
Title: The metabolist imagination : visions of the city in postwar Japanese architecture and science fiction / William O. Gardner.
Description: Minneapolis : University of Minnesota Press, 2020. | Includes bibliographical references and index.
Identifiers: LCCN 2019027156 (print) | ISBN 978-1-5179-0623-8 (cloth) | ISBN 978-1-5179-0624-5 (paperback)
Subjects: LCSH: Architecture and biology—Japan—History—20th century. | Visionary architecture—Japan. | Metabolism in architecture (Movement). | Architecture and literature. | Future, The, in literature. | Science fiction, Japanese—History and criticism.
Classification: LCC NA2543.B56 G37 2020 (print) | DDC 720/.47—dc23
LC record available at https://lccn.loc.gov/2019027156

Contents

Acknowledgments

I am grateful to many people and institutions who have supported me throughout the research and writing of this volume. Preliminary research was supported by an ACLS/SSRC/NEH International Area Studies Fellowship and an institutional affiliation with Keio University. During this research year, Tatsumi Takayuki of Keio University was a wonderful host and generously introduced me to writers, critics, translators, and fans in the Japanese SF community. I am also grateful to the late Komatsu Sakyō and the late Kawazoe Noboru for granting me interviews and to Otobe Junko of IO Corp. for innumerable forms of assistance with my research. I would like to thank the Swarthmore College Provost's Office for supporting subsequent leaves and research activities as well as a grant from the Constance Hungerford Faculty Support Fund for a subvention to include color photographs in this volume. Librarians and archivists are the unsung heroes of any research project and I particularly appreciate the responsive and resourceful support I received from Sandra Vermeychuk and her colleagues in the interlibrary loan staff of Swarthmore College, as well as the many other librarians who assisted along the way.

I would like to thank Tatsumi Takayuki, Midori Yoshimoto, and Jonathan Abel for their feedback and encouragement as editors of special journal issues where early versions of some materials in this volume were published. I also appreciate Mary Knighton, Bob Rehak, and Mutsuko Smith for their critical suggestions on the manuscript or portions thereof. I am especially grateful to Marc Steinberg together with one additional anonymous peer reader for the University of Minnesota Press for their very helpful comments that guided me during the revision process. Thanks go to Ken Tadashi Oshima, Midori Yoshimoto, Ōwada Toshiyuki, and Mia Lewis for advice and assistance regarding illustrations, as well Vincent D. Feldman for permission to include his wonderful photographs. I would also like to thank Jason Weidemann and the staff of the University of Minnesota Press for their support of this project and their editorial assistance. Any mistakes and shortcomings in the volume are entirely my own.

The opportunity for teaching collaborations provided invaluable intellectual sustenance while I was working on this project, and I would like to thank my coteachers Koyama Tadashi, Carola Hein, Tomoko Sakomura, and Alexandra Gueydan-Turek, as well as all my colleagues and students at Swarthmore College. Finally, I express my deep gratitude to my wife, Frances Tate, for sharing my enthusiasms for cities, architecture, and literature (as well as music and cats) and for all of the love and joy she brings to my life.

Introduction

The sprawling horizontal city remapped onto a set of giant, vertical, helix-shaped structures, dispersed and surrounded by green countryside, with recyclable, moveable housing pods plugging into the helix framework. Industrial cities floating "like a cairn of newly crystalized gems" off the Pacific coast of Japan, linking, expanding, shrinking, and shifting their locations according to economic demands. The family home reimagined as the mutual docking of capsules belonging to migratory, autonomous individuals. Architecture becoming liquid, invisible, indistinguishable from images. A second, virtual city overlapping the physical city. The capital of Japan flooded from melting polar ice caps, sunk into the ocean in a massive tectonic subduction, vanished under an electromagnetic cloud, wiped out by biological and nuclear weapons. A mysterious hit man founds a City Demolition Industry, Inc.; junk-eating mutants overtake Osaka; Hiroshima is returned to ruins; a swarm of self-replicating housing capsules spreads through Tokyo like a plague.

These are some of the scenarios of the future city, ranging from to utopian to apocalyptic, to be discussed in this book, which will examine the intersection of architecture and science fiction in postwar Japan. Some are proposals by postwar architects, some are the stories of professional science fiction authors, and some are fictional scenarios written by architects.[1] In the coming chapters, I will juxtapose architecture and fiction as two interrelated forms of artistic simulation. The architect imagines an intervention in the human and natural environment: the architectural plan, whether drawn, modelled, or described verbally, will propose a change, however minute or grandiose, in the existing natural/constructed environment and the lives of its imagined inhabitants. Similarly, as Judith Merril and Darko Suvin suggest, we can view fiction, and especially SF—science fiction or speculative fiction—as a form of imaginative simulation, positing a change or novelty in the natural, built, or social environments and tracing its narrative consequences.[2] Placing these two forms of artistic speculation side by side, I will argue, changes our view of both architecture and fiction: modern architects can be reassessed as authors of narrative, while we can discover a richer context for the role of science fiction authors in imagining the interactions of built and natural environments and their consequences for human lives. Furthermore, this study's pairing of architecture and SF from the recent past presents us with early formations of issues that are urgent to our own time, from the relationship of information science to our evolving physical and social constructs, to the very capacity of the human species to survive our own interventions in the environment.

In this study, the works of Japanese architects and science fiction authors converge in the exploration of futurity, or *mirai,* as well as their repurposing of the past. Indeed, during the High Growth Era in Japan, peaking with the 1970 Japan World Exposition in Osaka (henceforth referred to as the Osaka Expo), discourses of *mirai* (the future; literally the "not-yet come") proliferated through architectural projections of the "future city" *(mirai toshi)*; proposals for "future studies" *(miraigaku),* a new, interdisciplinary field of intellectual inquiry; and activity in the burgeoning literary genre of science fiction or SF, which took the future as its special temporal and thematic province. At the same time, the traumas of the past were rescripted onto the future through the motif of "ruins" in both architecture and science fiction. The future city in ruins, a recurring theme of the period, was simultaneously a reassertion of history, an apocalyptic prediction, and an incubation bed for yet another future.

While architecture and literature constitute fields that are rarely subjected to sustained analysis in a single work, I will argue that the work of the Metabolist group of architects investigated here includes a significant narrative dimension that especially invites this pairing: beyond the momentary form of buildings or urban designs that might be represented in drawings, models, or finished projects, the Metabolists were interested in the processes of change, growth, and decay and imagined architecture as a means of understanding and designing such dynamic processes. Thus, architecture could be approached as a temporal form, responding in part to the new diachronic possibilities of computer simulation but also linked to the temporality and tropes of narrative. With this foothold in narrativity, then, the writings and plans of the Metabolists are an especially fruitful object of comparison with their contemporary narrative arts, and I believe that this comparison will offer new perspectives on the evolution and imagined possibilities of postwar cities and both the visionary and critical aspects of science fiction.

This shared investment in futurity and narrative, which we could term a theoretical connection, is the primary basis for my joint investigation of postwar Japanese architecture and science fiction. However, there is a second, no less intriguing, basis for this juxtaposition, and that is the actual historical social connections between postwar architects and authors, within a broader international social and intellectual network that included academics, critics, artists, and government officials. For example, as detailed in chapter 4, science fiction author Komatsu Sakyō, Metabolist architecture critic Kawazoe Noboru, and the young architect Isozaki Arata each were responsible for different areas of the "Theme Zone" of the 1970 Osaka Expo, working on an architectural site that accommodated both the rationalistic site design by master architect Tange Kenzō, as well as the exuberant, irreverent Tower of the Sun monument by artist Okamoto Tarō. At the same time, Komatsu and Kawazoe, together with economist Hayashi Yūjirō, anthropologist Umesao Tadao, and media theorist Katō Hidetoshi, cofounded the Future Studies Research Group (later the Japanese Association for Future Studies) and jointly articulated theories of the coming "information society" that influenced Tange's works, such as his book *Nihon rettō no shōraizō* (The future image of the Japanese archipelago, 1966), in addition to numerous bureaucratic white papers and governmental urban planning and development initiatives, many of them at least partly realized in the real world, and promoted variously as "wired cities," "technopolis," "teletopia," or "new media cities," as I will outline in chapter 5. Conversely, as I will discuss in chapter 6, contemporary critiques of the "information society," as well as criticism of ambitious state construction projects that had metastasized into a pork-barrel "construction state," together with a rediscovery of the vernacular street architecture being destroyed by this "construction state," are all incorporated into the fictional works of anime director Oshii Mamoru, particularly his two *Patlabor* films of 1989 and 1993. Thus, I will argue that architecture and science fiction (taken broadly to include both literary and visual narratives) deserve to be considered together not only for their shared investment in artistic simulation but also for their complex historical interactions through both social and intellectual networks. While the current study takes into account only one historical corner of these broad networks, I hope that it will stimulate future inquiries into other aspects of these transmedial and interdisciplinary relationships.

Postwar Japan and *Metabolism 1960*

Large portions of nearly all of Japan's major cities were reduced to ashes and rubble by the incendiary and atomic bombs of the Second World War; yet the cities reemerged, in more or less of a chaotic fashion, to become denser and more populated than ever before. This study begins with the proposals put forth fifteen years after the war's conclusion in the manifesto *Metabolism 1960: The Proposals for New Urbanism*, in which a group of young architects offered bold visions for reimagining the city at a time when high economic growth rates and large-scale government investments in industrial and urban infrastructure seemed to encourage daring solutions to the problems of rapid urbanization, including housing shortages, gridlock, and environmental degradation.

The underlying idea of Metabolism, as outlined by the group's opening manifesto as well as subsequent writings by the contributors, is that architecture and the city should not be conceived as permanent but that architects and urban planners should design the city and the building in such a way as to remain open to the processes of growth, decline, and transformation. While this stance can be seen as part of an international reaction against totalizing modernist ideas of urban planning and architecture, as will be discussed below, it also reflects the historical legacy of a constantly rebuilt and transforming Japanese cityscape that faced frequent destruction by fires, earthquakes, and other natural as well as anthropogenic disasters. Metabolism was also informed by the flexible, modular forms of traditional Japanese architecture, in which "fittings" such as windows, shutters, doors, interior walls and screens, and tatami flooring components, set within a more permanent wooden framework, could be replaced or altered according to cycles of wear, the demands of weather and season, or changing living patterns.[3] However, the young architects of the Metabolist group were not interested in merely extending the building materials and techniques of traditional architecture into a modern context but rather in extrapolating from the underlying principles of traditional architecture to propose new designs with new methods and materials, across a variety of scales from the personal home to massive housing and industrial complexes, to the scale of the city and beyond.

The bold proposals by the Metabolist group resonated with other radical, utopian architectural proposals underway or soon to be unveiled in other locales, such as Paris-based Yona Friedman's Mobile Architecture, Dutch artist Constant Nieuwenhuys's New Babylon, and the Plug-in City and other proposals by Peter Cook and the Archigram group in Great Britain—proposals that also emphasized the potential for spontaneous change in urban design and often featured combinations of an infrastructural frame and changeable parts in a similar fashion to their Japanese contemporaries, with whom they were in frequent contact through publications as well as personal exchanges. As noted by architectural historian Simon Sadler, the appearance of these futuristic avant-garde groups in Europe, contesting the orthodoxies of the modernist postwar International Style, coincided with a revival of interest in the first, prewar wave of architectural avant-gardes, from the retrieval of idiosyncratic utopian projects and eclectic, organic forms featured in Ulrich Conrads and Hans-Günther Sperlich's book *Phantastiche Architektur* (Fantastic architecture, 1960), to a new assessment of Futurism in *Theory and Design in the First Machine Age* (1960) by Reyner Banham, the British architectural critic who would be a key interpreter and supporter of Archigram as well as an influential commentator on Metabolism.[4]

The architecture of the space age was also a key intertext for the new avant-garde in Europe and America, as well as Japan. To the architects of Archigram, for example, the giant scale, lattice framework, and moveable parts of American and Soviet rocket assembly buildings and launchpads were an inspiration for such mid-1960s design projects as Ron Herron's Walking City and Peter Cook's Plug-in City, while the astronaut's space capsule and space suit were sources for designs such as Warren Chalk's Capsule Home, David Greene's Living Pod, and Michael Webb's Cushicle and Suitaloon.[5] In Japan, Metabolist architect Kurokawa Kishō compared his own terrestrial capsule designs to the life-support environments for astronauts, drawing on the conceptual repertoire of cybernetics that developed in close proximity to the U.S. space program, while Isozaki Arata cited his experience touring NASA's Mission Control Center in the United States in 1967 as inspiration for his design of the cybernetic environment of the 1970 Osaka Expo's Festival Plaza.[6] While the space age forms an important international context, however, I should add that both the architectural works and the science fiction works I will examine here are oriented toward imagining the future of life on planet Earth. Although outer space is a significant topos in many works of Japanese as well as Euro-American science fiction, the present study will be Earth oriented—indeed, the imagination of the planet Earth as a socially and ecologically interconnected entity will be the subject of chapter 3.

As I will detail in my fourth chapter, the worlds of Metabolist architecture, the space age, and science fiction collided most spectacularly in the Japan World Exposition held in Osaka in 1970. Conceptualized from an early point as the "core of a future city," the expo grounds featured a site design by Metabolist mentor Tange Kenzō and showcased innovative buildings by many of the Metabolist architects. The Cold War "space race" was also a key subtext to the expo, as the popular American and Soviet pavilions, respectively, featured a moon rock recently collected by the Apollo 12 astronauts and a life-size model of a Soyuz 4 spacecraft. Science fiction authors also played a role in the planning of the expo site and contributed to the content of individual pavilions—none more so than Osaka-based SF author Komatsu Sakyō, who participated in numerous expo planning committees and helped to design a portion of the Theme Zone display under Tange's direction. The concept of futurity *(mirai)* as a field of inquiry connected the architectural project of the expo (future city/*mirai toshi*) with the practice of future simulation endemic to science fiction, as well as the nascent field of future studies *(miraigaku)*. Tours of the expo site were included in the Second International Futures Research Conference, held in Kyoto in April 1970, as well as the International Symposium of Science Fiction held in Japan in August and September 1970, which included such international literary figures as Brian W. Aldiss, Arthur C. Clarke, Judith Merril, Frederik Pohl, and Julius Kagarlitsky. Komatsu played a key behind-the-scenes role in facilitating ties and exchanges between the three spheres of future studies, science fiction, and the expo.[7] As I will explore in chapters 4 and 5, the Osaka Expo was not only a showcase for utopian visions of the future but also a lightning rod for critics who questioned the technocratic premises of future studies and the coming "information society" that many futurologists predicted.

I will discuss the architectural theory and practice of the Metabolists in more detail in chapter 1, together with an examination of fictional writings composed or inspired by this architectural group. As a preview of some of the themes running throughout this study, however, and in order to place the Metabolist projects in a broader perspective, I will briefly examine here the connections between architecture and science fiction with regard to three motifs prominent in Metabolist architectural projects and writings: megastructures (over land and sea), capsules, and apocalyptic cities.

Megastructures

As an extrapolation of the urbanization and population growth of the nineteenth and twentieth centuries, perhaps the most common motif in science fiction depictions of future cities is the basic image of height and size: cities as great forests of skyscrapers or the city arranged and condensed and into a single giant edifice—the megastructure. Arguably the most iconic representation of the towering city in science fiction is the central New Tower of Babel of Fritz Lang's groundbreaking film *Metropolis* (1927). Lang's vision of the dense cityscape of the film was inspired in part by the skyscrapers he witnessed on a trip to Manhattan, while the central tower, headquarters of the city's despotic ruler, borrows from the iconography of the Tower of Babel as depicted by Pieter Bruegel the Elder. As a single building serving as a platform or framework for multiple functional components of a conventional city, including industrial machine halls below ground and airplane landing pads encircling the upper floors, the New Tower of Babel could indeed be said to meet the technical definition of megastructure as defined by architect Maki Fumihiko (see below). The tower in Lang's film also functions as a social allegory: the elite capitalist ruling classes occupy the spacious and classically inspired upper reaches of the building, while the dark bowels of the building are occupied by laborers operating the industrial machinery of the city in slave-like conditions. In Japanese science fiction, the iconography and class structure of Lang's tower is echoed in Satō Haruo's prewar dystopian work "A Record of Nonchalant" (Nonsharan kiroku, 1929), as well as screenwriter Ōtomo Katsuhiro and director Rintarō's animated film *Metropolis* (*Metoroporisu*, 2001), which was inspired by Lang's work as well as Tezuka Osamu's early manga of the same name (1949).[8] The themes of Lang's film—attraction to and fear of technology, the excitement and the anxiety provoked by the soaring, gigantic modern city, and the social fears and conflicts attendant on differences of class, race, and gender—continued to reverberate through science fiction films and texts of subsequent decades, including those examined in this study.

In the realm of modern architecture, the most influential, utopian proposals for cities of high-rise buildings integrated into a comprehensive city plan are undoubtedly the works of Swiss-French architect Le Corbusier, including his Ville Contemporaine (Contemporary city, 1922), Ville Radieuse (Radiant city, 1924–33), and plans for Voisin (1925) and Algiers (1930–33, which featured his design for a single megastructural building combining a roadway and linear city at Fort L'Empereur), together with his Unité d'habitation (Housing unit) first realized in Marseille in 1952.[9] Le Corbusier influenced the development of architecture and city planning throughout the world through the instrument of the Congrès Internationaux d'Architecture Moderne (CIAM, founded in 1928), which promoted functionalist approaches to city planning—such as the "efficient" division of urban spaces into differing zones for work, dwelling, and leisure—while the Unité d'habitation was taken as the prototype for innumerable postwar housing projects. Despite, or perhaps because of its broad dissemination, functionalist urban planning and the associated "international style" of modernist architecture attracted a wide range of critiques, from the Situationist International in Europe, which sought to recover the force of individual agency, spontaneity, creativity, and political resistance in the face of the totalizing, managerial impulses of the functionalist city, to Jane Jacob's polemic *The Death and Life of Great American Cities* (1961), which questioned the effects of large-scale American urban planning projects on the actual street-level quality of life of city dwellers.[10] In the narrative arts, critiques of functionalism ranged from Jaques Tati's film satires *Mon Oncle* (1958) and *Playtime* (1967) to New Wave science fiction author J. G. Ballard's dystopian *High-Rise* (1975). Criticism from within CIAM's own ranks led to the dissolution of the organization in 1959.

The proposals of the Metabolist architects, as well as the other 1960's avant-gardes mentioned above, represent both a continuation of and a reaction to the influence of Le Corbusier. On the one hand, the Metabolists inherited from Le Corbusier and CIAM the idea of the architect as designer not only of buildings but of cities, capable of responding to urban crises or even reengineering the very social order through innovative, bold urban designs; Metabolist mentor Tange Kenzō himself participated in the final CIAM meeting in Otterlo, Holland, in 1959. On the other hand, even within CIAM's ranks the previous generation of functionalist city plans were increasingly criticized as inflexible, hierarchical, and authoritarian. Rather than inhabiting someone else's grand design, the critics argued, individual citizens should be given more autonomy to develop their own patterns and spaces for dwelling, work, and play. Metabolism responded to these conflicting influences by incorporating the potential for change, growth, and adaptation into their designs—indeed, by attempting to design the processes of change itself.[11]

Nevertheless, in keeping with the grand Le Corbusian gesture, many of the projects proposed by the Metabolist architects are notable for their sheer size—in fact the coining of the very term *megastructure* has been attributed to Metabolist architect Maki Fumihiko.[12] Maki defines the megastructure not merely as a very large building but as a "large frame in which all the functions of a city or part of a city are housed."[13] Referring to the writings of his senior colleague Tange Kenzō, Maki presents a further distinction between the megastructural frame and "discrete, rapidly changeable functional units which fit within the larger framework." In other words, the frame is designed to accommodate change and individual adaptation; frame and "functional units" are designed for differing temporal or metabolic cycles.[14] This type of megastructural design was featured in numerous proposals by Metabolist architects, including Kikutake Kiyonori's Tower-Shaped Community (1959) in which recyclable housing units plug into a cylindrical core, as well as Kurokawa Kishō's Helix City Plan for Tokyo (1962) and the related Floating City Kasumigaura, in which the framework, which also contained the transportation infrastructure, was based on the double helix structure of the DNA molecule.[15] Incidentally, this project was one of several that pointed to the Metabolists' interest in the issue of scale—that is, homologies between structures, both organic and man-made, of vastly differing scales—an issue that I will explore further in chapter 1.

In addition to designs of towering megastructures that soared into the sky, the Metabolists also dreamed of cities stretching across the water. In the Metabolist manifesto, Kikutake described his vision of a transfer from the "civilization of the continents" to the "civilization of the sea." This shift would be catalyzed by his proposal for Marine City, starting as floating manufacturing plants and developing into multifunctional cities with space for human communities on the surface and fish breeding grounds below the surface (Plate 1). The cities would be free to travel across the ocean or attach themselves to land as necessary, ceaselessly crystalizing into new forms.[16] As architecture scholar Zhongjie Lin points out, Kikutake's proposals for cities over the sea coincide with a resurgence of the idea of humans living in marine environments (usually under rather than over the water) in SF works such as Kenneth Bulmer's novels *City under the Sea* (1957) and *Beyond the Silver Sky* (1961) and Frederik Pohl and Jack Williamson's *Undersea Trilogy* (1954–1958).[17]

A year after the Metabolist manifesto, Tange Kenzō unveiled his ambitious Plan for Tokyo 1960, in which the city extended across the waters of Tokyo Bay on a linear access, perched on top of a giant, bridge-like concrete latticework. Tange's was not the first futuristic plan for Tokyo Bay: in 1959, the Council for Industrial Planning had proposed a Neo-Tokyo plan nearly filling the bay with artificial islands built with ground loosened by the underground explosion of an atomic bomb. After this proposal, Metabolists Ōtaka, Kurokawa, and Kikutake, as well as Tange, all weighed in with their own proposals for extensive developments across the bay. While none of these massive projects were completed, Tokyo governor Suzuki Shun'ichi's later plans for a Tokyo Teleport Town (1986) on infill spanning the inlet of Tokyo Bay closest to central Tokyo were partially realized, leaving traces of "futurity" (arguably already appearing as retro-futurism) across the new Odaiba waterfront, including the Yurikamome automated guideway transit line, the National Museum of Emerging Science and Innovation (Nihon kagaku miraikan, 2001) and the Fuji Television Headquarters Building (1996) designed by Tange Kenzō, which echoes Metabolist frame-and-capsule conceptions with its spherical observation pod set into a lattice of vertical columns and horizontal corridors connecting the building's two main towers (Figure 1).[18]

As Thomas Schnellbächer argues, the ocean has also been a recurrent topos in postwar Japanese science fiction, from the Pacific

Figure 1. Tange Kenzō, Fuji Television Headquarters Building (1996). Photograph copyright Vincent D. Feldman.

monsters of the *Godzilla* film series (1954–), to the project to develop a race of aquans to inhabit the rising oceans in Abe Kōbō's *Inter Ice Age 4* (*Daiyon kanpyōki*, 1959), to the resurrection of the Pacific battleship as a starship in in Miyamoto Reiji's manga and anime series *Space Battleship Yamato* (*Uchū senkan Yamato*, 1974–83).[19] Among the works to be discussed in this study, floating megastructures (dubbed "megafloats"), reminiscent of Kikutake's Marine City and related projects, are built to recolonize Japan's territorial waters after the submersion of the Japanese archipelago in Komatsu Sakyō and Tani Kōshū's *Nihon chinbotsu dainibu* (Japan sinks: Part two, 2006). In addition, Tokyo Bay is imagined as the site of "Neo-Tokyo," Project Babylon, or New City Center construction projects extending or resurrecting the currently existing city in Ōtomo Katsuhiro's *Akira* (Manga, 1982–90, film 1988), Oshii Mamoru's *Patlabor: The Movie* (*Kidō keisatsu patoreibā*, 1989), and Masaki Gorō's *Vīnasu shitei* (Venus city, 1992).

As Schnellbächer suggests, the recurrence of the Pacific as a topos in postwar science fiction indexes a continued struggle with the legacy of prewar Japanese imperialism, which was imaginatively supported by an extensive literature of adventure stories and proto–science fiction featuring Japanese technological prowess as well as personal valor and patriotism in expanding Japan's empire across the waters of the Pacific. From this perspective, could the compulsively repeated gesture of imaginative colonization of Tokyo Bay, as found in Tange's Plan for Tokyo 1960 and other historical proposals, as well as the fictional works mentioned above, represent a scaled-down version of Japanese imperialism available for ideological transference or critique, just as the colonization of outer space presented a laboratory for extending or critiquing Manifest Destiny and American imperialism in the U.S. space program and American science fiction narratives?

Indeed, architecture critic Yatsuka Hajime emphasizes the continuity in expansionist, ambitious architectural and urban design between the prewar and wartime colonization efforts in Taiwan and Manchuria led by Gotō Shinpei, and the national building efforts of the Metabolist group, with Tange, who debuted as a student architect in 1942 with his prizewinning design for a Greater East Asia Co-prosperity Sphere Monument at the foot of Mount Fuji, serving as a key transfer point between these two political and architectural moments. Yatsuka argues that with international colonization no longer a possibility, the only domains available for expansion to relieve population pressure in the postwar era were the sky and the ocean, which became the special provinces of Metabolist design.[20]

Together with this imperialist genealogy, another aspect connecting the megastructural tendency of Metabolism with the ideologies and practices of the Japanese nation-state is their shared interest in large-scale infrastructure projects. While the most iconic Metabolist megastructural projects, such as Kikutake's Marine Cities or Tange's Tokyo Bay Project, were never realized or supported by the State, many of the Metabolist ideas and urban diagnoses influenced bureaucratically guided national infrastructure projects, and Metabolists such as Kurokawa participated directly in government-funded research and planning initiatives.[21] During the High Growth Era, ambitious architectural and planning initiatives such as those promoted by Tange and his disciples dovetailed to some extent with the ruling Liberal Democratic Party's efforts to stimulate the economy through large-scale construction projects and, more boldly, to remold the Japanese archipelago and its distribution of population and economic resources through the restructuring of transportation, communication, and industrial infrastructures. For example, while they differ in many key aspects, the visionary scale of applying urban planning methods to the entire Japanese archipelago establishes Tange's book *Nihon rettō no shōraizō* (The future image of the Japanese archipelago), from 1966, as an important precedent for Prime Minister Tanaka Kakuei's best-selling book *Nihon rettō kaizōron* (Plan for remodeling the Japanese archipelago) from 1972.[22] Tanaka's book, released during his successful election campaign for prime minister, offered a diagnosis of urban overpopulation and overdevelopment and a proposal to reallocate national development resources to rural areas; to critics, it was seen as a blueprint for the structure of political patronage and public collusion with large private construction companies that came to be known as the *doken kokka* or "construction state."

Moreover, despite the ecological consciousness of the Metabolist architects (which I will discuss in chapter 1), to their critics the Metabolists' conception of the impermanence of architecture was complicit with the wastefulness of prevailing construction practices in the High Growth Era and beyond. As architect Miyauchi Kō stated in 1983, "Metabolist thought, which envisions buildings and cities as devices of cellular replacement *(taisha shōchi)* is nothing other than a theoretical reflection of the 'scrap and build' mentality of the High Growth Era, which endlessly generates environmental pollution."[23] I will explore these contentious issues of Metabolism, the imperial imaginary, and the "construction state" as they intersect with SF literature and film through my discussion of *Japan Sinks* (*Nihon chinbotsu*, 1973) and its sequel in chapter 3 and in my final chapter, focusing on *Akira* and *Patlabor*.

Capsules

After the megastructure, a second architectural form I will discuss in this study is the capsule. Returning to Maki's definition of the megastructure as composed of a framework and "discrete, rapidly changeable functional units," we could see the capsule—a self-contained, prefabricated unit capable of being plugged in or removed from the framework—as merely one of the two possible elements in this type of megastructural design. The most famous built example of capsule architecture, Kurokawa Kishō's Nakagin Capsule Tower (completed in 1972), exemplifies this idea through the pairing of central tower cores providing infrastructure and access and prefabricated steel capsules, the dwelling units, bolted to the cores. Nevertheless, there are several elements to the idea of the capsule, as proposed by Kurokawa and other architectural theorists, that are worth exploring beyond the basic dyad of framework and capsule. These include the qualities of enclosure and mobility, as well as the capsule's function as a cybernetic node in a wider information system.[24]

In keeping with the root meaning of the term in the Latin *capsula*, a small box or case,[25] enclosure is the basic quality and function of the capsule as architectural form: the capsule functions as a carefully calibrated membrane between the inhabitant and the outside world. For example, an article on the creation of capsules by the design firm GK, headed by Metabolist group member Ekuan Kenji, stresses homeostasis or the maintenance of equilibrium as the first defining quality of the capsule. Drawing on the language of cybernetics, GK explains that the capsule seeks, through artificial means, to achieve a balanced, sustainable relationship between the occupying organism and the surrounding environment, particularly in cases, such as a deep-sea environment or a rapidly moving vehicle, where the inhabitant would have difficulty surviving the environmental conditions through natural means.[26]

The vogue for the capsule as an architectural form in the 1960s is closely tied to the development of space capsules capable of protecting an astronaut from the radiation, temperature extremes, and vacuum of outer space. Nevertheless, we could ask, as an architectural form proposed for contemporary, terrestrial cities, what is the necessity for a membrane protecting the inhabitant from a hostile environment, beyond the sheltering functions of more traditional types of housing? References in the literature surrounding Metabolism explored in this volume, such as the urban ills of pollution and noise—including the "pollution" or "noise" of "information overload"—together with the dangers of nuclear and biological warfare, and even catastrophic climate change, suggest some possible answers to this question. Indeed, in the shared Cold War environment of the nuclear arms race as well as the space race, the "capsule" architecture of Japan can be seen as a cognate to other artificial, enclosed environments in postwar modern architecture, such as the House of the Future designed by Alison and Peter Smithson in 1956, which architectural historian Beatriz Colomina describes as "a kind of bomb shelter" engaged in a pitched defense against "all forms of contamination" from the outside.[27]

Yet, in addition to the defensive aspects of the capsule form, for Kurokawa and his Metabolist peers the capsule is endowed with a positive valence: rather than merely function as a protective shell, the capsule will provide a technological prosthesis for its inhabitant to survive and thrive in the social and economic environment of the "information society." Indeed, the capsule form reflects, responds to, and contributes to the development of this society, which is posited as increasingly atomized into autonomous individuals and small groups forming flexible networks in the place of previous large social organizations.[28] For Kurokawa, the capsule is foremost a form of "cyborg architecture," whereby the capsule functions as a feedback mechanism helping the capsule dweller to filter unwanted information (its "defensive" function), but also, as a technological prosthesis, the capsule will help the user to obtain useful information and to barter their own "creative information" in an extended information marketplace.[29]

For the Metabolists, mobility is another key aspect of the capsule form; in addition to space capsules and submarine vehicles, the mobile home or camper—a product of modern industrial design serving as a catalyst for new postwar lifestyles—was also an object of fascination for many 1960s architects and taken as a prototype for the capsule dwelling of the future. As discussed earlier, the capsule was often posited as part of a dyad of capsule (conceived to be relatively temporary and mobile) and supporting framework structure or megastructure (designed to be of longer temporal duration). However, writing in 1969, while serving on the team tasked with fitting various display capsules into the megastructure of Tange Kenzō's grand "space frame" roof covering the Theme Zone of the Osaka Expo, Metabolist theorist Kawazoe Noboru wrote that despite the promise of greater flexibility, the pairing of capsule and megastructure in effect made capsules "as unfree and immovable as a butterfly caught in a spider's web." Therefore, he called for a reconception of the city as a "free arrangement" of capsules liberated from the "totalitarian" domination of the megastructure.[30] Similarly, Kurokawa imagined the capsule as a dwelling for "*Homo movens*," a new stage of humanity that would be increasingly nomadic. While the ultimate form of such mobile capsules is not made explicit, Kurokawa imagines the "docking" of capsules as an expression of flexible social aggregations of autonomous, mobile individuals—from the creation of a household to the docking of individuals in a city center to create a new social space—the "metapolis"—for education, commerce, or leisure.[31]

Summarizing these various potentials of the capsule, Kawazoe writes that, while they seem to deepen the atomization of the enclosed self, capsules will also function as a point of engagement with the world as part of a technologized network or system. Referring to Victor Hugo's aphorism that the printing press and its product, the book (a pocket-sized expression of the individual), would destroy the cathedral (a grand architectural expression of the collective), Kawazoe predicts that the capsule will ultimately lead to the destruction of the city itself.[32] Architecture historian Lara Schrijver's analysis of the capsule form, while primarily focused on the case of Archigram and the European avant-garde, seems to reach a similar conclusion when she writes that "the truly radical nature of the capsular environment is . . . not about self-enclosure but about expansion. . . . The 'bubble' is about expansion into the environment, and in its ultimate form, dissolving into the technological mediascape," leading to the "fundamental disappearance of architecture as a solid, built environment."[33] I will discuss similar formulations regarding the "dissolving" or liquification of architecture and the Japanese city in chapter 5.

It is striking that 1972, the year of completion of Kurokawa Kishō's Capsule Tower, is also the year of the debut of Nagai Gō's manga and anime *Mazinger Z*, considered to be the first instance of an anime or manga robot piloted by a human pilot, and thereby the progenitor of an extensive genre of mecha (aka giant robot, mobile suit) anime featuring the combination of human pilots and "giant robots," including such subsequent serial works as *Mobile Suit Gundam* (1979–), *Macross* (1982–), *Patlabor* (1988–), and *Neon Genesis Evangelion* (1995–).[34] The mecha in these series are typically piloted by a young male *(shōnen)* pilot, enveloped within the womb-like protective space of the "robot," whose capacity for heroic, adult "masculine" action such as warfare is technologically enhanced. The mecha, even more literally than Kurokawa's capsule, is a type of "cyborg architecture," a combination of vehicle, clothing, dwelling, and weapon. While not usually a permanent abode, the mecha imaginatively fulfills the three aspects of the capsule outlined above: enclosure, as a protective shell or membrane; mobility; and the function of a cybernetic node in an information network. To this extent, the mecha motif also resonates with the writing of media and architectural theorist Lieven De Cauter, who has recently revived the discussion of the capsule as an architectural form in order to interrogate contemporary social, medial, and urban structures. In my final chapter, with reference to De Cauter's capsule theory, I will explore the mecha as imaginative architecture and its relationship to postwar social and geopolitical history, in the form of Oshii Mamoru's two *Patlabor* films (1989 and 1993), and discuss how the artist Yanobe Kenji has appropriated the forms of the capsule and the mecha in an ongoing engagement with Metabolist ideas and the mecha culture of Japanese manga and anime.

Apocalypse

The final imaginative motif I would like to introduce here, after the megastructure and the capsule, is the idea of the apocalyptic city: the future city in ruins, the city to be destroyed. The destruction of the city, especially the capital of Tokyo, is a familiar aspect of many Japanese science fictions across many media, including films, novels, manga, anime, and video games. Indeed, it is difficult to argue with historian William M. Tsutsui's claim that "in the years since World War II, fictional apocalypse has been visited upon Tokyo more frequently . . . than any other location on the globe."[35] The most iconic avatar of such destruction is undoubtedly Godzilla, who first emerged from dark Pacific waters to menace Tokyo in director Honda Ishirō's film *Gojira* for Tōhō Studios in 1954. Godzilla has engendered many interpretations over the course of a long film career—from the embodiment of nuclear dread, to the reemergence of repressed colonial memory, to the spirit of Japanese Pacific war dead, to a postwar champion of Japanese common men and women. In the context of this study, perhaps the most salient aspects of Godzilla's iconography are the interlinked qualities of the monster's serial reappearance and his role as destroyer of architecture.

Godzilla reemerged from the Pacific on a regular basis to raid the cities of Tokyo or Osaka, or to battle other monsters with much collateral damage to the cityscape, over the course of fourteen sequels to the original *Godzilla* between 1955 and 1975; over a dozen additional films followed a series "reboot" in the 1980s through the present day. In the original film, Godzilla ravishes sites of Japan's postwar industrial infrastructure—the engines of Japan's economic recovery: power plants and power lines, oil refineries, factories, and freight transportation centers, all typically positioned on shoreline areas—before attacking the symbolic heart of the Japanese nation-state, the National Diet Building (completed in 1936). Subsequent films feature destruction of Tokyo Tower (1958), a prominent symbol of postwar reconstruction, while in the later series, a scaled-up version of Godzilla destroys new landmarks of the bubble-era construction boom, such as Tange Kenzō's towering Metropolitan Government Building in Shinjuku (1990), which merely a year after its completion was fictionally destroyed in *Godzilla vs. King Ghidorah* (1991). Architecture critic Yatsuka Hajime describes this destruction of symbolic constructive sites as a type of "anti-urban ritual" symbolically assaulting the hubris of modern Japanese political, business, and architectural elites.[36] Nevertheless, this wanton destruction is also accompanied by the unseen reconstruction of the city, or "reset" of the urban landscape in the intervals between films. As Tsutsui notes, "Tokyo thus took on a 'self-healing' quality, as the presumed multiple rebuildings of the city were accomplished without any human agency."[37] Similar cycles of on-screen urban destruction and off-screen reconstruction were featured in such weekly television series as *Ultra Q* (1966) and *Ultraman* (1966–67) as well as postmodern variations on the monster film such as Anno Hideaki's anime *Neon Genesis Evangelion* (1995–96).[38]

In her recent study *Apocalypse in Contemporary Japanese Science Fiction,* Motoko Tanaka discusses the distinction between linear conceptions of time featured in the Zoroastrian and Judeo-Christian apocalypse as exemplified in the Book of Revelation and cyclical views of time and apocalypse such as those found in the Hindu and Buddhist traditions.[39] While she observes both conceptions of time operative in modern and contemporary Japanese science fiction narratives, her study repeatedly notes the importance of cyclical or "spiral" conceptions of apocalypse to these works. Certainly, the example of Godzilla and fellow Tōhō monsters' attacks on a spontaneously regenerating Tokyo, occurring as regularly as an urban ritual or religious festival, seem to suggest a circular conception of apocalypse.

In terms of the architectural theories discussed in this study, I would argue that the core conceptions of Metabolism, predicated on a comparison of human constructive activity and biological processes such as cellular replacement and regeneration, are fundamentally circular in nature.[40] Furthermore, architect Isozaki Arata's personal extrapolation of these ideas in the form of the "incubation mechanism" by which ruins lead to future cities—or rather, future cities *are* ruins and vice versa—demonstrates a profoundly apocalyptic, cyclical imagination. However, rather than analyzing the religious dimensions of this cyclical conception, I will focus on the connections between the cyclical conception of ruins and historical experience, particularly the postwar generation's experience of ruined Japanese cities.

This conception of "ruins" as both past and future, and the related apocalyptic vision of science fiction author Komatsu Sakyō are the subjects of my second and third chapters. Just as the planning scale of Metabolist architects stretches from megastructure to megalopolis to the global "ecumenopolis," so the imagination of "ruins" and "apocalypse" in Komatsu's work stretches from the scale of the individual, to the city, to the archipelago, to the planetary. Indeed, as I explore in chapter 3, Komatsu's work features prominent displacements and inversions of local and global, center and periphery, within a dialogic form that juxtaposes cosmopolitan and nationalistic discourses under the shadow of disasters that are planetary in scale.[41]

Architecture and Science Fiction

Despite their shared interest in representing future modes of life, the relationship between science fiction and architecture has not been thoroughly charted: regarding SF film in particular, architecture scholar David T. Fortin writes that "while these two cultural siblings have been ceaselessly linked since SF film's emergence at the turn of the past century, there has curiously not been a focused and comprehensive academic study exploring the relationship between them."[42] Fortin's own study, *Architecture and Science-Fiction Film: Philip K. Dick and the Spectacle of Home,* steps into the breach with a survey of previous writings on architecture and science fiction, as well as a focused study of domesticity and architecture in the fictions of Philip K. Dick and the film adaptations of his work. Similarly, while it is not focused exclusively on architecture, Scott Bukatman's exploration of subjectivity, technology, and the cityscape in *Terminal Identity: The Virtual Subject in Postmodern Science Fiction* takes a densely textured critical approach that productively relates cyberpunk prose fiction and film to contemporary cultural theory. Bukatman's second chapter on "terminal space" in particular provides a cogent critical model that interrogates the spatial aspects of both literary and cinematic science fiction, to which I will refer in chapter 5. Nevertheless, despite such compelling studies as those of Fortin and Bukatman, the relationship between science fiction and architecture remains both poorly mapped and undertheorized.

The sources discussed in the current study will be both visual and verbal. Architecture, in preparing (ostensibly) for an end product of built space that is experienced both visually and somatically (by a body positioned in and moving through space), typically proceeds through a series of preparative stages that are primarily visual: plans, drawings, and models, rendered with either traditional analog or digital drawing and modeling tools. These preparatory visualizations are closely related to the visualization of unbuilt or imaginative spaces in other media: painting or printmaking, magazine and book illustration, comic books, animation, and film sets. As noted examples of fantastic or "futuristic" cities in such visual media, we could cite the cover illustrations of science fiction magazines such as *Amazing Stories*, the comic book drawings, animation, or film design work of Moebius, Oshii Mamoru, or H. R. Giger, or the matte paintings and scale-model sets of such films as *Metropolis* or *Blade Runner*, and we can trace mutual influence and shared visual motifs between architectural drawing and these visual media. These intermedial relationships with respect to the visualization of architecture and cityscape could productively be the basis of a study of the media of manga, anime, and CGI rendering that have increasingly come to dominate Japanese cultural production and its international reception.[43]

However, while my study will explore such visual intermedial relationships, it will be fundamentally concerned with conceptual, discursive, and narrative connections and will hinge on written texts by architects, critics, and fiction authors. I will argue that Metabolist architectural theory and science fiction are invested in similar techniques of imaginative simulation, which are related to the development of simulation itself as a concept and technique with the rise of information technology, thus moving architecture beyond the purely visual and into the narrative mode.

In their discussion of simulation and architecture, Andrea Gleiniger and Georg Vrachliotis point to a historical shift: while simulation in architecture once referred to visual modes of presentation, with the advent of computer modeling simulation becomes a methodological and strategic instrument that could posit and test evolving relations between buildings, their users, and their environments as a dynamic system. In terms of temporality, this shift constitutes "a leap from timeless to time-contingent technology."[44] As indicated by Abe Kōbō's pioneering science fiction novel *Inter Ice Age 4* from 1959, or by architect Isozaki Arata's essay "Invisible City" from 1966, the possibility of computers functioning as tools for modeling the behavior of complex systems—simulating the interactions of built environments, city dwellers, and environmental factors such as natural disasters or climate change—was on the conceptual horizon as early as 1960, although it could not yet be fully implemented from a technological perspective.[45] The forthcoming chapters will explore the idea of simulation as it connects the narrative form of science fiction with the temporal aspects of Metabolist architectural theory and as it extends into the imagination of virtual cities created by information technology and inhabited by virtualized subjects.

Outline of the Study

By introducing a temporal element into architecture and urban design, the Metabolists opened a pathway connecting architecture and fictional narrative, which I will begin to explore in my first chapter. As an introduction, I will provide a brief overview of the situation of cities in postwar Japan through 1960, the year in which the Metabolist manifesto was presented to the World Design Conference in Tokyo, and examine some of the chief proposals of Metabolist architects, focusing on the concepts of "metabolism" and "scale," together with the urban forms of frame, capsule, megastructure, and megalopolis. I will then investigate the intersection of architectural writing and literary fiction by examining writings by architects that combine fictional elements with the architectural essay, as well as science fiction author Komatsu Sakyō's *Kūchū toshi 008* (City in the air 008, 1969), a novel for young readers that explicitly incorporates elements of Metabolist architecture. I will argue that fictional narrative offered the possibility of simulating the city's conditions and development under various conditions, connecting the idea of "simulation" as described by Isozaki Arata with the work of the science fiction "novum" proposed by Darko Suvin.

While both the genre of science fiction and architectural proposals of the Metabolists and their associates would seem to be resolutely oriented toward the future, a kernel of the past reasserts itself in both architectural and fictional works of the postwar period: the ruin. In terms of historical experience, the motif of the ruin points to the ruins of Japanese cities destroyed by the Allied forces' incendiary bombs and atomic blasts over Hiroshima and Nagasaki. Moreover, the ruin appears not only as a fragment of the traumatic past but as a harbinger of the potential for an apocalyptic future, remaining semihidden within the reality of the present. Isozaki describes this coexistence of the ruin with the constructive projects of the present and future in terms of a sine wave going in and out of phase, the ruins blinking in and out of the visual field with the waves of time. In my second chapter, I will examine the motif of ruins in the work of Isozaki Arata and in the essays and fiction of Komatsu Sakyō, particularly his essay "Haikyo no kūkan bunmei" (Civilization of the space of ruins, 1964) and the novels *Nihon apacchi zoku* (The Japan Apache tribe, 1964) and *Virus: The Day of Resurrection* (*Fukkatsu no hi*, 1964). I will argue that for both Isozaki and Komatsu, the ruin not only represents the persistent trauma of the past but is also a source of creativity, allowing them to embrace the potential of simulation and contingency.

My examination of the apocalyptic imagination in Komatsu Sakyō's work continues with chapter 3, encompassing his best-known work, *Japan Sinks* (1973), its sequel, *Japan Sinks: Part Two* (2006), as well as *Virus: The Day of Resurrection* (1964) and *Shuto shōshitsu* (The capital vanishes, 1985). I will show how these works often create conditions of exile and inversions of traditional roles of center and periphery by simulating the disappearance or annihilation of such organized political, social, and cultural entities as the capital city of Tokyo, the Japanese nation in its postwar geopolitical existence on the Japanese archipelago, or even the entire Cold War system of nation-states. These works, I will argue, attempt to go beyond the categories of city and nation-state to evoke a planetary consciousness, consistent with Komatsu's interest in global environmental issues, including the impact of biological and nuclear weapons as well as the possibility of catastrophic climate change. However, far from celebrating the emergence of an effective planetary consciousness and system of governance in response to such threats, Komatsu's works often highlight the gaps in global communication and the role of Cold War and post–Cold War geopolitics in creating information monopolies that can threaten effective responses to global crises. Nevertheless, while Komatsu's disaster novels do imagine human resilience to global catastrophe, this imagination is dominated by highly patriarchal formulations as the active roles in understanding and responding to disaster are inevitably assigned to males, while women are delegated reproductive roles in biologically preserving the species.

If Komatsu's works such as *Virus: The Day of Resurrection* and *Japan Sinks* reveal the apocalyptic scope of his imagination, it is important to also recall his positive engagement with the production of the 1970 Japan World Exposition in Suita, Osaka, which presented to the world an optimistic vision of a "future city," based on the principle of "Progress and Harmony for Mankind" and featuring a futuristic transportation system and information technology infrastructure, as well as exuberant, innovate architecture and public art. The expo environment and its supporting discourse were created through the collaboration of many architects, artists, and planners, including Tange Kenzō, Isozaki Arata, and the Metabolist architects, together with Komatsu Sakyō and his study group "Thinking the Expo." In my fourth chapter I will explore the evolution of the expo's discursive themes and physical environment, examining both their utopian aspects as well as the dissonant elements of anxiety and criticism regarding the present and future that could not be fully repressed despite the expo's cheerful and optimistic veneer.

A prominent aspect of the staging of the 1970 Osaka Expo was the extensive use of electronics, including computerized information terminals, computers controlling the sounds and video systems of individual pavilions, and giant robots in the expo's public performance area assisting with lighting, sound, and staging effects. Moreover, beyond the most visible aspects of robotics and computer systems, one of the goals of the expo planners was to use newly emerging information technology to control the various infrastructural functions of the expo site, particularly to monitor the massive crowds of visitors and facilitate their movement around the grounds. This can be seen as one aspect of the expo planners' attempt to create a model of a "core of future city," in which technology could help to create more efficient flows of people, goods, and information through an increasingly dense and crowded urban environment—a new operating system, so to speak, for an urban environment suited to the coming "information society." However, to critics, the expo's use of information technology, combined with a security apparatus designed to carefully manage a state-sponsored event for an international audience, seemed a harbinger of an emerging "managed society" in which spontaneity, freedom of expression, and political action and speech would be increasingly subjected to the technocratic control of political and economic elites.

In my fifth chapter, I will examine the idea of the "liquid city" or "invisible city" in which physical architecture becomes subordinated to the flow of energy and information in an environment dominated by electronic media. I will follow the development of the discourse on the "information society" and the related critique of the "managed society" as they intersected with the planning of the 1970 Osaka Expo and extended to city-planning initiatives and debates over public space in the subsequent decades. Furthermore, I will trace the shifts in the discourse around the penetration of information technology and media into urban space in the 1980s and 1990s, exploring architectural responses to the increasingly consumer-oriented culture of the late twentieth century, and the growing international "techno-orientalist" association between the global information and media future and the Japanese city. This association reached its apogee in the 1980s and 1990s with the cyberpunk movement, represented by such cinematic and literary works as Ridley Scott's *Blade Runner* (1982), William Gibson's *Neuromancer* (1984), and Masaki's Gorō's *Venus City* (1992). I will observe how the issue of "control" persists in debates about the mediatization of the city, from the critiques of the "managed society" to the emergence of cyberpunk, even as the focus of such imagined control shifts from a centralized government bureaucracy to more diffuse agents of multinational capital. In addition, I will trace how the idealized mobile subject inhabiting this cyber city transforms from the commuting masculine "salaryman" occupying the pods of Kurokawa's capsule hotel, to the imagined young female "urban nomad" temporarily sheltered in Itō Toyoo's Pao, to the gender-shifting, racially passing avatars of the virtual city in Masaki's work.

My final chapter will examine the lingering traces of Metabolist discourse and themes in the films of two prominent animators, Ōtomo Katsuhirō's *Akira* (1988) and Oshii Mamoru's *Patlabor* (1989) and *Patlabor 2* (1993), as well as the sculptures and performance art of Yanobe Kenji from 1990 through 2003. I will show how Ōtomo's *Akira* employs visual and thematic motifs extremely close to those of the Metabolists to present both dystopian and utopian apocalyptic visions to a generation of viewers born into the ostensible peaceful and prosperous realm of bubble-era Japan. Next, I will explore how Oshii's *Patlabor* offers a meta-architectural critique of the constant demolishing and reconstruction of Japanese cities, through an imaginative staging of the many postwar proposals to expand the city of Tokyo over Tokyo Bay, and how his *Patlabor 2*, through the figure of the mecha or human-piloted robot, offers a critique of media and technology that resonates with urban theorist Lieven De Cauter's recent reworking of the 1960s architectural discourse of the "capsule." Finally, I will discuss how artist Yanobe Kenji revisits Metabolist themes and landmarks, particularly the site of the 1970 Osaka Expo, which are explored in his work as the "ruins of the future." Yanobe's work offers a connection from Metabolism to the current post-bubble, post-Fukushima era, expressing the complicated relationship of a disillusioned present to a utopian future of the past.

The works of Ōtomo, Oshii, and Yanobe thus demonstrate the continuing relevance of Metabolist ideas and provide an occasion to reflect on the legacy of the postwar architectural imagination vis-à-vis our current social, cultural, and environmental conditions. Together with the works of their Metabolist and SF predecessors, these works pose such questions as: How does the combination of atomized "capsule" and information "network" endemic to modern society affect our social and political vision? Will the "software" of information exchange and processing underlying our public and private spaces be an instrument of liberation or control? How can we understand our own lives and living environments amid the historical waves of construction and ruins? Can we imagine apocalypse to be both "instantaneous" and "gradual," both singular and cyclical? Can we envision the consequences when the scale of catastrophe expands from city to archipelago to planet, when the inhabitants of entire nations or continents become refugees? As architects and city planners increasingly acknowledge the normality of disaster and the temporal contingency of urban space through discourses of "resilience," the questions raised by over a half-century of the Metabolist imagination are all the more compelling today.

1 City Visions

Metabolism and Science Fiction

The Japanese urban landscape was in a great state of flux circa 1960, the year in which a group of young architects unveiled the manifesto entitled *Metabolism 1960: The Proposals for a New Urbanism*. Only fifteen years previously, at the end of the Second World War, much of the urban landscape had been reduced to ashes and rubble: it is estimated that 40 percent of the urban areas in Japan's sixty-six major cities had been destroyed, including 65 percent of residences in Tokyo, 57 percent in Osaka, and 89 percent in Nagoya—three cities struck extensively by the Allied incendiary bombing campaigns.[1] After Japan's surrender, shantytown "barracks" and new construction emerged quickly in the bombed-out urban zones. In Tokyo, the Metropolitan Government drew up ambitious plans to restructure the city with the introduction of broad boulevards, extensive greenbelts and green corridors, and population distributed to satellite cities, but few aspects of the plan were actually implemented—instead, reconstruction and redevelopment emerged pell-mell, largely following the pre-1945 street grid.[2]

During the Allied occupation (1945–52), the occupation authorities requisitioned a broad corridor of still-standing buildings in the central Marunouchi district and adjacent areas, as well as approximately one thousand private residences for officers, while for soldiers and staff large, gated communities resembling American suburbs were built on the former Yoyogi Parade Ground (renamed Washington Heights) and on a former airfield in Nerima Ward (Grant Heights).[3] While some of the occupation transformations of Tokyo were short-lived, such as the labeling of major roads in the capital as Avenues A–Z and Streets 1–60, others were lingering, such as the 208 American military facilities, including Washington and Grant Heights, which remained in the capital even after the U.S.–Japan Security Treaty formally ended the occupation in 1952.[4] These remaining footholds of American military power, connected to an extensive archipelago of U.S. military bases throughout Japan, were one focus of anger for the thousands of citizens who occupied the capital to protest the renewal of the U.S.–Japan Security Treaty in 1960, the same year as the Metabolist manifesto's release.

After a dip in population due to wartime evacuation, the population growth of Tokyo and other urban areas accelerated during the postwar period from the significant pace it had already seen in 1920s and 1930s,[5] and there was a scarcity of housing for repatriated soldiers and civilians returning from rural evacuation, as well as migrants seeking work opportunities in the city. From the mid-1950s, economic recovery and intensified industrialization, much of it concentrated in the Pacific Belt Area connecting Tokyo, Osaka, and Fukuoka, initiated the unprecedented High Growth Era, with annual increases in GNP approaching or surpassing 10 percent for much of the period between 1953 and 1970. Rapid urban growth also continued during this period: between 1955 and 1965, the population of Tokyo rose from 7.5 million to 10.3 million, and in the twenty years following 1950, the population density of greater Tokyo increased 70 percent.[6] As geographer Chauncy D. Harris observed in 1982 (on the cusp of a similar transformation in China), "In such a short period, no other major country has experienced so dramatic and thorough a transformation, such rapid urban and industrial growth, or comparable concentration of population and industry in major metropolitan areas and a highly localized industrial belt."[7]

Initially, public investment in the postwar period focused on large-scale projects for industrial sites and port development, as well as basic infrastructure such as electricity and water supply, while, as urban planning scholar André Sorensen notes, "there was corresponding little priority given to other considerations such as long-term patterns of growth, residential quality of life, social capital formation in the form of parks, libraries and recreation facilities, or the broader environmental consequences of industrial expansion."[8] However, by the late 1950s and early 1960s, near-crisis conditions of traffic congestion and poor maintenance of roads, overcrowded transportation systems, and an inadequate housing supply stimulated a new attention to urban planning and investment from both public and private sources. In 1955, the previous state-sponsored housing authority was reformed and expanded into the Japan Housing Corporation, which began an extensive program of new construction of multistory concrete housing blocks, or *danchi*. The National Capital Region Development Plan of 1958 removed the existing 31-meter building height restriction in central Tokyo, paving the way for skyscraper construction. Furthermore, the Residential Area Development Act of 1963 set the stage for the development of planned communities such as Tama New Town near Tokyo and Senri New Town near Osaka, where previously lightly settled areas were thoroughly transformed with large housing blocks, planned green spaces, shopping and recreation facilities, and new transportation infrastructure.[9]

However, it was the announcement in 1959 that Tokyo had been named host city of the 1964 Summer Olympics that spurred the greatest effort of planning, construction, and infrastructure development in the Japanese capital. The Olympic construction boom included the creation of 138 kilometers of new roads and eight new subway lines supplementing Tokyo's existing three lines. The Metropolitan Expressway Corporation was established in June 1959 and overlaid a network of five new massive elevated expressway routes over the city, alternately tunneling under or bridging over top of existing streets and waterways. In addition to these massive new expressways, cutting-edge transportation infrastructure was established in the form of the Tokyo Monorail connecting the existing Yamanote railway loop with Haneda Airport, as well as the Tokaidō Shinkansen bullet train connecting Tokyo Station and Shin-Osaka, which began operations just days before the start of the 1964 Summer Olympics.[10] Architect Tange Kenzō was entrusted with the design of the symbolic focal point of the Olympics, the Yoyogi National Gymnasium, erected on the site of the former Washington Heights housing development for occupying American forces, which was only fully returned to Japanese sovereignty in the Olympic year of 1964. Tange's design, still a major architectural landmark of Tokyo, featured an innovative double-comma shape and the world's largest suspension roof at the time (Figure 2).[11]

Thus, from one perspective, the year 1960 found Tokyo on the brink of an international Olympic celebration of Japan's national sovereignty, engineering prowess, and economic recovery. However, the urban transformation and accompanying physical displacements of

Figure 2. Tange Kenzō, Yoyogi National Gymnasium (1964), detail (Harajuku entrance). Photograph copyright Vincent D. Feldman.

the Olympics construction boom coincided with extraordinary political turmoil centered on the renewal of the U.S.–Japan Security Treaty in 1960, which signified to its critics continued military and political dependence on the United States within a bipolar Cold War system. As many as five million students, workers, and other citizens participated in the protests against the treaty's renewal, culminating in tens of thousands of protesters surrounding the Diet Building in Tokyo in May and June 1960.[12] While not successful in preventing renewal of the treaty, these protests initiated a decade in which all aspects of the Japanese political, economic, and academic establishments would be subject to radical questioning from the left, including the environmentally and socially heedless pro-growth policies of the government and its bureaucratic managers, together with the business interests

with which they were closely allied. For many critics, the Olympic construction boom itself was symptomatic of the collusion of state and business interests that ignored the true interests and political voices of the people.[13]

Such was the tumultuous state of the Japanese cityscape and body politic circa 1960, when Japan hosted the World Design Conference in Tokyo, a conference of the international design community that drew approximately 250 architects and designers from twenty-seven countries to Tokyo.[14] In the preparations for this conference Asada Takashi, professor of architecture and assistant at Tange Kenzō's architecture laboratory at the University of Tokyo, assembled a study group of young architects and designers to produce a theoretical statement "originating in Japan but applicable to the world in general."[15]

This was to result in the publication *Metabolism 1960: The Proposals for a New Urbanism,* distributed at the conference, which propelled the group of architects to international prominence.[16] The bold designs offered in this manifesto were a young generation of architects' attempt to address many of the urban problems described above: overcrowding, poorly planned urban infrastructure, the loss of green spaces, and even the hierarchical, top-down nature of architecture and city planning themselves.

Asada's group of "Metabolists" included architecture critic Kawazoe Noboru; Kikutake Kiyonori, a young architect who had already published a series of futuristic proposals for a Tower-Shaped Community and Marine City; Kurokawa Kishō (a.k.a. Kurokawa Noriaki), then a graduate student in Tange's lab; Ōtaka Masato, an assistant to the modernist master architect and Le Corbusier disciple Maekawa Kunio; Maki Fumihiko, then a professor of architecture at Washington University in St. Louis; Ekuan Kenji, an industrial designer; and Awazu Kiyoshi, a graphic designer.[17] While Tange Kenzō was absent from much of the World Design Conference preparations because of his tenure as visiting professor at MIT for the 1959–60 academic year, he returned to serve on the executive committee of the conference and, after his return, began preparations for his revolutionary Plan for Tokyo 1960, a linear city to be built over Tokyo Bay, which was unveiled in January 1961 on a special New Year's broadcast on the NHK national television network. Assisting Tange on the preparations for this plan were the young architects Kurokawa Kishō and Isozaki Arata. Isozaki, who developed ties to leftist activists, critics, and artists from the avant-garde scene of the Sōgetsu Art Center in addition to his affiliation with Tange's lab, was not a contributor to the Metabolism manifesto but emerged as a key interlocutor, as collaborator, rival, and critic to Tange and the Metabolist group. He published his own futuristic urban design, City in the Air, in 1961.

In this chapter, I will discuss the ideas of the future city proposed by the Metabolist architects, their mentors Tange and Asada, and their peer Isozaki Arata, focusing on the concept of metabolism. I will examine this concept through the architectural forms of frame and capsule, as well as the Metabolists' interpretation of scale, together with the urban forms of megastructure and megalopolis. In addition, I will explore the affinity between Metabolism and science fiction, examining hybrid architectural-literary texts such as science fiction author Komatsu Sakyō's *Kūchū toshi 008* (City in the air 008, 1969), Kawazoe Noboru's "Dai-Tōkyō saigo no hi" (The last days of Greater Tokyo, 1961), Isozaki's "City Demolition Industry, Inc." (Toshi hakaigyō, KK, 1962), and "The Logic of Uselessness" (Muyō no ronri, 1971) by Itō Toyoo, an architect of the generation following the Metabolists.[18] Through its imaginative probing of the nature of the "future city," in its emphasis on emergence, transformation, and adaptation, and its theoretical engagement with apocalypse, the Metabolist movement, broadly defined, was especially suited to the temporality of narrative forms. The literary tradition of science fiction, like the nascent medium of computer modeling, offered architects the possibility of simulation of the future, in which specific variables of a given "reality" could be altered and the ensuing results could be worked out imaginatively; alternately, it could serve as a medium for criticism and philosophical exploration outside of the conventional architectural media of drawings, models, and buildings. By examining a number of such simulations, criticisms, and philosophical explorations in the current chapter, and throughout this study, I hope to reveal underappreciated affinities between the disparate artistic media of architecture and literary fiction.

Metabolism

The central idea of metabolism is to conceive and design buildings and other urban forms not in terms of built, completed, or potentially completed plans or structures but rather as entities capable of constant ongoing processes of metamorphosis, just as the material of a living organism undergoes a constant process of birth, growth, decay, and replenishment. In the Japanese text of the Metabolist manifesto (which was printed in both English and Japanese), the biological term *shinchin taisha*, designating the constitutive and sustaining chemical and physical processes in a living cell or organism, especially the intake of nutrition and expulsion of waste, is employed to describe this concept, alternatively with the romanized *metaborizumu*. The Metabolists' emphasis on change in urban form was simultaneously a reflection of the Japanese historical experience of frequent urban destruction and rebuilding, a diagnosis of the current fluid situation of global cities, and a search for a new working method amid a worldwide questioning of comprehensive modernist urban planning signaled by the dissolution of the Congrès Internationaux d'Architecture Moderne (CIAM) in 1959. Elaborating on the ideas of the Metabolist manifesto a year later, Kawazoe Noboru commented that even in the words "city planning" "one senses, with uneasiness, a certain tendency to imagine the city as something neat and orderly like a checker-board." Instead, for Kawazoe, the salient characteristic of the contemporary city is "precisely its capacity for changing day by day, for undergoing rapid transformation." "For example," he continues, "the rapidity of the metabolical changes in Tokyo in particular is without a parallel. If we are to formulate an idea of the city of the future, we must, I think, find it within this mobility, this ceaseless transformation." Thus, rather than striving for a fixed form or "master plan," architects and city planners should strive for a "continuous program," whereby "not a single part should be visualized as capable of completion; each part should be so designed that intense metabolic changes can take place freely inside it." Ultimately, Kawazoe concludes, "the city will be an organic being capable of encompassing all metabolic changes."[19]

As a method for designing building and cities capable of change, many Metabolist designs focused on a distinction between structural or framing elements that would be relatively stable (if expandable) and elements of shorter duration that could be more quickly replaced according to the life cycles and patterns of use of the inhabitants. Kawazoe glosses these two elements as "attachment points" of longer duration and "parts" of shorter duration; Maki's definition of megastructure, cited in the introduction, similarly proposes a division into the two elements of "framework" and "discrete, rapidly changeable functional units."[20] In the Metabolist manifesto and elsewhere, Kikutake Kiyonori refers to the more transient parts of his Metabolist scheme as "move-nets" of varying scale from "Human life Move-nets" such as kitchen move-net, bath move-net, etc., to "Family life Movable house," to "Urban life Mova-block."[21] As one of the illustrations of this "move-net" conception, Kikutake offered his plans for the Tower-Shaped Community for five thousand residents: a cylindrical tower composed of a concrete core and 1250 replaceable steel living units (Plate 2). In a typically organic metaphor, the replacement cycle of the living units, which would be recycled for new families at the end of one period of occupancy, is compared to the annual budding and falling of the leaves of a tree.[22]

The most famous built example of a Metabolist design exemplifying Kawazoe's distinction between "parts" and "attachment points" is Kurokawa Kishō's Nakagin Capsule Tower, completed in 1972 (Figure 3). The supporting structures or "attachment points" of this structure were provided by two steel frame and reinforced concrete tower cores, eleven and thirteen stories high; the "parts" were 144 prefabricated steel capsules, assembled in a factory that normally manufactured shipping containers, plugged into the two towers at the rate of five to eight per day of construction. Each capsule was outfitted with a unit bath, desk, air conditioner, and television and audio equipment that were prefabricated and assembled in advance at the factory. The capsules were attached to the core independently, with only four high-tension bolts, so that they could be easily removed or replaced as the function of the building evolved. The capsules were independent spaces, 2.5 x 2.5 x 4 meters in dimension, designed to provide a hotel space or pied-à-terre in central Tokyo for travelling businessmen, although the architect noted that, in the future, the capsules could be given special functions such as living room, kitchen, bedroom, etc., and linked through access doors to provide a more spacious apartment.[23]

For Kurokawa, the capsule form was more than a design expedient but rather was a central facet of a comprehensive architectural philosophy and vision for the future of society. In his "Capsule Declaration," published in 1969, Kurokawa wrote that the capsule form is emblematic of a newly evolving, nomadic modern lifestyle of "*Homo movens*." "People will gradually lose their desire for property such as land and big houses," Kurokawa asserts, "and will begin to value having the opportunity and the means for free movement. The capsule means emancipation of a building from land and signals the advent of an age of moving architecture."[24] Like a spaceship surrounding an astronaut, the capsule is an "environment particular to itself."[25] Far from being an anonymous or homogenous space, for Kurokawa the capsule will be an expression of the individualism of its occupant—a "highly independent shelter," "determined by the free will of individuals," where "the inhabitant can fully develop his individuality."[26] In practical terms, Kurokawa envisioned a "selective mass-production

Figure 3. Kurokawa Kishō, Nakagin Capsule Tower (1972). Photograph copyright Vincent D. Feldman.

system" whereby capsule interiors would be broken down into functional units, such as toilet, bath, and kitchen units, and individuals could customize their capsules by selecting and combining these units.[27] Furthermore, the advent of capsule living will stimulate the development of a new family system, described as the antithesis to the traditional patriarchy—an association of autonomous individuals, whereby "family relationships between a couple, parents, and children will be expressed in terms of the state of docking of many capsules of individuals' spaces."[28] Finally, as will be discussed further in chapter 5, for Kurokawa, the capsule is also "cyborg architecture," in which man, machine, and space form a "new organic body."[29]

Scale, Megastructure, and Megalopolis

Though perhaps more abstract than the Metabolists' writings and designs for "move-nets" and "capsules," a particularly salient feature of the Metabolists' works for this study is their conception of spatial and temporal scale, which is often modular, organic, and capable of extending far beyond the confines of a single building. The major retrospective exhibition, *Metabolism: The City of the Future*, organized at the Mori Art Museum in 2011, highlighted the importance of "Asada's Scale," a scheme developed by the Tange Lab member and Metabolist mentor Asada Takashi.[30] Asada's Scale was an attempt to envision and calibrate the range of space from subatomic particles to galaxies, based on the exponential increase or decrease of the unit of the size of an adult human. The exhibition notes argued that Asada's Scale prefigured the intention announced in the Metabolists' manifesto to seek commonalities between processes of growth and decay through a vast range of scales, from molecular to galactic. Indeed, Kawazoe's opening statement for the 1960 Metabolist manifesto began with the assertion, "We regard human society as a vital process—a continuous development from atom to nebula."[31] Significantly, Asada himself participated in relief activities immediately following the atomic bombing of Hiroshima. According to the commentary on Asada's Scale in the Mori exhibition catalog, "The fact that the micro collision of atoms could blast away a whole city on the macro level had a great influence on Asada."[32] This comment points to the significance of Asada's Scale not just in encompassing the vast range of sizes between subatomic particles and galaxies but in foreshadowing the discovery of similarities and interrelations between units of widely varying scales.[33]

In his "Metapolis: The Hishino Plan" ("Teijū tan'i keikaku no rinen to hōhō"), published in 1967, Kurokawa Kishō employed exponentially varying metabolic temporal cycles or "time modules" operating in different parameters of urban space, or "space modules," thereby stressing the need for dynamic plans that accommodated multiscalar modules of both time and space.[34] Examples would include the differing temporality or metabolic cycle associated with spaces for living (which might be the relatively short span of a human generation, measured by a "time module" of 25 years) versus different temporalities in the spaces for association and monumental cultural facilities (which should be planned for multiple human generations, in time modules of 125 and 625 years, respectively) and spaces of nature (whose "time module" is posited at 15,000 years). Kurokawa's scheme thus stressed the need for dynamic plans that accommodated multiscalar modules of both time and space.[35] Just as in the Metabolist manifesto statement of Kawazoe, Kurokawa references the cosmic as well as the molecular scale: on the cosmic scale, he defines the metabolism of cities and architecture as a "control mechanism" for both entropic and negentropic processes, which might not only seek order out of chaos (negentropy) but also sometimes seek "a shift to a more complicated, dynamic, and uncertain state from a state of fixed classical order," concluding that, "just as the universe as an open system accepts new stars and creates what Ludwig Boltzmann called the 'state of disequilibrium,' we can be rescued from the ever-increasing disorder and cold if cities and buildings have an open structure."[36]

The Metabolists also responded to a new international vocabulary of urban scale, applied to existing cities as well as urban planning and futuristic visions, that was emerging in the 1960s. In 1957, geographer Jean Gottmann applied the term *megalopolis* to describe the continuous stretch of urban and suburban areas from Boston to Washington, D.C., which he presented as a new "super-metropolitan" phenomenon beyond the sum of its parts that served as a "hinge" of the national economy, proposing that "megalopolis heralds a new era in the distribution of habitat and economic activities."[37] Greek urban planner Constantinos Doxiadis extrapolated on this idea in the following decade with his idea of the ecumenopolis, in which the megalopolises of the world would coalesce as a "continuous system" in the future into a single planetary city.[38]

Metabolist theorists applied this vocabulary to the Japanese archipelago in their works. In his 1966 book, *Nihon rettō no shōraizō* (The future image of the Japanese archipelago), Tange Kenzō not only outlined the characteristics of the "Tokaidō Megalopolis" emerging between Tokyo and Osaka but also applied clearly Metabolist vocabulary to his diagnosis, referring to the Japanese archipelago as an "organic structure" *(yūkitai kōsei)*. "I would like to posit that Japan is still in its childhood, when its metabolism *(taisha)* is intense," Tange wrote. "Or perhaps we should view it as still in the prior incubation phase. Therefore, I think that its cellular division and metabolism *(shinchin taisha)*, and the circulation and flow that result from that, show us that, on the whole, it is headed in the correct direction of development."[39] Furthermore, Tange posited that the growth of an information- and communications-based society would establish the distributed "nervous system" capable of transforming the archipelago's urban areas from a megalopolis to an ecumenopolis. Similarly, Kurokawa deployed the concepts of megalopolis and ecumenopolis extensively in his 1967 Hishino plan cited above. Just as he posits exponentially increasing "time modules," Kurokawa identifies an exponential set of "space modules," from house, through "metapolis," metropolis, megalopolis, ecumenopolis, and finally a yet-to-be-realized "cosmopolis." Kurokawa conceives his Hishino "metapolis" (a plan for a "New Town" site near Nagoya) as a "super-urban unit" designed to function through cybernetic mechanisms as a working part of the global ecumenopolis.

The Metabolist attention to "scale" can also be seen in the sheer size of many of their proposed projects—in their attention to the "megastructure" as well as the "megalopolis."[40] The ambition of such projects was often framed in terms of breaking the logjam of conventional, purportedly ineffective urban planning, and to bypass the chaos of dense streets, zoning regulations, and convoluted land ownership issues, seeking solutions outside of the existing urban framework.[41] For example, in the introduction to his Tower-Shaped Community proposal for the Metabolist manifesto, Kikutake wrote of the "state of confusion and paralysis in metropolitan cities" and singled out Tokyo in particular as a diseased body: "Tokyo, a huge city, is worn out with bad sickness. She has lost the proper control of city, because of her mammoth like scale. . . . The limitation of the horizontal city has far passed over from the ability of function of transportation and the living standard. The new harmful tissue like cancer is spreading over the city."[42] Thus, Kikutake proposed to transpose this horizontal sprawl onto the vertical "tower-shaped" community, while the surplus space freed by this vertical development could be planted with trees to freshen the air and the roads that formerly "wriggled around among the lots" could be plotted in straight lines connecting tower communities.[43] As described in the introduction, another of Kikutake's proposals, the Marine City, opened the possibility of urban development beyond the limitations of the land itself, through floating industrial cities that could attach themselves to existing industrial port cities or even move across the open water. Indeed, floating cities and megastructures of varied designs were projects to which Kikutake returned repeatedly over the course of his career.[44]

Kawazoe, as well, promoted the concept of "artificial land," which would serve as a consolidated, planned basis for individual habitations, thereby liberating the remaining land as public property or allowing it to revert to its natural state. Through such expedients, Kawazoe speculated, "it would be no idle dream to think that Tokyo would revert to its past form as the Musashino Plain, and that the people would be able to delight in natural woods and brooks."[45] Thus both Kikutake and Kawazoe embraced the seeming paradox of liberating the natural environment through the construction of huge, highly artificial structures. Meanwhile, Isozaki Arata proposed a different solution to urban sprawl: building on top of the existing city with his City in the Air (1961). This series of interlocking megastructures would rise above the existing city grid on a set of pillar-shaped cores, each a mere 10 square meters in diameter. As Zhongjie Lin describes, "When the cores rose above the 31-meter level, that is, the skyline [i.e., the former height restriction] of old Tokyo, cantilevered members began to grow horizontally out from the cores in various directions. These cantilevers extended useable spaces for housing and offices, forming self-contained human habitats in the air. The whole image was like a few gigantic trees growing up from a dense forest of shrubs."[46]

In March 1966, a number of such megastructural proposals were collected, imaginatively assigned to specific locations in the Tokyo area, and depicted in utopian fashion through lyrical watercolor and ink illustrations in the popular illustrated magazine *Taiyō*. These include Tange's plan for Tokyo Bay, Ōtaka Masato's urban subcenter built on artificial ground in Shinjuku (developed in collaboration with Maki Fumihiko), Kikutake's Tower-Shaped Community in Shibuya, Kurokawa's Helix City situated in the central Marunouchi district (Plate 3), and Kurokawa's prefab housing blocks integrated into a green "garden city" environment in the suburban "new town" of Tama Hills (Plate 4). This special magazine feature, appearing roughly at a midpoint between the World Design Conference of 1960 and the 1970 Osaka Expo, presented many of the ideas of Metabolism to a general Japanese audience. Reprising and extending the lineup of contributors to *Metabolism 1960*, the special feature included an interpretive essay by Kawazoe Noboru, layout design by Awazu Kiyoshi, and artwork by professional illustrators Terashima Ryūichi and Yamamoto Tadayoshi.[47]

Perhaps one of the most dramatic, and certainly one of the most detailed, proposals to emerge in the Metabolist era was Tange Kenzō's Plan for Tokyo 1960, which offered a comprehensive plan for extending the city of Tokyo over Tokyo Bay. It was introduced to the Japanese public in a special broadcast on the NHK national television network on New Year's Day 1961. Nevertheless, Tange's was not the first proposal for large-scale development in Tokyo Bay. Responding to crowded conditions in the existing city and seeking new opportunities for economic development, the private think tank and lobbying group Industrial Planning Committee (IPC, Sangyō Keikaku Kaigi) had already proposed a Neo-Tokyo Plan in 1959, in which fully two-thirds of Tokyo Bay—600 million square miles—would be covered with land freed by the underground explosion of a nuclear bomb in Chiba Prefecture (across the bay from Tokyo) and used to house industrial and commercial facilities, a new airport, residential areas and green space, and a new expressway and rail route across the mouth of the bay.[48] This, in turn, stimulated a number of alternative plans for Tokyo Bay development, including plans by Kikutake, Kurokawa, and Ōtaka Masato, as well as Tange.[49] In contrast to the IPC's Neo-Tokyo Plan, Tange's Plan for Tokyo 1960 proposed to preserve the waters of the bay itself while extending the city across the bay not by conventional (or nuclear-generated) landfill but by building a new "linear city," an elegant looped chain of elevated expressways, infrastructure, and civic buildings bridging across the bay, feeding out at right angles to a grid of secondary freeways that were punctuated at regular intervals by A-shaped megastructures, situated on a system of cores and pilotis anchored on the bay floor. These tiered, tent-like structures would serve as artificial ground for residents to build their own houses (Plates 5 and 6).[50]

The Plan for Tokyo 1960, however, was not just a plan for the development of Tokyo Bay. Rather, responding to the rise of the automobile and the problems of urban congestion, and imagining a new national economy based on more efficient circulation of people and information, Tange proposed to change the entire orientation of the capital city. In an information- and service-based economy, Tange argued, "the circulation that occurs before and after production, as opposed to the production itself, is becoming a more and more important part of the economic process."[51] Thus, from the congested former castle town laid out in a series of concentric rings, Tange's plan would reorient Tokyo around a new linear axis, in which the expressway system crossing the bay would extend across the core of the old city and eventually as far west as Mount Fuji. Drawing an organic metaphor from the repertoire of Metabolism, Tange laid out the stages of development of this linear city in an extended comparison to the growth of a spine and nervous system of a vertebrate animal.[52]

Tange's plan was not adapted by the Japanese government and, like many of the most ambitious Metabolist proposals, was never realized. Nevertheless, his bold scheme had a major impact on architectural circles both within and outside of Japan. In his book *Megastructure: Urban Futures of the Recent Past* (1973), the influential British architecture critic Reyner Banham praised Tange's plan as "one of the most heroic visions of town planning to appear in this century," marking a "definitive break with all previous urban design concepts, however vast," and "a work of art in its own right that can be left to stand up for itself as a monument to a particular intersection of time and national culture."[53] Other commentators, however, including architects Maki Fumihiko, Peter Smithson, and Christopher Alexander, criticized Tange's design as inflexible, overly hierarchical, and aggrandizing of the authoritarian role of planners and bureaucrats—as Smithson bluntly put it, "centralized, absolutist, authoritarian."[54] While Tange's plan stands as an early vision of the development of Japan as a post-industrial, information-based economy, the debate over the plan anticipated subsequent debates over bureaucratic management and control in such a society.

Architecture and Fiction 1: Komatsu and Kawazoe

Since Metabolist theory emphasized process over product, it could be argued that the traditional architectural plan or model—or even a constructed building at any point of time—could never be the final or best representation of Metabolist architectural ideas. As Kawazoe writes, "Our proposals are nothing more than mere segments of an image, or else mere suggestions about the directions and the methods to be taken. There can be no 'final point' at which the city will one day arrive in its development."[55] Rather, by stressing the processes of becoming, transforming, and even disintegrating, the Metabolists introduced a narrative element into their architectural theory, and indeed several figures associated with Metabolism, including Kawazoe and Isozaki, used narrative literary forms to express their ideas. In the remainder of this chapter, I will examine several written narratives that highlight the architectural ideas of the Metabolists and their peers.

With the nascent development of information technology and computer modeling, one form that architecture and city planning could take, as an alternative to the conventional drawing, model, or urban "master plan," was that of computer simulation. This possibility especially intrigued Isozaki Arata. Isozaki imagined that even the most utopian, fantastic urban schemes could be tested against reality conditions on a simulation program, and the results could usefully inform the planning process. With his typical provocative rhetoric, and referring obliquely to Kikutake's Marine City as well as his own City in the Air, Isozaki described such a simulation process as follows:

> Now impractical, fantastic city models can be produced only through the systems process. And, even if such a model is totally disparate and incompatible with urban reality, once it has been expressed as a model, simulation becomes possible. This means that, through computers, its possibilities become linked with the possibility of flow into the actual city. Under such conditions, considerations of totality, creation of visual order, and

> formal unity lose significance. But all kinds of cities can be planned: City on the Sea, City in the Air, Labyrinth City, City for the Dead, and so on. In the process of expressing these ideas in models and manipulating them so they overlap with the real city, the designer acts as a pilot and must not be swayed by his own fixed, preconceived concepts, since he is dealing with constant mutual response between reality and hypothesis. His city-designing resembles push-button warfare.[56]

While computer simulation is one way of introducing the temporal element into architectural schemes, several architects associated with Metabolism were also drawn to literary forms as an alternative method of expressing their ideas. Like computer modeling, literary forms can allow for a process of simulation, which can include the meeting of base assumptions of reality with an element of the unfamiliar—in terms of Darko Suvin's well-known theory of science fiction, the introduction of the "novum" to "the author's and implied reader's norm of reality." Suvin defines the novum as a novelty or innovation that is "'totalizing' in the sense that it entails a change of the whole universe of the tale," thus becoming the key variable interacting with the given environment in a future simulation.[57]

In addition to narrative simulation, literature can also offer elements of social critique, satire, or absurdity not usually associated with conventional forms of architectural presentation. Isozaki resorted to literary forms at several points in his career, including the oracular, poem-like text "Fuka katei" (Incubation process), published in the art journal *Bijutsu techō* in April 1962 (discussed in chapter 2), and the nearly Dadaistic parable "Toshi hakaigyō, KK" ("City Demolition Industry, Inc."), published in the architecture journal *Shinkenchiku* in September of that same year.[58]

Outside of the works by architects and architecture critics, science fiction author Komatsu Sakyō's work of juvenile fiction *Kūchū toshi 008* (City in the air 008, 1969), written during the period when the author was collaborating with Kawazoe, Kurokawa, and other Metabolist architects in the production of the Osaka Expo, is perhaps the most straightforward representation of Metabolist architecture in literature. The novel features a utopian description of a twenty-first-century lifestyle in which mobile housing units plug into a helix-shaped megastructure surrounded by greenery and clean air. In footnotes to the main text, Komatsu specifically references Kurokawa's Helix City Plan for Tokyo 1961 and also introduces concepts developed in Kikutake's "move-nets" as presented in *Metabolism 1960*.

Komatsu's work foregrounds a concern for the loss of green space through urban sprawl in postwar Japan and offers an optimistic vision of the future in which the young protagonist moves with his family from the crowded old city to his new plug-in home on the helix city (named Aozora or "Blue Sky"), where "the sun's light, clean air, the blue sky, and green trees belong to everyone."[59] The story is told through the eyes of its youthful protagonist and evokes a sense of wonder as the boy and his sister explore the gigantic building and its surroundings. Later chapters also explore familiar science fiction tropes of robots, moving sidewalks, "air cars," rockets, and visits to an underwater city, a space station, and the moon, each chapter with footnotes explaining the current state of science and engineering underlying the novel's futuristic vision. A stop-motion animation version of *City in the Air 008* was broadcast on NHK from 1969 to 1970. As architectural historians Igarashi Tarō and Iso Tatsuo argue, this broadcast, together with the 1970 Osaka Expo itself, had a strong impact on a generation of Japanese children's imagination of the bright future ahead.[60] Nevertheless, the novel's utopian vision, clearly tailored for a young audience, provides a striking contrast to Komatsu's apocalyptic tales such as *Nihon apacchi zoku* (The Japan Apache tribe, 1964), *Virus: The Day of Resurrection* (1964), and *Japan Sinks* (1973), which will be discussed in the upcoming chapters.

The apocalyptic themes in Komatsu's fiction were anticipated by a short narrative, "Dai-Tōkyō saigo no hi" (The last days of greater Tokyo), which Kawazoe Noboru contributed to the journal *Kenchiku bunka* in 1961. In the introduction to this piece, Kawazoe describes the work as a "history of the future in the form of a science fiction story" (kūsō kagaku shōsetsu modoki no miraishi). This narrative made explicit reference to a number of the Metabolists' proposals, including an expansion over Tokyo Bay along the lines of Tange's Plan for Tokyo 1960 and the development of floating city structures reminiscent of Kikutake's Marine City. Kawazoe divides his future history into several phases, each of which is distinguished by the interaction of social and environmental factors and an architectural *novum*. In the end, the natural environment itself becomes the *novum*, providing an apocalyptic conclusion to Kawazoe's narrative.

The first phase encountered by the city in Kawazoe's story is a "period of struggle with government" (1961–65). Echoing the recent history of massive demonstrations against the U.S.–Japan Security Treaty, in this scenario student demonstrations throughout the city take advantage of the capital's vulnerability to traffic congestion, leading to gridlock and urban paralysis, and gradual realization of the need for urban planning solutions. This leads to the second stage, the "period of struggle with technology" (1965–80), in which technological solutions are sought, such as advanced electronic systems to monitor and control flows of traffic through the city, as well as the construction of giant parking structures outside of an urban core reserved primarily for pedestrians, such as those proposed by Louis Kahn for Philadelphia in the late 1950s.[61] Toward the latter half of this phase, building on the increased credibility of urban planning solutions, architects respond to continued urban growth and begin to create a new grid of megastructures over Tokyo Bay, similar to that proposed by Tange in his Plan for Tokyo 1960.

These innovations are tested by a series of natural disasters in the third phase, "period of struggle with nature" (1980–2010), including an earthquake that destroys much of the old city and reveals the vulnerabilities of its electronic control systems, as well as a typhoon that damages much of the new city built over the bay. Furthermore, increased seismological and volcanic activity worldwide compounds the buildup of carbon gasses in the atmosphere caused by human activity and leads to a gradual rise in the oceans' water level. This prompts new interest in Kikutake's proposals for cities over the water, and floating parks, stadiums, and factories begin to appear. At the same time, a belated understanding of the importance of the environment and appreciation of the role of water in sustaining human communities lead to the establishments of new parks, green zones, canals, and waterways across the old city. However, the gradual advance of water over the contours of the city cannot be reversed, and by the final phase, "period of spiritual struggle" (2010–50), the residents of Tokyo come to realize that the city must in large part be abandoned.

Thus, Kawazoe unveils a prescient vision of the capital's vulnerability to climate change brought on to a combination of natural processes (increased volcanic activity) and man-made factors (the accumulation of carbon gases in the atmosphere). Kawazoe writes:

> This fate did not belong to Tokyo alone: New York and London were the same. The three great cities of ten million people born to human civilization in the 20th Century all stood on the precipice of extinction. International conferences were convened one after another. Until this point, some geophysicists held the optimistic view that as carbon gases built up, plant life would also increase and would absorb these gasses, and the metabolic balance of the earth would somehow allow it to avoid catastrophe, but that metabolic balance had been destroyed by humans. In other words, just as the three great cities were the product of 20th Century Civilization, so they would have to bear on their backs the sins of the 20th Century.[62]

Kawazoe's essay not only adapts the science fiction form to present a chilling early vision of the effects of climate change, it offers a kind of "meta-metabolist" narrative in which successive architectural "solutions" are placed in a dynamic feedback circuit with the Earth's environmental systems.[63]

Architecture and Fiction 2: Isozaki and Itō

For Kawazoe, the narrative form allows him to explore temporality in a way that a conventional essay or presentation of architectural plans could not; but nevertheless, the narrative form is still used to convey a series of concrete architectural ideas. By contrast, in "City Demolition Industry, Inc." from 1962, the narrative allows Isozaki Arata to move outside of the realms of architectural drawing or even expository writing to unleash a Dadaistic metacommentary on the position of the architect and the practices of architecture and urban planning. (Like Kawazoe's "The Last Days of Greater Tokyo" as well as Itō Toyoo's text below, Isozaki's story might be said to be less "pure" narrative fiction than a hybrid of architectural essay and fiction.) Among other subversive ideas, Isozaki's story suggests that the faithful implementation of city planning, the proposal of utopian urban ideas, or the building of massive housing blocks would in fact be effective means of destroying the city's functionality and self-image. "Put city planning into practice," the narrator advises, "and you will find it an excellent means for throwing the city into turmoil and stultifying its energy."[64]

The story is narrated in the first person. The narrator (later identified as "Arata") tells of meeting his alter ego "S." (later identified as "Sin" *[Shin]*, an alternative reading for the same Chinese character as "Arata"). S. is a former professional hit man who gave up his profession when, after looking at daily statistics of urban traffic accidents, he concluded that hit men cannot compete with the city itself in its efficiency in committing murder. Therefore, he has founded a new company, the eponymous "City Demolition Industry, Inc.," in order to destroy his rival, the city, and to establish a "civilization in which elegant, pleasant and humanistic murder can be carried out easily."[65] S. shares with the narrator the prospectus for his new urban demolition business, which outlines the methods for destroying the city. These include: (1) physical destruction of the city, "using all possible means including human power, dynamite, atomic and hydrogen bombs"; (2) destruction of the city's functions, carried out by "the aggravation of traffic confusion through the systematic abolition of traffic signals, etc., the encouragement of illegal construction, the dropping of poison into water reservoirs, the disturbance of communication networks, the total abolition of the house number system," and "the immediate and complete enforcement of all legal city planning provisions"; and (3) the "destruction of images," which paradoxically entails "the encouragement of proposals for Utopia city planning in the future, the enforcement of city improvement and a solution to the housing shortage by the mass-construction of public corporation-style residences," and "the elimination of all calamities in the cities including traffic accidents."[66]

In the remainder of the story, the narrator and S. argue over various aspects of the proposal, including whether cities are merely abstract ideas and whether or not the physical destruction of the city is even possible, debating the examples of Tokyo and Hiroshima, which were turned to ashes only eighteen years before but had been resurrected like a pair of phoenixes. The narrator expresses some jealousy toward S., who, since he is a killer rather than a planner or architect, can carry out concrete action, while as an architect "I make concrete proposals, concrete countermeasures, and improvements on them," yet "I am made to feel ever more keenly the impossibility of putting my proposals into practice."[67] Thus Isozaki uses this fictional medium to express his professional misgivings and ambivalences, as well a darkly satirical vision of the entire enterprise of city planning, less than two years after he had participated in one of the most ambitious urban planning exercises of all, Tange Kenzō laboratory's Plan for Tokyo 1960.[68] At the same time, the story's unresolved, underlying theme of destruction versus construction will be addressed in different forms in Isozaki's other works, including the poem "Incubation Process" and the photomontage "Hiroshima Destroyed Again in the Future," in chapter 2.

Roughly ten years later, an architect from the next generation, Itō Toyoo (born 1941), would also use a hybrid essay and fictional medium to announce his appearance as an independent voice on the architectural scene and to express his criticisms and ambivalences about the current state of architecture and the city. Itō worked for Kikutake Kiyonori Architects from 1965 to 1969 and founded his own studio, Urban Robot (a.k.a. URBOT), in 1971. That same year, he published the essay "The Logic of Uselessness," which architect Thomas Daniell describes as a "theoretical statement, practical manifesto, cultural diagnosis, science-fiction homage, satirical short story and implicit critique of his peers and predecessors."[69] The essay/story describes the Urban Robot office's first three architectural designs, URBOT-001, -002, and -003, as autonomous agents spawned by the city: capsule-like shelters shelled in aluminum, which become independent, sentient protagonists in Itō's narrative.

Although the text never mentions Kikutake, Kurokawa, or other Metabolist architects by name (instead referencing Archigram's Plug-in City and the California vernacular designs of Charles Moore and Joseph Esherick), the URBOTs and their philosophical quandaries as narrated in the story seem to be in large part a reaction to Kurokawa's "Capsule Declaration" and ongoing Nakagin Capsule Tower project. In addition to borrowing the basic architectural form of the capsule itself, as well as its implied inhabitant of a highly independent individual or nuclear family, Itō's text engages with Kurokawa's conception of the capsule as "cyborg architecture" that would be equipped to "transmit, receive and feed back information at any time,"[70] as well as the conceptions of the computerized future city promoted at the Osaka Expo a year earlier:

> From what URBOT could gather, if developments continued to extend in the same direction, Tokyo's fate would be to take on the form of a "mechanistoria": a city endowed with vast, extensive management mechanisms under the perfect control of a "town brain" comprising large-scale computers and robots equipped with all manners of information devices.
>
> There within dwelling capsules that acted as information terminals, each individual person would have sex, eat and sleep.[71]

However, while feeling the pull of such a conception, Itō's URBOT-001 ultimately resists the urge to incorporate any such informational devices:

> If URBOT were able to function as an elite next-generation architecture—one of a group of competent urban robots, acting as a terminal within an individual dwelling as well as serving as a community information portal—this would result in an integrated human-machine system. . . . However, while sensing the appeal of having powerful information devices installed within himself, URBOT was hesitant. It was similar to the desire to avoid becoming a businessman in a major corporation. His hesitancy was not an ideological confusion arising from being inserted in an enormous administrative apparatus, but was provoked by the non-mechanical, non-technological, irrational emotions that roiled within him. . . . In his eyes, the image of a "mechanistoria" informational city was nothing more than the collective illusion of a homogeneous world, where as he could only feel reality in those spaces that transmitted the warmth of human breath and corporeality.[72]

Thus, Itō presents us with the paradox of a potentially cybernetic "Urban Robot" who refuses to plug into the city's information systems; instead, the URBOT is described as a dysfunctional unit with "recessive heredity" whose existence is based on the "logic of uselessness."

In narrating the evolution of the URBOT series, Itō's text makes explicit reference to Stanisław Lem's 1964 science fiction novel *The Invincible*. In Lem's novel, the crew of an interstellar spaceship encounters a planet that has been taken over by small, autonomous, self-replicating machines, capable of swarm-like mass behavior. The crew uncovers a history of evolutionary struggle between two rival "species" of autonomous machines, or in Lem's terms, a "necroevolution" of inanimate matter, of which the swarming microbots are the apparent victor.[73] Itō draws a parallel between the imagery of Lem's world and "the incredible ongoing expansion of the bizarre urban future that is named Tokyo," as follows:

> Comprising a countless number of uniform cuboid cells, it [Tokyo] gives the impression of an eternal battle between vertically extending steel-framed skyscrapers and low-rise concrete dwellings covering the ground surface. This battle ends with the victory of the skyscrapers, equipped with advanced control mechanisms and innumerable capsules clinging to their scattered, soaring steel frames, like an abundant grape harvest spilling from overflowing shelves. Below is a concrete desert of crumbling white sand endlessly stirred by a freezing wind, the remnants of abandoned capsules buried in the sand like rotting fruit. While people contort their bodies within the cramped capsules, encircled by all manner of information terminals, peals of eerie vibrato laughter may be heard between the thickets of metal trees.[74]

In this disturbing vision, combining realistic observation and fantasy, contemporary Tokyo is already a dystopian science fiction futurescape. Itō's essay/story ends with the necroevolution of his own URBOT units, having taken over the city in a bizarre capsule apocalypse:

> Independent URBOT-003 units are buried in the desert-like vacant lots of Tokyo. As if bubonic plague had struck the city, the scene is of a spreading contagion weaving through the crevices between skyscrapers, covering the roads, covering the plazas, covering the rooftops, covering the expressways. I want you to imagine the appearance of innumerable home-sized capsules with metallic gold cladding emitting a lingering, dull light at sunset in smog-covered Tokyo.[75]

Rather than helping humans to survive in an apocalyptic environment, modern architecture in Itō's fantasy *is* the apocalypse. His dystopian vision is of an entirely artificial, denuded, and polluted landscape populated by self-replicating architectural capsules—far indeed from Komatsu's story, derived from the Metabolist architects' most utopian visions, of architecture coexisting with nature in the park-like city of Blue Sky.

Thus, not only through drawings, architectural models, and built projects, but also through their writings spanning essay and fiction, the architects and writers in the Metabolist network produced a fascinating range of architectural visions—from the utopianism of Kikutake's Tower-Shaped Community and Marine City, Tange's Plan for Tokyo 1960, or the plug-in Helix City Komatsu borrows from Kikutake and Kurokawa, to the deadpan, nihilistic critiques of Isozaki, to the apocalyptic visions of Kawazoe and Itō. I will explore the tension between utopianism and apocalypse in the works of Komatsu and Isozaki further in the upcoming chapters. As for Itō, despite his exclusion of informational devices from his Urban Robots in his opening manifesto (as well as his early built works such as the White U House of 1976), the younger architect later became known for his writings on "architecture for the simulated city" and his ambitious, sensitive incorporation of information technology in such signature architectural works as the Tower of the Winds (1986) and the Sendai Mediatheque (2001), as I will discuss in chapter 5.

2 Ruined Cities

Isozaki Arata and Komatsu Sakyō

> As I stood amidst the ruins of Nagoya, the third largest city in Japan, there was nothing but scorched earth for as far as I could see. In contrast to the desolate surroundings, the blue of the mountain range on the horizon was dazzling to the eyes.
>
> . . . I belong to the fourth generation [of modern Japanese architects], whose point of origin is the defeat and destruction in the war. For this reason we are sometimes called the Charred Ruins School. In the heart of all the members of this generation are the traumatic images of events that took place when we were in our formative childhood years: the sudden, tragic destruction of Hiroshima and Nagasaki by atomic bombs and the virtually total reduction of cities and buildings to ashes.
>
> **—Kurokawa Kishō, "The Philosophy of Metabolism"**

> The things that might have served as a prototype were reduced to rubble by the B-29 incendiary bombs of World War II. Everything I had considered enduring and immutable in architecture was obliterated, one building after the other. The ruins were unlike the romantic ruins of European cities. Those places were in their present condition long before I ever saw them. The war ruins were created before my very eyes, instantaneously. But, even destroyed, the cities persisted.
>
> **—Isozaki Arata, "Invisible City"**

Taken from central texts in each architect's oeuvre of written works,[1] the quotations above point to the importance of "ruins" to the personal mythology of two key figures of the 1960s architectural avant-garde. The "ruins" here, needless to say, are not the forgotten vestiges of an ancient civilization but the charred remains of daily life as it was lived on the Japanese home territories before and during the Second World War. Such witnessing of the devastation wrought by the atomic bombings of Hiroshima and Nagasaki, as well as the B-29 incendiary bombings that leveled vast portions of major cities such as

Tokyo, Osaka, and Nagoya in the final stages of the Second World War, is offered as a primal, foundational experience for the two architects and as a key to understanding their works to come.

Similarly, author Komatsu Sakyō has offered the experience of witnessing the fire-bombings of Japanese cities, as well as the enduring afterimage of the "ruins" themselves, as a primal foundational scene influencing his subsequent works and worldview:

> What of that bizarrely pure and simple scene of ruins, with its overwhelming sense of reality? It was like an absolute scene of the end of time, space, and history. And even now, perhaps those ruins are the only absolute reality, and the many works of humans and the prosperity that followed—expressways, skyscrapers, the din of crowded commercial districts, the countless modes of transportation and the pleasure-seeking of men and women—perhaps these are only a mirage, floating on top of those absolute ruins?[2]

With these remarks, Komatsu frames the viewing of ruins not only as a formative personal experience but as a world-historical event and even metaphysical experience, casting a shadow over subsequent postwar "reality." As I will discuss below, Komatsu's positing of the war ruins as an "absolute reality" transcending the works of postwar reconstruction offers an important insight into Komatsu's thematic and methodological predilections in his science fiction and disaster narratives.

Architect Kurokawa Kishō's reference to the "Charred Ruins School" in his remarks above also links his generation's architectural innovations to the literary work of the *yakeato-ha,* the "Burnt-Out Ruins School," or *yakeato sedai,* "Generation of Charred Ruins." This "school" or "generation" emerged as a literary-historical construct in the late 1960s after being first proposed by Nosaka Akiyuki (1930–2015), best known for his tragic fictionalized depiction of the incendiary bombings of the Kōbe area, *Grave of the Fireflies* (*Hotaru no haka,* 1967).[3] A common definition of the Charred Ruins School as those belonging to the Showa "single-digit" generation—that is, born between 1926 and 1934—would include Komatsu (1931–2011), Isozaki (born 1931), and Kurokawa (1934–2007).[4] This was a generation that spent their formative years under the regime of total war, yet were generally too young to be sent to the front, and who experienced the end of the war and occupation as adolescents. One could say that the experience of witnessing "charred ruins" constitutes a generational origin myth, articulated in various ways by Komatsu, Isozaki, and Kurokawa. However, what I will be concerned with in this chapter is less the traumatic experience of the war and its role in a generation's personal mythology but instead the importance of "ruins" themselves as a philosophical category and a source of creativity to Isozaki, Komatsu, and their associates.

Of course, the contemplation of ruins has also played an important role in European visual culture, literature, and thought, as Isozaki alludes to when he cites the "Romantic" ruins of European cities. From the rediscovery of classical ruins in the Baroque and Neoclassical eras, such as the Roman ruins painted by Salvator Rosa (1615–1673) or etched by Giovanni Battista Piranesi (1720–1778), to the medieval ruins treasured in the Romantic era, such as Tintern Abbey as depicted by J. M. W. Turner (1775–1851), the contemplation of ruins in modern European culture has often been a means of meditating on the relationship between past and present, the rise and fall of empires, or the tension between the constructive will of humans and the natural forces of time and decay.[5] Yet, as Isozaki's remarks suggest, the discourse of the "burnt-out ruins" school centers not on ruins of antiquity but on contemporary ruins, "created," writes Isozaki, "before my very eyes, instantaneously." For members of the Charred Ruins School of Japan, then, the contemplation of ruins involves not so much a mediation on the passage of time and the incremental processes of entropy but the possibility of modern urban landscapes and lived experience transforming into ashes and rubble overnight.

Moreover, in contrast to the massive crumbling stones typical of Romantic ruins, Komatsu notes how few physical remnants remained after the atomic and incendiary bombings:

> Many people will remember this—how truly "nothing" the charred remains of Japan were. Particularly, we should pay attention to how, before the war, [Japanese] cities were almost all made of wood, unlike the concrete architecture of today. Every form in the city was reduced to smoke and flames, and disappeared into the atmosphere without a trace. No vestige remained of tradition, culture, or everyday life. As far as the eye

> could see, you could only make out the faint pattern of roads through charred earth. Perhaps it is so difficult to recognize these as "ruins" because the city of wood is so easily rebuilt, or so easily absorbed into nature. This is clearly different from a city of stone such as Machu Picchu, which survived for four hundred years on an unknown mountaintop, or the adobe buildings of the ancient Orient, or the stone temples of the Parthenon.[6]

The ephemerality possessed even by the ruins themselves, as figured in Komatsu's remarks above, points to a significant paradox in the writings of the charred ruins generation. On the one hand, for Komatsu, ruins are the "absolute" or "original" reality, a concept that he will explore in both personal and metaphysical terms in his essay "Haikyo no kūkan bunmei" (Civilization of the space of ruins, 1964). On the other hand, the survival of ruins is extremely precarious. The ruins barely exist as physical traces; they are easily rebuilt and easily absorbed into nature. Isozaki's remarks point to a similar paradox: "Even destroyed," he writes, "the cities persisted." Isozaki continues by citing the example of Hiroshima: "It was virtually completely annihilated. But not long after the atom bomb, its urban entities began to reemerge. Today it is a bigger city than ever before."[7]

For Komatsu and Isozaki, then, ruins are both absolute and transcendent and precarious and invisible: flickering in and out of phase, overlaid on top of the alternate reality of economic recovery and newly emergent cities. They are both the past and the future: formative personal experience and blueprint for an "always already" future apocalypse. Ruins are also a generative site of creative energy: for Isozaki, ruins are the "incubation mechanism" for future cities, for Komatsu, they are the source of a vital, viral dynamism personified by the protagonists of his early novel *Nihon apacchi zoku* (The Japan Apache tribe, 1964). However, even as they are a source of creative energy, ruins are also an apocalyptic destiny: As Isozaki writes, "Future cities are themselves ruins." For Komatsu, superimposing new ruins on the reconstituted cities of the present and near future, through the varied apocalyptic devices of mutant insurrection, bioweaponry catastrophes, nuclear war, seismic disasters, climate change, and alien-encounter anomalies, was a kind of life's work. After a brief overview of the role of "ruins" in Isozaki's architectural theory, I will examine Komatsu's apocalyptic imagination in two of his earliest novel-length fictional narratives, *The Japan Apache Tribe* and *Virus: The Day of Resurrection* (*Fukkatsu no hi*, 1964).

Isozaki, Ruins, and "Incubation"

As suggested by the quotations above, the writings and building projects of the Metabolist group of architects and their associates, including their mentors Tange Kenzō and Asada Takashi, as well as their sometime collaborator Isozaki, were marked by the traces of "ruins" of incendiary bombs in the Second World War. The first major postwar project of Tange Kenzō was his plan for the reconstruction of Hiroshima, including the Hiroshima Peace Memorial Park and Museum (1949–50), which can be seen as an important event in the prehistory of the Metabolist school. These plans, which include an arch-shaped memorial cenotaph as well as Tange's modernist architectural landmark, the Peace Memorial Museum, are oriented along a sight-line axis pointing toward the "atomic bomb dome," the ruins of the Hiroshima Prefectural Industrial Promotion Hall near the bomb's hypocenter—thus enshrining through urban design what has become the most recognizable Japanese "ruin" of the Second World War.

Likewise, as pointed out by art critic Sawaragi Noi, the prehistory of the Metabolist group includes the collaboration of Asada Takashi, a second important Metabolist mentor, and critic Kawazoe Noboru in the production of a special issue of the journal *Shinkenchiku* on architecture and living conditions on the tenth anniversary of the atomic bombings, entitled "Ten Years under the Atomic Bomb: Japanese Architecture and Architects 1945–1955."[8] Kawazoe's subsequent essay, "Material and Man," from the 1960 Metabolism manifesto, begins with a discussion of the possibility of nuclear war, as well as the nuclear anxiety that harms people's minds like a form of "radiation."[9] In this essay, Kawazoe celebrates the optimism of architects and their trust in "tangible objects" as an antidote to nuclear anxiety. Nevertheless, he enjoins architects to place their faith not only in materials but also in energy and change itself and to learn from the natural processes of metabolism whereby "every piece of matter is a dynamic body ever changing and developing," in order to "create something which, even in destruction will cause a subsequent new creation." This "something," he concluded, "must be found in the form of the cities we are going to make—cities constantly undergoing the process of metabolism."[10]

Although he did not participate in the production of the 1960 Metabolist manifesto, several of Isozaki Arata's writings seem to elaborate on concepts raised in this work, particularly the relationship between "destruction" and "subsequent new creation" proposed in Kawazoe's essay. Nevertheless, Isozaki's graphic and textual works often take these themes into darker, more provocative, or even satirical territory. These include the photomontage *Hiroshima Ruined Again in the Future,* produced for the installation *Electric Labyrinth* at the 1968 Milan Triennial, in which futuristic megastructures grow "like weeds over the blasted landscape of Hiroshima" (as described by Koolhaus and Obrist)[11]: an image in which the devastation of Hiroshima is "imagined as a future scene of megastructures in collapse" (Plate 7).[12] This sardonic exhibit was an extension of Isozaki's earlier montage *Incubation Process,* published in the art journal *Bijutsu techō* in 1962, in which the sketch of a future cityscape (Isozaki's own City in the Air: Shinjuku) is interwoven with what appear to be classical stone ruins. This illustration was accompanied by a poetic text, which concluded with the following lines:

> Future cities are themselves ruins
> Our contemporary cities, for this reason, are destined to live
> only a fleeting moment,
> Give up their energy and return to inert material
> All of our proposals and efforts will be buried,
> And once again the incubation mechanism is reconstituted.
> That will be the future.[13]

As Isozaki summarized in a later commentary, "Both images [*Hiroshima Ruined Again in the Future* and *Incubation Process*] aim to portray cities in the recurring cycle of growth and death and both sought to represent the way cities self-destruct."[14] The architect recapitulated this idea in his noted essay "Invisible City" (1966), again linking the idea of the "future city" with the image of "ruins": "The future city is not unrelated to the charred ruins that are the original form of the city. The city of the future introduces its ultimate condition into the present moment. Design, or architecture, becomes reality when it overlaps with its own extinction. The future city is ruins."[15]

This understanding of cities and buildings at any given point in time as mere cross sections amid the "recurring cycle of growth and death" coincides with Isozaki's focus on fluidity, flux, and process, articulated further in the essay "Invisible City": "Today, the urban environment continues to increase in fluidity. Viewed in terms of the time axis of transformation, the city is in a liquid state of constant organic reproduction and division. . . . We have before our eyes fragments of cities in the process of flux. The fragments constantly shift into succeeding phases. In a city of this kind, where exterior appearances move and change without cease, process alone is trustworthy."[16] Thus, in order to respond to the need to design "process" rather than "exterior appearances," Isozaki was particularly interested in the possibilities of computers in simulating and designing the temporal evolution of cities.

However, for Isozaki, the idea of the city's fluidity amid the cycles of growth and death was an ambivalent one. On the one hand, it allowed the architect or urban planner, through such tools as computer simulation, to attempt to intervene in the city's metamorphosis and to imagine urban forms in terms of both their "future" *(mirai)* and "ending" *(shūmatsu)*.[17] However, in its darker moments, such as the photo collage *Hiroshima Ruined Again in the Future,* Isozaki's urban eschatology *(shūmatsuron)* seems to question whether the catastrophic possibilities of the city can lie within the realm of even technological "process planning." Rather, they summon the possibility of change that is not merely fluid and organic, as one might imagine from the organic metaphors Isozaki himself frequently employed in his writing of this period, but instead sudden, convulsive, and apocalyptic. This darker aspect of Isozaki's work would offer, in his own words, "a critique of modern city planning which only depicts a rose-colored utopia."[18] Later, looking back at his position at the time, Isozaki attempted to distinguish his viewpoint from the Metabolists' idea of organic change and regeneration, which he characterized as being dominated by "harmony" and "smooth order": "I was in agreement with most of what they [the Metabolists] said but I could not see eye to eye on one cardinal point: drawing a direct analogy between organic metabolism and architectural composition. For rather than being systemic, change is dramatic and destructive, lying outside the bonds of human control. It is the result of complicated accumulations of overlapping, unforeseeable coincidences."[19] Such "dramatic and destructive" change was also the focus of the imaginative career of Isozaki's exact contemporary, science fiction author Komatsu Sakyō, who articulated his own discourse of "ruins" in his fiction and essays.

Komatsu, Ruins, and the "Play of Combination"

Near the time that he was releasing his first two full-length novels, *The Japan Apache Tribe* and *Virus: The Day of Resurrection*, Komatsu expanded on his discourse of ruins in an essay entitled "Haikyo no kūkan bunmei," (Civilization of the space of ruins, 1964). In this essay, Komatsu makes it clear that for him, "ruins" refers not only to the state of Japanese cities after the Allied bombings but also to the psychological and spiritual state in which the Japanese war effort and wartime society were completely overturned—the "battle front" and "home front" transformed to "ruins" by the emperor's radio address announcing Japan's surrender.[20] Komatsu particularly focuses on the brief period between surrender and the establishment of the new postwar regime as a historical vacuum or a "rent" in the fabric of time and lived experience. "From the end of the war until the 'post-war' had begun—after the aerial bombings had ceased, and before the 'everyday life' that had vanished in the faraway mists had returned—there was a very brief period of emptiness, when the mating of scrap and ruins occurred. . . . It was as if we were born into this space of ruins without any trace of cause or effect." Furthermore, for Komatsu, the ruins are an "original condition" *(shigen jōtai)* with a power capable of asserting a primal reality and overturning or negating the following years of postwar progress:

> This "original condition" has the meaning of the negation of the flow of all time, and all historical development. It has the effect of denying all "development" and "progress" of the last nineteen postwar years, all postwar "recovery" and "change"—not only for Japan, but in terms of world history, denying all genealogies of civilization and value, and returning them to zero point—in other words, returning them to the condition of those ruins.[21]

For Komatsu, the space of ruins, or the rent in the fabric of lived experience, is also an "order-less," nonhierarchical space dominated aesthetically by the grotesque and the absurd. Amid the ruins of fire-bombed Kōbe and Osaka of his youth, he cites the experience of seeing one leg of a grand piano jammed into the bowl of a toilet, or the upper body of a bespectacled, bearded gentleman immersed in a pond, perfectly preserved as in life, while his lower body was swollen and burnt to a crisp, with his charred penis protruding up toward the sky. This was also the space for cruel and anarchical children's play—Komatsu recounts children building "barrack" shanties out of the refuse of the bombings only to burn them down for play, or watching younger children in the burnt-out ruins taking turns shooting a dog tethered to a telephone poll with a pistol.[22] Later in the essay, he extrapolates from these experiences a more abstract quality of "the space of ruins," which can turn all "productive" activity into mere "play": the most serious topics become the punch lines of jokes; revolution and war become "playing revolution" and "playing war."[23]

Building on these observations, Komatsu proposes a theory of "the space of ruins" that could be equally read as a theory of SF (science fiction or speculative fiction). Within this space, "things that happened" *(atta koto),* "things that might happen" *(ari-eru koto),* and "things that could never happen" *(ari-enai koto)* are all equals. Furthermore, in the "non-Euclidean geometry" governing the "space of ruins," the three temporalities of past, present, and future are only random points or segments placed at will on a line, and any segment of this line can be erased or superimposed with another. "This can be a most interesting play of combination," Komatsu writes. "You are free to make it a game by introducing a set rule into the combination, or you are free to do without rules. . . . From the 'endless play of combination' possible in this space, one can discover any number of things that are 'valid' or 'useful' to reality."[24] This "endless play of combination" in which the realism of "things that happened," the simulation of "things that might happen," and absurd and grotesque "things that could never happen" comingle is abundantly evident in Komatsu's first two full-length novels, *The Japan Apache Tribe* and *Virus: The Day of Resurrection.*

The Japan Apache Tribe

The preface to *The Japan Apache Tribe* begins with an idyllic vision of postwar reconstruction—the successful, harmonious, and even beautiful rebuilding of the urban landscape, and its economic and social underpinnings, in Osaka, Japan's second largest city—narrated in the first-person voice of the novel's author:

> Recently, I was standing on the outskirts of Osaka Castle, looking at the view of the Suginami District of the Eastern Ward in the twilight. Before my eyes stood rows of factory roofs, and to the left, i.e. to the south, there was a beautiful park that had been completed several years before. Across the elevated tracks right in front of me, the tightly packed cars of Osaka Loop (formerly the East Castle Line) carried commuters to and fro; above the city streets neon signs began to glow; and the peaks of the Ikoma range faded into the eastern night sky. This was a completely peaceful evening vista in the great metropolis.[25]

However, Komatsu quickly interrupts this idyllic scene by superimposing it with the memory of the war—specifically, the gigantic Osaka Army Arsenal complex that formerly occupied this territory—and the rubble and chaos that were left in the wake of the American B-29 bombings that struck the complex:

> And yet—
>
> At one time, these were the largest and most terrifying "ruins" in all of Osaka. Before the War, this was a munitions factory for the Army, and during the war it was repeatedly bombed, and it turned into a mountain of rubble—concrete and iron bars as far as the eye could see. Collapsed fences and twisted beams obstructed the view; rubble and chunks of concrete denied one's feet any purchase on the ground. Finally, with the end of the war, weeds three meters high grew everywhere, hungry wild dogs roamed about, and it turned into an accursed territory, where it was said that those who ventured inside rarely returned alive.[26]

Tellingly, Komatsu's book does not begin with the contemplation of actual ruins—recall that what is actually before the narrator's eyes is a scene of peaceful postwar construction—but rather the imaginative conjuring of ruins, invoked out of the past of traumatic wartime memory. Into this landscape of remembered ruins, Komatsu projects the memory of the "Apache"—soon to be the protagonists of his outrageous tale—scrap thieves who plundered the ruins of the munitions factory during the roughly ten-year span before the area was fully redeveloped.[27] According to the narrator, these scrap thieves "imbibed their anarchical energy from the ruins themselves, and their very lives depended on the rubble."[28] However, noting the city's gradual recovery from the war and the erasure of even the most stubborn remnants of wartime destruction, the narrator asks where the ruins and their inhabitants, this "tribe" of Apache with their "fierce energy," have vanished. He answers that the ruins, with their "evasive anarchical spirit," "flood of energy," and their "boundless potential," are still alive within himself. "Therefore," he writes, "I decided to write down the tale of the 'Apache'":

> This was no longer just the tale of that group of scrap thieves, but a tale of the "ruins" themselves. And, perhaps, it is not the prettified site of the ruins we see today, but another future—another possibility—of the ruins themselves. This preposterous, fanciful tale is a "Postwar" that still lives stubbornly on, inside of me.[29]

In the pages that follow, Komatsu indeed presents the reader with "another future," out of the ruins—an alternate "postwar history" in which the ruins and their anarchical "Apache" inhabitants reconquer Japan.

The "Apache" in Komatsu's tale not only live amid the ruins of the Osaka Army Arsenal, they literally live *from* them. In his fantastical alternate postwar history, the scrap scavengers living amid the ruins have been confined to a broad, fenced-off no-man's-zone on the site of the bombed-out arsenal and, deprived of other sources of sustenance, have rapidly evolved digestive systems capable of digesting scrap metal—that is, they have developed a new postwar "metabolism" based on the bodily absorption of "ruins." Moreover, they have embraced the identity of "Apache"—a label bestowed by journalists on their real-life counterparts to convey the scrap thieves' outlaw, renegade status. Based on their knowledge of ethnic stereotypes and clichés from Hollywood Westerns, the "Apache" in Komatsu's tale have taken pseudo–Native American names and set up their own tribal society. Komatsu thus spoofs the consumption of American "junk" culture in the postwar years including and following the American-led Allied occupation. The powerful survival instincts of the "Apache" allow them to adapt their identities from the detritus of Americanized popular culture, just as their bodies are forged from the debris of the American bombs and the destroyed wartime regime.

With their new cultural and dietary adaptations, the tribe members live more or less happily on the grounds of the former arsenal, until the government attempts a total extermination campaign. Forced to flee their iron-rich homeland, the "Apache" must find a new mode of survival as a truly alien and threatening ethnic minority in the midst of Japanese urban society. However, while humans in positions of power generally see the "Apache" as a threat, the *ferro-tification* of Japan proceeds almost virally, as many on the margins of society across Japan begin eating metal and enter into alliance with the "Apache" tribe. After many twists in their fate, the "Apache" declare total war on the humans and eventually overturn the government and destroy Japanese civilization as we know it.

In an interview in the book *SF e no yuigon* (A last testament for SF, 1997), Komatsu describes Karel Čapek's *War with the Newts* (1936) as one of the inspirations for writing *The Japan Apache Tribe*. Komatsu cites as inspiration the novel's satiric humor, as well as its apocalyptic narrative, in which a race of anthropomorphic salamanders, initially enslaved by human beings, proliferate and overthrow their human captors. However, Komatsu also asserts a critical difference from Čapek's work:

> What's a little different from Čapek, though, is this: [in *War with the Newts*] there's a salamander who walks upright, and since it's quite clever, [the humans] begin to train it, and realize they can exploit it however much they want, just like a laborer, and they can even freely send it into battle since it isn't human. After that the salamanders become gradually stronger and more intelligent. In Čapek's novel, it's all written from the perspective of the humans, first in using the salamanders as slaves, then in depicting them as a kind of monster who destroys mankind.
>
> But, in our case, we lost the war. Seeing it from the viewpoint of the Allied Forces—the whites—it might just be that *we* are the salamanders. So, finally, when asked "will you die as humans?" we replied, "we want to live, even as monsters (*bakemono*)." That's the key phrase for the novel.[30]

This assertion of the will to live amid the ruins, "even as monsters," and indeed the assumption of the viewpoint of the "monster," lies at the heart of Komatsu's novel. Nevertheless, the novel conveys a high degree of ambivalence about the "Apache," who are living a primal existence without the emotional or cultural niceties of "human" civilization—a "civilization" that is also revealed to be authoritarian, hypocritical, and exploitative.

As indicated in his essay, "Civilization of the Space of Ruins," the ruins represent for Komatsu a posthistorical topos or an "original condition" outside of history, indeed a denial of historical narratives of progress or triumph, "denying all genealogies of civilization and value," as Komatsu writes, whether the technical progress of Enlightenment civilization or the triumph of the Japanese Empire. Similarly, the scrap-eating, emotionally coarse, and culturally ersatz identity of the "Apache" is a type of posthuman identity, redolent of Alexandre Kojève's description of postwar American consumer society as a posthistorical, posthuman "Animal" existence, free from the historical struggles and trials of the spirit that Kojève's Hegelian vision identified as uniquely human.[31] For what appears to be a simple, ludicrous fable, Komatsu's narrative actually carries a deceptively complex tone, simultaneously celebrating the "evasive anarchical spirit," "flood of energy," and "boundless potential" of the "Apache" and yet retaining an undercurrent of unease at the defeat of the humans and their both rapacious and tender "civilization."

As Park Yu-ha and Tatsumi Takayuki discuss, the historical Osaka "Apache" on which Komatsu's satire is based, a marginal community who inhabited the ruined grounds of the Osaka Army Arsenal and made a living in part by selling the scrap metal they scavenged within, were associated strongly with ethnic Koreans, a significant ethnic minority who were comprised of both economic migrants and conscripted laborers during the period of the Japanese Empire and many of whom remained in Osaka and other Japanese cities in the postwar era. This Korean ethnicity is emphasized in Kaiko Ken's fictional account of the Osaka Apache, *Nippon sanmon opera* (Japan three-penny opera, 1959), which preceded Komatsu's tale, as well as Yang Sok Il's subsequent novel *Yoru o kakete* (Through the night, 1994), which also focuses on the Osaka Apache.[32] In Komatsu's tale, however, the Apache are socioculturally marked as working-class Osakans but not marked as Korean: instead, ethnic Koreans are displaced in the tale to a trading post just outside the fenced-in no-man's-zone. In other words, the conquest of this marginal tribe over the territory of Japan and its human population only occurs after Komatsu displaces the ethnically Korean scrap collectors to a further marginal position outside of the homeland of the novel's "Apache" or mutant protagonists. Therefore, the novel not only introduces us to Komatsu's strategy of geopolitical dis-placement through his conquest of Japan by the outré Osakan Apache tribe but also draws our attention to question of the limitations or hidden re-placements of this strategy through the double marginalization of Koreans from the Apache tribe.

Virus: The Day of Resurrection

At first glance, the writing style and tone of Komatsu second full-length novel, *Virus: The Day of Resurrection* (1964), could hardly have been more different from *The Japan Apache Tribe*. In contrast to the farcical tone of Komatsu's first novel, which is punctuated with colloquial Osaka dialect recalling Komatsu's apprenticeship as a writer for satirical radio news presentations drawing on the Osaka tradition of *manzai* comedy, *The Day of Resurrection* establishes a tone of high seriousness, mixing international intrigue and scientific exposition in following an international cast of characters as they react to the outbreak of a deadly virus. Indeed, its contemporary/near-future setting (spanning 196X–73), its attention to technical scientific details, its context of Cold War geopolitics, and its blurring of the spy novel and hard science fiction genres, all anticipate the development of the "techno-thriller" in Anglo-American fiction, particularly Michael Crichton's *The Andromeda Strain* of 1969, considered a foundational text of the techno-thriller genre, which also explored the theme of a deadly outbreak of an extraterrestrial microorganism.

In the case of Komatsu's novel, the deadly virus in question is likewise derived from an extraterrestrial organism, which has been modified in an American military lab as part of the U.S. bioweaponry research program and henceforth stolen from the lab and traded on the international weapons black market. After an airplane carrying the stolen virus crashes in the Italian Alps, the organism is released and rapidly begins to spread disease across human populations. Moreover, the deadly organism is capable of fusing with or "hijacking" other viruses and appears in numerous guises as different viral outbreaks occur simultaneously across the globe. Komatsu's novel tracks the world's dwindling population centers as scientists and politicians attempt to respond to the outbreaks, with various degrees of denial, self-deception, and ineptitude. Finally, only a small population of humans remains in Antarctica, where the extremely cold temperatures have insulated the members of various Antarctic research stations from the contagion.

However, it is at this point that the true audacity of Komatsu's novel is revealed: his will be the tale of not just one global apocalypse but two, with the world suffering a gratuitous second death. It turns out that in an instance of Cold War paranoia the White House has installed an automatic missile defense system to defend against a Soviet nuclear attack. When a massive earthquake strikes Alaska, the missile defense system mistakes the earthquake for a nuclear attack. With the United States completely depopulated and no one in the White House to disengage the automatic system, a full-scale automated exchange of nuclear missiles between the United States and the Soviet Union is initiated, despite the best efforts to defuse the automatic missile system by the Japanese scientist Yoshizumi, who was able to predict the upcoming Alaskan megaquake.

Regardless of the novel's extensive trappings of realism, the narrative excess of the double-apocalypse plot of *The Day of Resurrection* encodes an underlying absurdity and black humor, true to the grotesque aesthetics of ruins outlined in Komatsu's essay "Civilization of the Space of Ruins." Indeed, the 1980 film version of the novel, directed by B-movie maestro Fukasaku Kinji, emphasizes the black humor of this scenario: the mise-en-scène of the film features the grotesque skeleton of an American general seated at helm of the underground nuclear defense control room, seemingly controlling the events from beyond the grave in spite of Yoshizumi's attempts to disengage the atomic missile system. Throughout Komatsu's novel, structures of hate, hubris, and irrationality overcome the safeguards of the expected autopoetic maintenance of human civilization, returning humanity to the open-ended zero point, the "original condition" of ruins, outside of history. Yet, as the novel's title suggests, *Fukkatsu no hi*, or *The Day of Resurrection* is, equally with *The Japan Apache Tribe*, a tale of survival: the final scenes of the novel feature Yoshizumi, who was spared a direct hit from the nuclear missiles in the underground bunker below the White House, reuniting with the remaining survivors from Antarctica after an epic solo trek from the ruins of Washington, D.C., to the tip of South America. Ironically, the nuclear irradiation of the globe has stimulated the growth of counterviruses that help to destroy the deadly germ agents behind the first apocalypse. The ruins of civilization are reset as a new "incubation mechanism."

Just as Isozaki's photomontages show the simultaneity of the future and the past, of future cities and ruins, so too Komatsu's work returns repeatedly to the "zero point" of ruins, in which constructive activity and the will to survive are locked in an elaborate cyclical dance with apocalypse. For both Isozaki and Komatsu, current reality must be viewed as superimposed on "ruins" as both a point of origin and locus of future return. In addition, the act of seeing "ruins" as the underlying reality frees them both to embrace simulation and contingency, the play of "things that could be" and "things that could never be" over the landscape of given contemporary reality. I will further examine Komatsu's simulations across a global scale in the following chapter.

3 Planetary Cities

Komatsu Sakyō's Disaster Fiction

In the preceding two chapters, my analysis has focused primarily on the city and how both architects and fiction writers have imagined the transformation of urban space under increasing pressures of population density, industrial and technological development, and apocalyptic risk. Indeed, we have seen in the visions of the Metabolists outlined in chapter 1 an understanding that population growth, urbanization, and connectivity could lead not only to the development of the megalopolis but beyond to an ecumenopolis, or groups of major world cities linked tightly together through the increasing travel and communications of their citizens. In the current chapter, I would like to further examine the work of SF author Komatsu Sakyō in terms of how it imagines the city per se and how it challenges the assumptions of modern life organized around the modern nation-state, bounded by a specific geographic territory, dominated by its capital and great cities, and for much of the twentieth century, organized around a Cold War system led by the United States and Soviet Union. In Komatsu's work, we see simulations of life with the capital city vanished, the geographical territory of the nation-state destroyed, or, as introduced in chapter 2, the entire Cold War system of nation-states wiped away amid a worldwide plague that spares only an international team of scientists on Antarctica.[1] These simulations often lead to inversions of center and periphery and the creation of conditions of exile—a process of imaginative deterritorialization that places nationalistic and cosmopolitan visions of human community into conflict.[2] Furthermore, Komatsu's narratives emphasize how complex global systems of communication, geopolitics, and scientific protocol intertwine with risk exposure and crisis response to tie together individuals from vastly different parts of the globe. In this sense, Komatsu's fiction seems to be striving for a "planetary" point of view, even though it also weaves powerful strands of nationalism and nostalgia into its dialogic tapestry.[3]

In her book *Sense of Place and Sense of Planet: The Environmental Imagination of the Global,* Ursula K. Heise argues for the need to transcend locally based environmental movements and ecological understandings in order to develop a vision encompassing interactions, networks, and shared risks that may be truly global in scale—a vision that she terms "eco-cosmopolitanism." "In a context of rapidly increasing connections around the globe, what is crucial for ecological awareness and environmental ethics is arguably not so much a sense of place as a sense of planet—a sense of how political, economic, social, cultural, and ecological networks shape daily routines."[4] In addition to offering a critical examination of how theorists from various fields have envisioned global interdependency through such heuristics as James Lovelock's Gaia hypothesis and Ulrich Beck's "world risk society," Heise also examines how such interdependency has been depicted in fiction such as Karen Tei Yamashita's *Through the Arc of the Rainforest* (1990), David Brin's *Earth* (1991), or Richard Powers's *Gain* (1998).

I would argue that Komatsu's works represent an early and sustained attempt at envisioning a planetary totality threatened by such processes as biowarfare, climate change, and sudden shifts in the earth's own internal dynamics—such as the convection currents in the earth's mantle responsible for the subduction of Japan in his magnum opus *Japan Sinks* (*Nihon chinbotsu,* 1973). Such "processes of global systemic transformation," Heise writes, pose a "challenge for narrative and lyrical forms that have conventionally focused above all on individuals, families, or nations," since they require "the articulation of connections between events at vastly different scales."[5] Komatsu's fiction takes up this challenge, probing the links between the predicaments and actions of characters in widely disparate locations and ranging in its perspective from that of isolated individuals and their daily decisions to the various regional as well as national identities that tie these individuals to society, to that of the planet Earth itself and the entire scope of geologic time.

This narrative propensity is abundantly evident in Komatsu's early masterwork *Virus: The Day of Resurrection* (*Fukkatsu no hi,* 1964).

The disparate characters in this story range from Professor Gregor Karlsky, a biochemical researcher working for the British Army, who inadvertently hands over a sample of a deadly virus to international arms smugglers, to Italian movie star Antonio Sevellini, who is the first person to come into contact with the virus after the smugglers' plane crashes in the Italian Alps, to Yoshizumi Toshio, a geologist assigned to the Japanese Showa research station in Antarctica. Sections of the narrative are even told—via an omniscient third-person narrator—with the Earth itself as protagonist, opening the story out to an expanded temporal scale of geological or cosmic time as well as an expanded spatial scale.[6]

Temporally, Komatsu's novel ranges backward and forward, starting with a prologue from a moment near the temporal climax of the novel (the near future of March 1973), after the deadly virus has wiped out most human life on earth, when Yoshizumi, surveying the coast of a deserted Japan from a submarine, nostalgically views the ruined city of Tokyo and the surrounding natural landscape of Tokyo Bay.[7] Subsequent chapters push the temporal setting back nearly a decade, to the incidents in winter 196X when the virus is leaked, to the subsequent spring, when outbreaks of disease begin to spread, to the following summer, when death and disease are rampant, and finally forward again to the following decade, when the lone survivors at the South Pole try to prevent a second global catastrophe, as discussed in chapter 2.

Throughout the crucial spring, while the plague is spreading, various authorities struggle to piece together the story of the missing experimental virus, seeking to reconstruct the full web of events from the preceding winter section. Tragically, however, no one is able to make the connection between the missing experimental virus and the plagues of disease that are spreading all around, and thus there is no chance that an effective antidote can be devised. Ironically, Komatsu situates a discussion of this failure of identification and diagnosis within a description of the many ways in which global communication had increased at the time of the novel's release in 1964—a litany of effects that resonate with Marshall McLuhan's contemporary theme of the "global village" and that, since the late 1980s, have been increasingly referred to as "globalization."[8] These include international communications networks that "lay wrapped around the globe like a net," relay satellites that bring scenes of foreign cities to local television screens, transportation networks of materials and supplies flowing in all directions, and financial networks tightly linking distant economies. As Komatsu writes, hints of a tariff hike in Washington can cause a plummet on the stock exchange in Tokyo, while "in Roppongi, Tokyo, you could learn the stats of yesterday's Dodgers game, and in Cairo, you could learn the details of that morning's earthquake in Alaska."[9]

However, speaking of the long time that it takes for characters within the *Virus* narrative to be able to make connections between disparate events related to the viral outbreak, the narrator stipulates, "the mass media had made the world of the twentieth century like the holes in a net, and even if people everywhere could learn about events happening all over the globe each day, there was still a regular organizational system and ranking of import in the reporting, so that things far removed from this established order tended to slip through the holes in the net."[10] Moreover, any individual will struggle to connect events in his or her daily life with distant and seemingly unrelated news items. The narrator illustrates this with the rather extreme example of the difficulty of connecting the death of a pet bird with the headlines regarding the death of Antonio Sevellini, which readers know was caused by the identical viral outbreak:

> Suppose that one fine spring morning, you find your pet Java sparrow, which had been fine the day before, lying cold on the bottom of its cage, even though you quite properly brought the cage in and put a cloth over it last night. If that were to happen, could you tie the death of your lovely pet bird to the fuss that had started ten days ago in the entertainment columns and celebrity magazines over the sudden death of the "hunk of the century" Antonio Sevellini in a car crash, a death which female fans worldwide were weeping their hearts out over now?[11]

Even discounting this extreme example, the narrator then speculates on how difficult it might be to link the sudden death of a friend in Japan to the headline, on the bottom of page two in the local paper, about a mystery disease in Taipei. Thus, the narrative emphasizes not only global interconnection—the chains of cause and effect that connect the British scientist, Italian movie star, Japanese geologist, and countless other characters—but also the gaps in connection: the incomplete links in the global networks, as well as—as we learn elsewhere in the narrative—the obstacles from nationalism, Cold War politics, interpersonal jealousy, insecurity, lack of curiosity, or failure of imagination that can prevent the free flow of information and the intellectual connections and conclusions necessary to truly understand the situation of the planet and its human population. "It was true," the narrator summarizes, "humans lived much farther apart from one another than everyone imagined."[12]

Thus, while Komatsu's works of the 1960s and 1970s strive to depict a planetary whole, they differ from other emerging depictions of global totality during these decades, such as McLuhan's "global village," Fuller's "Spaceship Earth," Lovelock's "Gaia," and the famous "blue marble" photograph of planet Earth taken by the Apollo 17 aircraft in 1972, all of which, in Heise's analysis, "relied on summarizing the abstract complexity of global systems in relatively simple and concrete images that foregrounded synthesis, holism, and connectedness." "The efficacy of these tropes," Heise continues, "depended not only on their neglect of political and cultural heterogeneity, . . . but also on a conception of global ecology as harmonious, balanced, and self-regenerating."[13] While Heise's characterization of the diverse conceptions of McLuhan, Fuller, and Lovelock may be something of an overgeneralization, clearly this characterization would not apply to Komatsu's work, which foregrounds the geopolitical frictions, the gaps in global connections, and a global ecology that is fragile and subject to sudden, catastrophic change.

Environment and Disaster

In his subsequent fiction and essays, Komatsu continued to explore environmental and planetary issues: the unexpected global interconnections and vulnerabilities to disasters and environmental crises that are simultaneously "natural" and "man-made," as well as the impediments to effective human responses to planetary threats. His 1967 collection of travel essays *Nihon taimu toraberu* (Japan time travel), coauthored with Metabolist architect Kurokawa Kishō, documented the impact of land reclamation, large-scale industrial development projects, transportation infrastructure development, and other massive state-sponsored development projects on the landscape throughout Japan. As will be discussed in the next chapter, Komatsu also raised ecological issues while commenting on the suppression of darker concerns about the future from the bright visions of a "future city" presented at the 1970 Osaka Expo, warning that man-made destruction of the "thermal balance" of the atmosphere and oceans might cause either a great advance of the oceans or a new ice age.[14] He later followed this warning with a book-length work of nonfiction, *Ijō kishō* (Abnormal weather, 1974). While focusing primarily on the scenario of global cooling, rather than the global warming that dominates the climate change discourse today, Komatsu's nonfiction work explores such issues as human effects on climate, the relationship of the ocean and atmosphere, the effects of climate change on human history, and the relationship of climate change to famines and epidemics.[15] Finally, the book concludes with a call for the establishment of an age of "earth government" *(chikyū seiji)*, including the forecasting of systemic changes in climate zones and their effects on ecosystems and agricultural output, while warning that such information should remain open to all and not fall prey to national monopolies or power politics.[16]

As Karen Colligan-Taylor and Karen Laura Thornber note in their pioneering studies of environmental literature in Japan and East Asia, several of Komatsu's short stories written during the period between the Osaka Expo and the publication of *Japan Sinks* address environmental issues while reflecting Komatsu's awareness of the emerging global environmental movement. In particular, the story "Seijaku no tsūro" (Silent corridor, 1973), which narrates a near-future couple's struggles with fertility issues that may have been caused by toxic chemical exposure, echoes Rachel Carson's *Silent Spring* with its title and includes a quotation from the Japanese translation of Carson's groundbreaking environmentalist text as a preface.[17]

Komatsu's increasing attention to ecology, as well as the spread of environmental concern and awareness in Japan in the early 1970s, provides an important context for the writing and reception of Komatsu's novel *Japan Sinks*, which became a runaway best seller on its publication in 1973 and was quickly remade into a successful live-action film. In their studies of Japanese disaster and apocalyptic fiction, Susan Napier and Motoko Tanaka both point to the inflationary oil shock of 1973, which ended the nearly twenty years of the High Growth Era, as context for the public embrace of *Japan Sinks*. Tanaka writes: "The novel functions to reveal the antithesis of the promising future that the Osaka Expo presented in 1970. It became so popular precisely because it represented the growing disconnect of many Japanese during the 1970's, as their cultural, economic, and political identity and stability came under attack from international pressures."[18] Tanaka's observation that *Japan Sinks* represents the antithesis of the promising future presented by the expo is astute, but a reduction of the novel to a reflection of generalized social anxiety in the midst of the 1970s economic downturn ignores the ways in which the novel's apocalyptic narrative relates to more specific contemporary fears about the vulnerability of human populations to catastrophic events, from the "instantaneous destruction" of nuclear war to the "gradual destruction" of environmental damage, as these two dangers were characterized in the Theme Zone of the Osaka Expo itself.[19] Furthermore, while the seismic disaster in *Japan Sinks* is neither anthropogenic nor directly related to climate change, it features the same type of sudden change in a fluid circulatory system (the earth's mantle) that was previously thought to be slow-moving and relatively stable, much as meteorologist Edward Lorenz, a pioneer of what would become known as chaos theory, warned might occur in the interlinked atmospheric and oceanic systems to produce sudden and unexpected shifts in the Earth's climate.[20] I would posit that Komatsu's exposure to new theories of atmospheric and fluid dynamics in his research on trends in emerging climate science influenced his *novum* in *Japan Sinks*: the conception of a sudden, catastrophic event in the mantle convection dynamics of plate tectonics, which was itself a relatively new frontier of earth science when Komatsu was writing his novel.

As I have discussed above with regard to *Virus: The Day of Resurrection*, Komatsu's work in the "disaster fiction" genre explores the dynamics of risk and catastrophe that endanger disparate human communities and continually reconfigure the relationship of humans to their environment. In her aforementioned study *Sense of Place and Sense of Planet*, Ursula Heise stresses the important role that the concept of risk has come to play in reshaping "the imagination of the global in its environmentalist as well as other dimensions," arguing that understanding of translocal risk has "galvanized" the environmental movement and has also become "an important theoretical lens with which to envision the emergence of new social movements and structures," pointing to the work of the environmental justice movement as well as the theoretical writings of Charles Perrow, Ulrich Beck, Anthony Giddens, and others.[21]

Both Komatsu's *Virus: The Day of Resurrection* and his subsequent novel *Japan Sinks* can be seen as studies in the dynamics of risk and disaster. *Virus: The Day of Resurrection,* for example, directly addresses the question of the interaction of complex systems in modern society and the extent to which the triggering of a major disaster is dependent upon the "coincidence" of the failure of multiple interlocking safety systems:

> Usually when something that we call a "major accident" happens, unfortunate coincidences accumulate to a nearly impossible degree, all manner of safety systems fail one after another, and the accident occurs. Go and read about the very first nuclear reactor accident in history in 1952 on Canada's Chalk River, or about the dam that burst in France. No, even without going that far out of your way, it will be enough to think about some big train derailment that is still fresh in your memory. . . . Even when an accident just barely avoids becoming a terrible tragedy, all is decided by whether the switch of coincidence is turned to the left or the right.[22]

As a further example, the narrator cites the case of the accidental dropping of a hydrogen bomb in North Carolina in 1957: of the six layers of safety apparatus to prevent such an accidentally dropped bomb from exploding, five had been out of order, and only one prevented the bomb's detonation.[23] These meditations on the dynamics of complex systems and the role of chance anticipate Charles Perrow's influential study *Normal Accidents: Living with High-Risk Technologies* (1984). In this work, Perrow proposes the concept of a "normal accident" or "systems accident" whereby an accident is provoked when multiple interlocking technical systems are coupled with such complexity and cohesion that not all aspects of the system interactions can be comprehended by the operators, so that "given the system characteristics, multiple and unexpected interactions of failures are inevitable."[24] In other words, the chance aspect of "coincidence" is combined with systemic coupling and systemic blind spots in such a way that major accidents are increasingly likely to occur.

Komatsu's *Virus: The Day of Resurrection* points not only to the strange role of "coincidence" in modern disaster but also to the difficulty of mapping the complex technical and human systems through which modern disasters unfold. The novel examines the failure of technical systems, such as bioweapons research protocol, but also the failure of the broader interlocking social systems of global politics, journalism, science, academia, and other human social connections. It is within these complex social systems that, as discussed above, no one is able to grasp the totality of the unfolding viral outbreak or effectively intervene in its spread. To this extent, *Virus: The Day of Resurrection* might be said to be an atypical science fiction narrative in that it lacks the exceptional, heroic figure of the scientist or intellectual who is able to make the crucial connections or recognize the underlying pattern necessary to prevent or even warn of the disaster. (It is only in the second part of the novel when Yoshizumi is able to help predict, if not prevent, a second apocalyptic disaster striking mankind.)

Japan Sinks, however, differs from *Virus: The Day of Resurrection* in that it includes the heroic and tragic figure of Professor Tadokoro, the eccentric geophysicist who is able to read the signs of the impending disaster and, moreover, to summon the imagination necessary to comprehend the unfolding dynamics and anticipate the full scale of the disaster when no one else is able to see it. For example, the following passage, a conversation with the protagonist Onodera, seems to not be directly related to the pending seismic event but helps to establish Professor Tadokoro's expertise at distinguishing patterns and emerging systems:

> "From my perspective, humans and plants and coral—all are the same. If they encounter some kind of protuberance, they'll wrap themselves around it. Even the earliest forms of life probably didn't just appear randomly in the water, but complex protein molecules must have first formed when a polymer colloid got caught on some sort of rough surface on the molecular scale, and adhered to it." . . .
>
> "What do you think? Insofar as they both set in place calcium carbonate and build a communal framework around it, could we really say that reef-building coral and humans who construct a modern city with concrete are all that different?"
>
> "I see . . ." Onodera nodded in assent for the first time. "If

> you look at it that way, the pattern of evolution for humans, and their future destiny, is already written in the four-billion-year history of life on earth."
>
> "Not only that! From the evolution of sub-atomic particles to the evolution of the universe, the stages are different, but there is some kind of extremely similar, shared pattern hidden there."[25]

This passage seems to anticipate the scientific interest in fractal dynamics—the generation of "self-similar" shapes on different scales throughout the natural and mineral worlds, from flakes of soap to clusters of stellar matter, as well as the complex systems theory of the following three decades.[26] It also echoes the cosmic vision outlined in the Metabolist architectural manifesto of 1960, which posits humans' built environment as part of a continuum from "atom to nebula," as well as the analogy, found in numerous Metabolist writings and designs, of growth patterns between modern architecture and organic processes such as the formation of coral reefs. Thus, in echoing the language of Metabolism, this passage hints at a countercurrent of constructive energy, on the cosmic and molecular as well as human scales, amid the wanton destruction foregrounded in the novel's narrative.

Tadokoro's comprehension of complex system dynamics allows him to make the imaginative leap that a subtle change in underlying patterns in the circulation of the earth's magma could result in a rapid "cascade" effect, producing unanticipated dramatic changes on the earth's surface. Komatsu, who based the science of his novel on extensive personal research and interviews with members of the scientific community, was undoubtedly tapping in to the science of dynamical systems, chaos theory, and complexity that was still just emerging in the 1970s. As these emerging sciences became more widely known, the cascading results of a minor event, such as those identified by Tadokoro, would be popularized as the "butterfly effect"—the idea that the flapping of a butterfly's wings could produce rippling effects on the atmosphere that could affect even distant weather patterns.[27] Furthermore, regarding the unprecedented scale of the catastrophe, Tadokoro repeatedly stresses that, given the vast and still unfolding scope of geologic time, just because something has not happened in the brief span of recorded human history does not mean that it is impossible. It is this ability to imagine beyond standard "risk analysis" to see the potential for truly catastrophic change that sets Professor Tadokoro apart from the surrounding characters.

Diaspora

The recognition and diagnosis of the unfolding disaster, however, is only one part of the narrative of *Japan Sinks*. The other chief narrative arc of the novel is the question of how the Japanese people will respond to the sinking of their homeland—whether the Japanese can survive as a "people" without the physical homeland of the Japanese archipelago—an issue that is taken up in further detail in the novel's belated sequel, *Nihon chinbotsu dainibu* (Japan sinks: Part two), co-written with Tani Kōshū and published in 2006, thirty-three years after the original best seller's appearance. *Japan Sinks* and its sequel are two of several Komatsu narratives that invert center and periphery: In *Shuto shōshitsu* (The capital vanishes, 1985), characters from the periphery must cope with the loss of the political, economic, and media center of Japan. In *Japan Sinks*, Japanese characters must survive the loss of the geographical center of Japan itself. And in *Virus: The Day of Resurrection*, the entire world population is exiled from six of the earth's continents, leaving only a small population on Antarctica to reconstruct human society.

By simulating various extreme inversions in the relationships between center and periphery, Komatsu's works provide an invitation to question the geopolitical, economic, and social status quo. Nevertheless, in counterbalance to their unsettling elements, his narratives often provide a conservative reassurance in the form of resilient patriarchal structures anchored by strong male political leaders, effective old-boy networks, and competent scientists and engineers who, while they may not be able to avert ultimate disaster, at least manage to overcome bureaucratic intransigence and mitigate the effects of disaster on the populace. Thus, while his stories issue a challenge to the complacency of the High Growth Era in Japan, they also encode in highly mythologized fashion the postwar reconstruction ideals of competent technocratic leadership, engineering know-how, and patriarchal social stability. More interestingly, perhaps, Komatsu's narratives also dramatize the ambivalence of postwar Japanese identity, presenting conflicting viewpoints of internationalism or "cosmopolitanism," cultural chauvinism, and resurgent nationalism in a dialogic form.[28]

Komatsu revisited a number of the themes from *Virus: The Day of Resurrection* and *Japan Sinks* in his twentieth book-length novel, *Shuto shōshitsu* (The capital vanishes, 1985).[29] This work offers a simulation of what would happen to Japan if the Tokyo metropolitan region suddenly vanished beneath a mysterious curtain of clouds and the rest of Japan had to learn to function, and to navigate complex Cold War geopolitical tensions, without the capital of Tokyo. Throughout the narrative, Komatsu draws acute attention to the vulnerabilities caused by the centralization of Japanese economic, political, military, communications, and cultural power in greater Tokyo. Furthermore, the novel presents a narrative of self-actualization of "provincial" characters, as characters marginal to the former center of power in Tokyo must step into the breach and assume leadership in dealing with the unprecedented crisis of Tokyo's disappearance. Such characters, many of them from the upper managerial ranks of the white-collar "salaryman" class, are represented first of all by the newspaperman Tamiya, a native of Kyushu who was educated in Tokyo and worked for a major national newspaper but quarreled with his bosses and eventually "dropped out" to become assistant editor of a local Kyushu newspaper. However, when the capital disappears behind the mysterious cloud, Tamiya not only seizes the opportunity for enterprising reporting on the story in the absence of Tokyo-based media outlets but, through his diligence and creative grasp of the situation, eventually becomes a key media aide to the new provisional government.

Indeed, Komatsu imagines a pivotal role for communications media in a post-Tokyo Japan, as the provisional government operates out of a high-tech hotel in Nagoya outfitted with cutting-edge network communications and information technology. Furthermore, the novel reprises the theme of the control of information itself as a key nexus of Cold War conflict and human survival (familiar from *Virus: The Day of Resurrection* as well as his nonfiction work *Abnormal Weather*). In *The Capital Vanishes*, the United States attempts to monopolize information about the strange cloud encircling Tokyo as a military secret, while several of the novel's protagonists try to evade this scenario by arranging an open international investigation of the enigma.

Nevertheless, the narrative of self-empowerment of characters marginal to the center of power has its limits. The peripheral networks that these characters forge to compensate for the lost radial links to the capital are constituted of the accumulated social capital of networks of university classmates and corporate associates: even when Tokyo is removed, the operations of power in the novel have a clubby, "old boy" affect. This "old boy" dominance is brought into further relief by the near total absence of active female characters in the narrative. The one limited exception is "Miiko" (Matsunaga Mieko), a Shōnan "surfer girl" and ultra-competent part-time secretary in the Atsugi research facility where some important early scenes transpire.[30] We are informed near the end of the novel that "Miiko" has also risen through the opportunities of the crisis and has become a valued "unseen support" member *(shitabataraki)* of the research team investigating the anomaly, but we are given her story merely as a summary and not as a fully narrated sequence of events.[31]

The loss of center explored in *The Capital Vanishes* is given even more dramatic form in *Japan Sinks* and *Japan Sinks: Part Two.* In the *Japan Sinks* narrative, the lost center is not only Tokyo but the entire Japanese archipelago, which sinks under the Pacific Ocean in a cataclysm of seismic activity. The two novels pose the provocative question of whether the Japanese people could survive as a diaspora and what it would mean to be Japanese if the geographic entity of Japan were to disappear, explicitly comparing the post-deluge Japanese exodus with the Jewish diaspora. Amid the crisis of ethnic or cultural succession posed by the loss of homeland, there is a strong emphasis on the issue of reproduction, and the female characters in the original *Japan Sinks* are depicted primarily in terms of their suitability to bear children and preserve the race, while patriarchal figures, such as the political sage Watari and the heroic submarine pilot Onodera, guide the national response to the disaster. Nevertheless, the bulk of the first novel is taken up by the narrative of the disaster of Japan's subvention under the Pacific and ends just as the last survivors are fanning out across the globe, so it remains to the sequel to explore what life in the post-archipelagic world will actually entail.

The sequel is set in a world twenty-five years after the subvention of the Japanese archipelago: that is, from the perspective of the sequel's release in 2006, it represents a "parallel present" of a world altered by the events of *Japan Sinks,* imagined to have occurred in the decade immediately following that novel's publication in 1973. Irrespective of the subvention of Japan and its effects on global politics and climate, many of the events in our world, such as the collapse of the Soviet Union and the development of the internet, have also occurred in the "parallel present" of *Japan Sinks: Part Two*. In the sequel, the Japanese people are scattered across the globe, often living in ethnically partitioned settlements and holding dual citizenships with their host countries and a Japanese government-in-exile, with Japanese governmental functions globally dispersed but provisionally headquartered in Australia. The novel follows characters in Papua New Guinea, Kazakhstan, and elsewhere as they struggle with issues of economic survival, maintenance of cultural identity, and neocolonial ethnic, political, and economic tensions with the natives of their host countries. In contrast to *The Capital Vanishes* and *Japan Sinks*, female characters have central narrativized roles among the multiple protagonists of *Japan Sinks: Part Two*. These leading female characters include Watari Sakura, a secretary to the Japanese prime minister, and Abe Reiko, an executive assistant to the U.N. High Commissioner for Refugees.

In response to the continued precarious position of the Japanese diaspora, the Japanese government led by Prime Minister Nakata has initiated two large-scale national engineering projects: the first being the "earth simulator," a supercomputer system in Australia devoted to predicting the climate effects of the subvention of Japan together with ongoing population shifts and development patterns. Secondly, government-sponsored engineers are secretly at work on the creation of a "megafloat" massive floating city in the waters formerly occupied by the Japanese archipelago, evocative of Metabolist architect Kikutake Kiyonori's futuristic proposals for Marine Cities. This "megafloat" project is launched in part to assert Japan's territorial claim to these waters in the face of increasingly aggressive Chinese exploration for possible undersea mineral wealth and other natural resources. The narrative presses to a climax as the earth's climate grows increasingly colder because of the lingering effects of the volcanic activity accompanying the sinking of Japan, and the "earth simulator" predicts the rapid arrival of a new ice age.

Toward the end of the novel, there is a climactic confrontation between Prime Minister Nakata and Foreign Minister Torikai that encapsulates some of the ideological tensions surrounding the future of the Japanese people. Nakata asserts an explicitly nationalist position with a plan to reconsolidate the increasingly attenuated Japanese diaspora, as well as to reclaim the home waters through the "megafloat" project. Torikai, however, articulates the position of "cosmopolitanism." He claims that historically, smaller social organizations have often had a stronger pull for the Japanese people than the nation-state. Furthermore, citing the examples of the ancient Phoenicians, the Chinese diaspora, and particularly the case of the Jewish diaspora, Torikai argues that, rather than clinging to the concept of nation, the Japanese should make use of their propensity to create cohesive social organizations at the subnational level and use their mercantile skill to survive through flexible global networks. Finally, he also offers a definition of cosmopolitanism as "the earth viewed from the cosmos" suggesting that this planetary vantage point is preferable to that of a narrow nationalism.[32] After this ideological confrontation, Nakata forces Torikai's resignation and enters into an alliance with the United States in order to offset the Chinese threat to the megafloat project. However, his trust is betrayed as the United States, following its own narrow national self-interest, tries to monopolize control of the predictive climate information generated by the "earth simulator"—a clear parallel to the role of the United States as information monopolist in *Virus: The Day of Resurrection* and *The Capital Vanishes*.

Like its predecessor *Japan Sinks*, the sequel sometimes reads like a dialogic narrativization of various essentialistic *nihonjinron*, or theories of Japanese identity. Indeed, according to Komatsu himself, one of his key intertexts while writing the original *Japan Sinks* was the bestselling *nihonjinron* text *The Japanese and the Jews (Nihonjin to Yudayajin)*, published by Yamamoto Shichihei under the name Isaiah Ben-Dasan in 1970.[33] As both Thomas Schnellbächer and Jessica Langer discuss, this *nihonjinron* rhetoric and the underlying problematic of Japanese national/cultural identity and its relationship to the "homeland" and diaspora is haunted by the language and experience of Japanese imperialism as well as the Japanese postwar experience of the American occupation and its ensuing political and cultural imperialism, making both *Japan Sinks* and its sequel very much postcolonial narratives.[34] Indeed, as Susan Napier suggests, a significant element of *Japan Sinks* is a revisiting of wartime trauma—the traumatic scene of ruins Komatsu has re-created throughout his fiction—as well as an act of mourning of the loss of the Japanese "nation" under wartime defeat and American cultural and political hegemony, and the re-imagining of Japanese national resiliency in its wake.[35]

Nevertheless, in *Japan Sinks: Part Two,* despite the idealistic theories offered by both Nakata and Torikai from the vantage points of nationalism and cosmopolitanism, the novel's description of life in the actual Japanese diaspora is fraught with tension and strife, particularly in the ethnic and class tensions between the segregated and security-guarded Japanese settler population and the native populations. Such a vision of tension and strife, for example, is provided through the eyes of the engineer Shinohara, who has been working on agricultural development and settlement projects in Papua New Guinea.[36] Inspiration for this section seems to be drawn not from an idealized narrative of the successful maintenance of Jewish identity through a centuries-old diaspora but from the contemporary realpolitiks of tensions between Israelis and Palestinians on the West Bank and occupied territories.

In his study *The Seven Beauties of Science Fiction,* Istvan Csicsery-Ronay Jr. analyzes the colonial adventure tale as one of the precursors of science fiction and identifies the recurring tropes in both genres of the "Handy Man" or problem-solving (and paradigmatically male) protagonist and the "fertile corpse" or foreign land where the Handy Man is tested:[37]

> The fertile corpse is the scene of the Handy Man's performance. It is usually not represented in human form, but as a region with strongly displaced qualities of female reproduction. It is fertile, because the Handy Man's manipulations induce it to yield bounty, ranging from sustaining food and natural resources to more intangible yields. It is a corpse because it is found to be insentient, the residue of a distributed life-force that has no consciousness. The Handy Man is able . . . to make this unconscious feminine body into a responsive, productive field.[38]

This paradigm of the Handy Man and fertile corpse seems to apply readily to the efforts of Shinohara and other Handy Man characters in Komatsu's tale to establish settler communities in Papua New Guinea and elsewhere to support their exiled people by bringing productivity to their new lands. However, both the intractable tensions of diasporic neocolonial relations with host communities as well as the broader narrative trajectory of an increasingly frigid and inhospitable planet belie the potential of the Japanese Handy Men to convert the planetary body into a productive field.[39] This narrative of infertility is further emphasized by the life story of Onodera, who has been separated from his companion from *Japan Sinks* and whose wife in the settler territories has died before bearing children. Thus, far more than the original *Japan Sinks*, the sequel is a novel of deassurance, questioning the potency of the patriarchal figures who provide hope amid catastrophe in *The Capital Vanishes* and *Japan Sinks*.

We have seen from these various examples the persistent play between center and periphery in Komatsu's work—in particular, the narrative strategy of obliterating the center, whether Tokyo or the entire Japanese archipelago, and observing the efforts of characters surviving outside the center to reconstitute "Japan" through peripheral networks. While such peripheral networks are given an advocate under the banner of "cosmopolitanism" in the person of Torikai in *Japan Sinks: Part Two*, countercurrents in the novel also lead us to question the ease with which the ideologies of both "nationalism" and "cosmopolitanism" can respond to the environmental and geopolitical challenges that abound in the novel's defamiliarized but very familiar postdiluvian parallel present.

In the examples from this chapter, I have also tried to highlight the importance of the themes of "scale" and "simulation" in Komatsu's work, connecting his work to the writings of the Metabolist architects and to such emerging, interrelated conceptual fields as cybernetics, systems theory, and chaos theory. In the case of "scale," the ability to recognize shared patterns and interrelationships between structures and events on the micro (local) and macro (global) levels connects the fictional Professor Tadokoro's theories in *Japan Sinks* with Kawazoe's opening prose of the Metabolist manifesto and with meteorologist Edward Lorenz's pioneering work in climatology. Similarly, the concept of "simulation" connects the work of the "novum" in Komatsu's SF (the supervirus in *Virus: The Day of Resurrection*, the geological catastrophe in *Japan Sinks*, or the disappearance of Tokyo in *The Capital Vanishes*) with the "push-button warfare" method of city planning imagined in Isozaki's essay "Invisible City," as well as with the computerized global climate simulation incorporated into the narrative of *Japan Sinks: Part Two* and implemented by the real-world scientific community as part of our fitful efforts toward global survival, starting from the mid-twentieth century and continuing to the current day.[40]

If the novels of Komatsu Sakyō were one "virtual" site of the intersection between science fiction, architectural theory, and information science, the Japan World Expo, held in Osaka in 1970, was another, "real-world" site of this interaction, which I will explore further in the two upcoming chapters.

4 Future City

The 1970 Osaka Expo

The dark vision of an apocalyptic "future city in ruins" articulated in the works of Isozaki Arata and Komatsu Sakyō, haunted by the traumas of the Second World War as well as the specters of Cold War conflict and environmental destruction, received its antithesis in the utopian vision of the "future city" offered in the Japan World Exposition of 1970, which was organized around the idealistic and optimistic theme of "Progress and Harmony for Mankind." Hosted by the city of Suita, Osaka, the Japan World Exposition (the Osaka Expo) was the first world's fair held in an Asian country, and it attracted a record 64 million visitors. Ironically, both Komatsu and Isozaki, whose apocalyptic writings I examined in the last two chapters, as well as Metabolist architects, designers, and theorists Kurokawa Kishō, Kikutake Kiyonori, Ekuan Kenji, and Kawazoe Noboru, in addition to Metabolist mentor Tange Kenzō, all played key roles in the design of the physical environment of the expo and the articulation of its themes. More than any novel, film, or animation from the period, I would argue that the Osaka Expo itself, as a collaboratively produced environment, was the most striking and significant science fictional presentation of a utopian "future city" to emerge in postwar Japan.

Through its integration of advanced technology, immersive multimedia environments, and eye-popping architecture, the Osaka Expo projected Japan as a simulation site for a future society. Indeed, many journalistic accounts heralded the expo as "*mirai no toshi*" (city of the future), just as the 1939–40 New York World's Fair had been cast as the "World of Tomorrow." At the same time, the Osaka Expo enacted an elaborate staging of Japan's relationship with the outside world, through massive "international" events such as the opening ceremony attended by the Shōwa Emperor. To a large extent, this effort was successful in promoting an international image of Japan that not only had recovered from the ravages of the Second World War but could be seen as an avatar of a high-tech global future: an emerging "techno-orientalist" vision of Japan that I will discuss at the end of this chapter. Together these national and international elements created a bubble of "progress and harmony" within a nation torn by virulent protests against the U.S.–Japan Security Treaty and the Vietnam War. Yet beyond the apparent optimism of the expo's theme, the futuristic visions underlying the articulation of its themes and elaborated in its architecture and display environments were considerably more complex. In this chapter I will examine the utopian aspects of the Osaka Expo as well as the elements of disharmony and the anxious possibilities for the future that underlay the expo's colorful veneer. In addition, I will explore how the expo became a physical as well as an intellectual node or connecting point for a diverse network of architects, authors, artists, and academics exploring issues of futurity (through the emerging interdisciplinary field of future studies) and articulating a vision of the coming "information society."

Science Fiction and the Osaka Expo

The connections between the Osaka Expo and science fiction were striking and multifarious. In addition to the creative and critical participation of Komatsu Sakyō, we can cite multiple examples of science fiction writers and artists involved in the expo. Such contributions include the Fujipan Robot Pavilion produced by the famous manga artist Tezuka Osamu; a farcical multiscreen science fiction film created by writer Abe Kōbō and filmmaker Teshigahara Hiroshi for the Auto Pavilion;[1] and the Mitsubishi Future Pavilion, realized by a team of science fiction auteurs including special effects wizard Tsuburaya Eiji of *Godzilla* and *Ultraman* fame, together with science fiction writers Fukushima Masami, Hoshi Shin'ichi, and Yano Tetsu, as well as illustrator Manabe Hiroshi, all working under the direction of producer Tanaka Tomoyuki from the Tōhō film studio (producer of *Godzilla*). This Mitsubishi Future Pavilion, one of a number of pavilions sponsored by private companies, presented an especially optimistic vision of the future of fifty years hence as a utopia of economic, technological, and natural resource "development" and "management." Moving walkways conveyed visitors through four different display rooms featuring giant screens and dioramas, seemingly torn from the pages of popular science fiction magazines: the first an imposing multiscreen chaos of storms, volcanic eruptions, and tsunami entitled "Japan's Nature"; the second, "Japan's Sky," featuring a space station and World Climate Management Center capable of controlling the earth's weather; the third, "Japan's Ocean," showing an underwater city, aquaculture "sea pastures," and underwater power generators; and the fourth, "Japan's Land," featuring a future city surrounded by greenery "in harmony with nature," with a model home sporting such near-future consumer items as a wall-hanging TV and a home computer.[2]

Furthermore, an International Symposium of Science Fiction, timed to coincide with the Osaka Expo, was held in Japan from August 31 through September 3, featuring events in Tokyo, Nagoya, and Ōtsu, as well as a tour of the expo site. Representing one of the first meetings between science fiction authors from both sides of the Iron Curtain, this symposium included authors Brian W. Aldiss and Arthur C. Clarke from the United Kingdom; Judith Merril and Frederik Pohl from North America; and Vasilii Pavlovich Berezhnoi, Yulii Iosifovich Kagarlitskii (aka Julius Kagarlitsky), Ieremei Iudovich Parnov, and Vasilii Dmitrievich Zackharchenko from the Soviet Union; joining Japanese writers including Komatsu, Fukushima, and Hoshi.[3]

Appearances of the Osaka Expo and the "expo" theme in Japanese science fiction works include Mayumura Taku's novel *Expo '87*, first published in 1968, which describes the competition among businesses to establish an edge in the entertainment, leisure, and information industries through their exhibits in a fictional Tokaidō Expo held in the twenty-years-hence future of 1987, and Tsutsui Yasutaka's satirical stories "Jinrui no daifuchōwa" (The great disharmony of mankind, 1970) and "Shinya no bankokuhaku" (The expo at midnight, 1970). The latter story provides a farcical take on Cold War theatrics of the competing American and Soviet Pavilions: an international spy battle erupts on the expo grounds, climaxing in the dome-shaped American Pavilion floating into the air as a flying saucer.[4] The Osaka Expo was also featured as a location for the *kaijū* (monster) film *Gamera vs. Jiger*, directed by Yuasa Noriaki (1970), and more recently played an important role in the best-selling manga *20th Century Boys* (Nijūseiki shōnen, 1999–2006) by Urasawa Naoki, as well as a film trilogy based on the manga (directed by Tsutsumi Yukihiko, 2008–2009). However, while these fictional characterizations of the expo are intriguing, in this chapter I will focus on the development of the Osaka Expo site itself as a locus of both collaborative and contending ideas about the future—in other words, the expo site as a multivalent, multiauthored "science fiction."

The Thinking the Expo Group and Origins of the Expo's Themes

The Osaka Expo was one part of a massive infrastructure development of the Suita region during the apex of the High Growth Era, which included the extension of the Hankyū Senri railway line (completed 1967), construction of the Meishin Expressway (1963–65) connecting Nagoya and Kobe, and the development of the Senri New Town, a planned development of over one thousand hectares adjacent to the future expo site, built to accommodate a population of 150,000, whose first units opened in 1962. The Ministry of International Trade and Industry (MITI) proposed the expo to the Bureau International des Expositions (BIE, International Exhibitions Bureau) in 1964 as a showcase for Japanese postwar recovery and modernization, as an economic stimulus, and as a catalyst for further infrastructure development in the Kansai region, just as the 1964 Tokyo Olympics had stimulated and showcased redevelopment for Tokyo and the Kantō region. Just as the Olympics had been criticized by the Japanese left as diversion from the protest movement that had galvanized over the 1960 renewal of the U.S.–Japan Security Treaty, the left also expressed suspicion over the Osaka Expo, especially as its scheduled opening coincided with the ten-year automatic renewal of the Security Treaty. Suspicion about the motives of the expo, together with critique of the ideology expressed by the event, fueled a lively and creative protest movement throughout the period of planning and execution of the fair.[5]

However, the announcement of the bid to host a World's Fair in Osaka was also met by constructive critical engagement from a group of Kansai-based intellectuals with connections to Kyoto University.

The study group Thinking the Expo (Bankokuhaku o kangaeru kai), founded in July 1964, was spearheaded by Kyoto University professor of anthropology Umesao Tadao, communication scholar and media theorist Katō Hidetoshi, and Osaka native and Kyoto University graduate Komatsu Sakyō, who was then working as a journalist and radio scriptwriter while beginning his career as a science fiction author. This circle, which became an important intellectual nexus connecting production of the Osaka Expo's central Theme Zone with the emergence of *miraigaku*, or future studies, in Japan, was initially formed around the journal *Hōsō Asahi* (Broadcast Asahi), published by the Osaka Asahi Broadcasting Corporation, to which Komatsu, Katō, and Umesao were frequent contributors. Indeed, the *Hōsō Asahi* editorial staff provided key logistical support throughout the development of the Thinking the Expo group, and the editorial trends of this journal, which were unusually ambitious for what was ostensibly a public relations magazine for a media company, provide important context for understanding the intellectual background and developing role of the Thinking the Expo group.[6]

From September 1963 through 1966, Komatsu contributed a regular series of articles to *Hōsō Asahi*, entitled "Eria o yuku" (Journeying across local areas), featuring reports on regional cultural history from across the Kansai region.[7] In addition to Komatsu's articles on Kansai geography and local culture, *Hōsō Asahi* featured numerous articles on anthropology and comparative cultural research by a number of members of the Kyoto University Institute for Research in Humanities, including Umesao, Katō, and institute codirector Kuwahara Takeo.[8] This institutional nexus serves as background to the expo's eventual thematic embrace, under the influence of the Thinking the Expo group, of a relativistic, multipolar humanism, which attempted to highlight the knowledge or "wisdom" *(chie)* of Asian and African cultures in the first World's Fair hosted by an Asian nation.[9]

Furthermore, given the importance of the concepts of "information" and the "information society" to the thematic development of the Osaka Expo, it is significant that *Hōsō Asahi* was the initial publication forum for Umesao's groundbreaking article "On Information Industries" in January 1963, which is credited for starting the journalistic boom of interest in information theory, "informatization" *(jōhōka)*, and the "information society" *(jōhō shakai)*. According to communications scholar Itō Yōichi, the actual term *information society*, which was not employed in Umesao's original article, was first used in a roundtable discussion published in *Hōsō Asahi* in January 1964, and the "information industries" *(jōhō sangyō)* were the subject of a series of articles in *Hōsō Asahi* from November 1964 through July 1966.[10] Thus, we can see that the members of the Thinking the Expo research group were at the forefront of thinking on information systems, computerization, and mediatization of contemporary society at exactly the same time as they were beginning to participate in this study group, and they continued to be active in the development of research and theorization on these topics simultaneously with their engagement with the expo throughout the late 1960s.

The members of the Thinking the Expo group researched the history of World's Fairs, paying particular attention to the thematic development of postwar expositions since the Brussels World's Fair of 1958, and studied the ongoing 1964 New York World's Fair and the planning for the 1967 Montreal Expo, in addition to exchanging ideas and critical opinions regarding the Japanese proposal. Concerned by the lack of vision expressed in MITI's initial proposal to the BIE, the group offered a series of public critiques that were to have a significant impact on the development of the expo. To summarize, the group argued: First, that the expo must not simply be a "trade show" designed to feature Japanese products and economic progress but instead must have clearly articulated themes and serve as a site for exchange of knowledge and information—including information on such complex global problems as, for example, pollution, material scarcity and distribution, and genetic erosion and diversity.[11] Second, expo planners should not overlook the significance of the expo as the first Asian World's Fair and must emphasize the participation of Asian and African countries. Third, the molding of the expo environment must not be carried out by conservative bureaucrats, but rather planners should give cutting-edge artists and architects free rein to realize innovative visions.

After a year of functioning as a voluntary, private research circle, the Thinking the Expo group attempted to convey its conclusions to the public, and to open them to further discussion and debate, in its first and only general conference, at the Osaka Science and Engineering Center on September 15, 1965, one day after the official announcement confirming that Osaka would be the host city for the 1970 Japan World Exposition.[12] While the Thinking the Expo group originally took its mission as pure research, or at most the provision of contextualization and constructive criticism from the outside, they were soon called upon to consult with local Osaka officials about the planning for the fair, and the expo's central planning committee adopted their suggestion to articulate a set of themes for the expo. Several of the members, including Komatsu and Katō, were soon drafted as theme committee members, together with Katō and Umesao's senior colleague from the Kyoto University Institute for Research in Humanities, professor of French Kuwahara Takeo, who was responsible for the final written draft of expo themes. Ultimately, the committee emerged with the optimistic, if often disparaged, theme of "Progress and Harmony for Mankind" (Jinrui no shinpo to chōwa). A subsequent subtheme committee elaborated this motto with an equally idealistic set of supporting themes, which positioned the official values of the expo squarely within the trajectory of economic development and consumer capitalism established by Prime Minister Ikeda Hayato's Income Doubling Plan of 1960: "Toward the Realization of a Richer Life," "Toward the Utilization of a More Bountiful Nature," "Toward the Design of Better Lifestyles," and "Toward Deeper Mutual Understanding."[13]

As will be discussed in the final chapter, the expo's embrace of "progress" also included promotion of the potential of the peaceful use of nuclear energy as a power supply: nuclear energy was featured prominently in such venues as the Electric Power Pavilion, sponsored by the Federation of Electric Power Companies. Indeed, the expo year of 1970 was a watershed year for nuclear power in Japan: the first plant to produce electricity commercially in Japan was the Osaka-based Kansai Electric Power Company's Mihama Nuclear Power Plant, commissioned in 1970, while the Tokyo Electric Power Company's Fukushima Daiichi Nuclear Power Plant first achieved criticality in 1970 and began to supply power commercially in 1971.

The theme "Progress and Harmony for Mankind" was later lampooned by Komatsu's science fiction colleague Tsutsui Yasutaka in his short story "Jinrui no daifuchōwa" ("The Great Disharmony of Mankind"). In this story, a mysterious "ghost pavilion," the Son My Village Pavilion, reappears every morning in different locations on the expo grounds. The name of this pavilion refers to the site of the mass killing of several hundred unarmed Vietnamese civilians by the U.S. Army in 1968, known in Japanese as the "Sonmi mura gyakusatsu jiken" (Son My Massacre) but better known in the United States as the My Lai Massacre. In Tsutsui's story, U.S. soldiers storm the hut-like pavilion every morning, killing women, children, and the elderly, but even though the local authorities collect the bodies and destroy the pavilion every afternoon, it reappears again the next morning. In addition, another ghost pavilion appears: the Biafra Pavilion, referring to the secessionist state declared during the Nigerian civil war of 1967–70, which was blockaded, leading to widespread famine and disease. In Tsutsui's story, refugees from this pavilion appear in the expo's various restaurants and cafeterias to beg for food. Finally, in an effort to expiate itself before the various national representatives inconvenienced by the ghost pavilions, the Japanese government offers to share the embarrassment by setting up its own "Nanking Massacre Pavilion." Needless to say, the stubborn reappearance of past and contemporary "disharmony" in Tsutsui's short story belies the utopian (or bureaucratic/consumer capitalist) attempt to create an artificial entertainment zone dedicated to "the harmony of mankind."

Nevertheless, despite the rose-colored sloganeering of the official theme satirized by Tsutsui and widely scorned in left-leaning media and intellectual circles, much of the discussion in the theme committee actually focused on the contradictions, disharmony, and danger in the world of the mid-1960s, including the Cold War, the threat of nuclear apocalypse, and problems of overpopulation, social inequality, and pollution. Indeed, even the official theme statement reflects these underlying concerns, albeit in a rather watered-down, bureaucratic form of prose:

> Nevertheless, when we look at the situation of the world . . . [we see that] mankind is beset by many forms of disharmony. Due to the high level of development of technical civilization, mankind today is undergoing a fundamental revolution in our entire way of life, but the many problems that arise from this are not yet resolved. Furthermore, in every region of the world, large inequities exist, and not only is the exchange, both spiritual and material, between each region clearly inadequate, but frequently, understanding and tolerance are lost and friction

> and tensions erupt. Even science and technology themselves, if they are applied incorrectly, hold the possibility of leading mankind to ruin.[14]

With its characteristic rhetoric of multipolar humanism, the text goes on to assert that wisdom to avoid such a dire fate and unlock the "prosperity of mankind" can be found not in one place but "wherever human beings can be found." "If the diverse wisdoms of mankind can be effectively exchanged and [allowed to] mutually stimulate each other," the text continues, "a higher level of knowledge can appear, and from the understanding and tolerance between different traditions, we can achieve the harmonious development of a better life for all of mankind."[15] Thus, the idea of contemporary "disharmony" forms the backdrop of the official expo theme of "harmony," and a subtle criticism of Western universalism underlies its expression, through the suggestion that the wisdom to solve mankind's problems can be found not in one single source (i.e., Western civilization and enlightenment) but throughout the world.[16] In addition, the text establishes international intellectual, artistic, and human "exchange" as a central goal of the expo—framing a key tenet of the Thinking the Expo group in a way that would influence the design and discourse surrounding the central Theme Zone of the expo site. Nevertheless, for the vast majority of visitors and critics, it was not the statement of the theme committee in its entirety but simply the bromidic "Progress and Harmony for Mankind" that was remembered as the official slogan of the event. The tension between the sunny exterior of the official slogan and the underlying debate over the articulation of more critical viewpoints would be repeated in other forms as the expo unfolded.

The Osaka Expo and Future Studies

The subtheme committee was significant as the meeting place between Komatsu Sakyō, Umesao Tadao, and Katō Hidetoshi of the Kansai-based Thinking the Expo group with Kanto-based architecture critic Kawazoe Noboru and economist Hayashi Yūjirō, all of whom were later active in the founding of *miraigaku,* or the Japanese articulation of future(s) studies. According to his own account, Komatsu suggested the idea of pursuing future studies in the course of a dialogue with Umesao in the *Shūkan Asahi* magazine soon after their return from North America to observe the preparations for the 1967 Montreal Expo. By Komatsu's account, this idea was quickly seized upon by Hayashi and Kawazoe, whose credentials as intellectuals with an interest in future societies were unquestionable.[17] Kawazoe, of course, was the editor and coauthor of the futuristic architectural and design manifesto *Metabolism 1960*, while Hayashi, as director of the Economic Research Institute of the national Economic Planning Agency in 1965, had coauthored an influential report on the lifestyles of the Japanese in the twenty-years-hence future of 1985.[18] Furthermore, in 1969, after his extensive contacts with the Thinking the Expo group members, Hayashi was to publish arguably the most popular and influential book of its era on the "information society," *Jōhōka shakai: hādo na shakai kara sofuto no shakai* (The information society: From "hard" to "soft" society).

In the fall of 1966, the Future Studies Research Group (Miraigaku Kenkyūkai) was founded by Komatsu, Umesao, Katō, Kawazoe, and Hayashi and expanded in 1968 into the Japanese Association for Futures Studies (Nihon Mirai Gakkai), which hosted the second International Futures Research Conference in Kyoto in April 1970.[19] While Komatsu later situated the genesis of Japanese future studies as a continuation of the work of the Thinking the Expo study group, future(s) studies and futurology had been percolating as an area of inquiry worldwide in the 1960s,[20] culminating in the first International Futures Research Conference in Oslo in 1967, which laid the groundwork for the establishment of the Futures Research Federation in 1973. The basis for this emerging interdisciplinary field was the belief that the future was no longer the province of idle speculation or religious prophecy but that trends in conceiving the future could be examined critically through historical and semiotic analysis, while new insights into possible and probable futures could be gained through such informational heuristics as data analytics and systems theory, modeling, and simulation.[21]

Thus, the Osaka Expo emerged as a convergence point in the articulation of ideas of the "future" in the context of the overlapping discourses of future studies, comparative cultural studies and ethnology, media theory and the "information society," and architecture and urban planning. In an article entitled "Bankokuhaku no bijon" (The expo's vision) for the *Yomiuri* newspaper in 1967, Kawazoe expressed the convergence of these issues and discourses as follows: "Japan is not only continuing its high growth. It is the society where population density and mediatization have progressed the furthest, and Japan itself has become a laboratory for a new civilization. Therefore, the Japan Expo is not only about the search for Japan's future, but has a [broader] significance in the history of civilization."[22]

Similarly, in the essay "Bankokuhaku kaijō keikaku," (The plan of the expo site: From survey to design) for the magazine *Kenchiku zasshi*, architect and urban planner Nishiyama Uzō, who collaborated with Tange Kenzō on the initial drafts of the site design, described the expo site as "a model for the city of the future" *(mirai toshi no moderu)*. Touching on many of the official themes worked out by the theme committee, Nishiyama writes:

> The concentration of population in cities is advancing at a rapid pace in our country, and it is said that soon the great majority of Japanese will live in a belt zone connecting Tokyo and Osaka. From a worldwide perspective, the living space of humans is, of necessity, in a trend towards urbanization. Due to this, however, pollution, natural disasters, and every form of paralysis, disharmony, and degradation of the living environment is also progressing. . . . To create a living space with a high degree of density, which would overcome the various faults that have appeared in contemporary cities, and to give people the physical experience of such a space—this would certainly give substance to [the ideal of] "progress and harmony" through the site design. This was the reason I endeavored to create the model of a "core of a future city."[23]

Toward this end, Nishiyama offered four principles for his initial site design: (1) to revive the "correct cycle of nature" in the face of contemporary environmental pollution through the design of recycling and purifying air and water systems and artificial lakes; (2) to create a central "festival plaza" where humans can have direct, face-to-face contact; (3) to develop advanced computerized systems to efficiently control the various functions of the site; and (4) drawing upon these systems, to effectively control the flow of the anticipated massive crowds of people in and out of the site.[24] While Nishiyama's involvement was curtailed after the early stages of the site design, and not all of his ideals were fully realized in the final site, his conceptualization of the expo site as the core of a "future city" infused the concept of the "future" even further into the rhetoric surrounding the site, and his drafts left important conceptual and physical traces on the evolving Osaka Expo site.[25]

Symbol Zone Design and the Architectural Translation of Expo Themes

As the expo planning progressed, the site was divided into spaces for national pavilions, corporate pavilions, peripheral areas, and a central Symbol Zone, where the themes of the expo would be articulated through architecture and design. After the initial drafts by Nishiyama, much of the final site design and execution was overseen by internationally recognized architect Tange Kenzō. Tange also contributed the central architectural feature of the site, the broad Festival Plaza open on the sides but covered by a grand "space frame" roof of prefabricated steel pipes and ball joints in a triangular lattice, topped by a lightweight, translucent polyester film (Plate 8). In part through the lobbying of the Thinking the Expo group to involve innovative artists in the highest levels of planning, the design of exhibition space in the central Symbol Zone and Theme Pavilion was turned over to artist Okamoto Tarō, who proposed the audacious Tower of the Sun, a totemic icon bursting through the roof of Tange's central Festival Plaza. This exuberant tower, with two winglike arms outstretched toward Tange's roof, was crowned by a metallic "Golden Face" reigning high above the roof and also featured a cubist-inspired "Face of the Sun" at the core of the tower facing frontward toward the plaza, a menacing "Black Sun" facing toward the rear, and a "Subterranean Sun" at the underground exhibition area. Okamoto's tower became the visual focal point of the entire expo space, and its primitivist, kitschy appearance was seen as an antithesis to the cool rationality of Tange's space frame design.

Also crucial to the conception and design of the site was the transportation infrastructure, as first described by Nishiyama above and then elaborated in Tange's later site designs. These infrastructure elements included moving sidewalks connecting the Festival Plaza to a radial set of subplazas, a monorail encircling the site, and portals connecting the site to outside rail and highway networks. As Hyunjung Cho summarizes, "The Symbol Zone, located at the core of the expo grounds, was compared to a 'trunk,' a central nervous system of facilities that transmits energy and water to various parts of an organism. The moving walkways extending to sub-plazas from the Symbol Zone were equated with the branches of a tree, and various pavilions were likened to colorful flowers blooming on the tree. Tange conceived Expo '70 as a living organism in which the constant but dynamic equilibrium of the space was coordinated by a vast central management and control system."[26]

Both the central Symbol Zone and the prominent transportation network were elements of the expo's thematic emphasis on circulation, encounters, and information exchange, which were conceived as illustration, instruction, and acclimatization for the dawning postindustrial "information age." In a discussion with Kawazoe Noboru published in the May 1970 issue of the journal *Shinkenchiku*, Tange develops several themes first articulated by the Thinking the Expo members:

> During the stage of an industrial society, world expositions had the cultural-historical significance of "exposing" physical things, such as technology and the fruits of scientific engineering. However, such a form [of display] doesn't have much meaning in the current age, in which we are progressing into an "information society." Rather than displaying hardware, or going to see it, isn't it more meaningful to create a software-like environment? Instead [of the old type of expo], we should gather together to exchange direct communication between people, each bringing our own cultures or non-physical traditions to exchange. Rather than an exposition, it would be a festival.[27]

Tange's remarks reflect the influence of the Thinking the Expo team's rhetorical emphasis on the importance of the expo as a site of communication and exchange rather than simply a display of goods. Furthermore, in his use of the key term *information society* to contextualize the social significance of the expo, he uses a term developed in part by the Thinking the Expo research group members and also employs the distinction between "hardware" and "software," used metaphorically to distinguish different sectors or stages in the development of society, that was popularized in Hayashi Yūjirō's book from a year before, *The Information Society: From "Hard" to "Soft" Society.*

In addition to articulating the conception of "information-age" architecture and design shared in various ways by many of the prominent contributors to the expo's design, Tange's remarks also testify to the emergence of the concept of "festival," which was not initially part of the expo's thematic framework. First proposed by Nishiyama and promoted by both Tange and Okamoto, the idea of the "festival" had different meanings for each figure. For Tange, the "festival" was "the interchange of human energy, the exchange of human wisdom and creativity."[28] For Okamoto, "festival" had a more anarchic, primal valance: "The Expo is a festival," he stated. "I don't think that expositions are fundamentally about learning various types of scientific knowledge. Rather, [they are a place where] surprise and joy are commingled, where old concepts and scientific knowledge are wiped away and tossed aside."[29]

The Symbol Zone, which represented a compromise or juxtaposition between Tange's and Okamoto's visions in execution of the expo's thematic program, elaborated the official expo theme of "Progress and Harmony" together with concepts of "exchange of information" and "festival" through its articulation of space. The official theme of "progress" was articulated through the "mandala"-like temporal and spatial layering of the Symbol Zone's Theme Pavilion architecture, with an Underground Exhibition space representing the "Past: The World of Origins," the Ground Level Exhibition, or "Festival Plaza" representing the "Present: World of Harmony," and the Aerial Exhibition installed in the giant space frame ceiling covering the vast Festival Plaza representing the "Future: The World of Progress." Finally, all three layers were interpenetrated by the Tower of the Sun, representing Okamoto's primal "Energy of Life."[30] Komatsu and Kawazoe, two of the subtheme committee members, were called upon to be subproducers for different regions of the Theme Pavilion: Kawazoe was responsible for the Aerial Exhibition representing the future, while Komatsu was tapped as subproducer for the underground exhibition, representing the past (which Komatsu and his colleagues interpreted on a cosmic scale, creating an environment that represented the development of atoms and the molecular building blocks of life, from proteins and nucleotides such as ATP to larger structures such as RNA and DNA, before moving on to depict the development of organisms, human beings, and human cultures).[31]

Notably, while the Underground and Aerial spaces featured extensive displays consistent with their themes of past and future, the Festival Plaza representing the present was intentionally kept largely devoid of display; rather, the giant roofed open-air plaza was the "hardware" shell to house public events and daily exchanges of people that were to comprise the "software" of the event. This emphasis on public spectacle and exchange was furthered by the placement of technological event "systems," designed by architect Isozaki Arata, most notably the giant robots "Deme" and "Deku," designed to control lighting, move stage components, and otherwise facilitate expo events (Plate 9). Furthermore, this conceptual emphasis on "software" and "information exchange" was intensified both in the Symbol Zone and throughout the expo's various pavilions by the omnipresence of sound and video projection, multiscreen displays, and other multimedia environments. Thus, in its conceptualization and realization, the expo site in general and its core Symbol Zone in particular could be called a proto "cyber city" designed to herald the advent of the "information age."[32] I will explore this "cyber city," its critics, and its progeny in Japanese architecture and science fiction further in the next chapter.

Emergence of the "City of the Future"

In addition to the mandala-like temporal-spatial arrangement of the Theme Pavilion in the Symbol Zone dramatizing the progression from past to future, many of the national and corporate pavilions also placed a heavy emphasis on temporality, specifically the emergence of the society of the future, in their architecture and choice of displays. This was generally in keeping with the tone of utopian future-thinking that had been a major component of world's fairs from the Crystal Palace of the Great Exhibition in London in 1851, through the World of Tomorrow exhibits at the New York World's Fair of 1939–40, to Moshe Safdie's progressive housing complex Habitat '67 and Buckminster Fuller's geodesic dome featured at the 1967 Montreal Expo.[33]

The two most popular national pavilions at the Osaka Expo, the American and Soviet Pavilions, both highlighted the exploration and future development of space, through the exhibit of NASA technology as well as a moon rock collected by the Apollo 12 astronauts in 1969 in the American Pavilion and a life-size model of a Soyuz-4 and other spacecraft in the Soviet Pavilion. The corporate pavilions, dominated by domestic Japanese pavilions, also featured various visions of the future, starting with the Mitsubishi Future Pavilion, as has been described above. Other corporate pavilions, especially the Sanyo Pavilion, Midori Pavilion, and Takara Beautilion, presented visions of future lifestyles and consumer products, including the celebrated "human washing machine" or ultrasonic bath pod in the Sanyo Pavilion, while technologies of the future, including flight simulators and wireless mobile telephones, were demonstrated in such pavilions as the Hitachi Group Pavilion, IBM Pavilion, and Electronic Communications Pavilion.[34]

However, arguably the greatest factor in creating the public image of the Osaka Expo as a "city of the future" would be the dense juxtaposition of innovative architectural forms, including Tange's Great Roof, the low inflated dome of the American Pavilion and aggressively pitched roof of the Soviet Pavilion, and, most especially, the contributions of the young Japanese architects and designers associated with the Metabolist movement, including Kikutake Kiyonori's Expo Tower and Kurokawa Kishō's Toshiba IHI Pavilion and Takara Beautilion, all interpenetrated by the futuristic transportation infrastructure of monorails and moving sidewalks—including "street furniture," monorail, and electric cars designed by Ekuan Kenji.[35] This was the eclectic architectural and design gestalt that would be extensively publicized in the Japanese press as the "city of the future" *(mirai no toshi)*.

In particular, the expo served as a major demonstration of the Metabolist theme of "capsule" construction—i.e., the establishment of a frame or core that can be fitted with prefabricated, modular, detachable capsules, evolving in shape and design as the life cycles and needs of the building's users change. These frame/capsule elements include the Aerial Exhibition illustrating the "World of the Future," in the central Theme Zone, featuring capsules designed by various architects from both inside and outside of Japan, which were "plugged" into Tange's space frame roof overhead of the Festival Plaza. These included "capsules for living" designed by Kurokawa Kishō and Kamiya Kōji, featuring ultramodern prefabricated kitchen, bedroom, and bathroom capsules; a plug-in model of a networked city (i.e., a city whose form is determined by information networks) designed by Maki Fumihiko; and architectural and urban design displays by European and American architects, including such key interlocutors for the Metabolist movement as Archigram (UK), Moshe Safdie (Canada), and Yona Friedman (Paris).[36] Scattered throughout the festival grounds were more examples of capsule/frame architecture, including Kikutake's Expo Tower, in which spherical polyhedron capsules used as viewing chambers were attached to a vertical space frame core, and arguably the most elegant of expo buildings, Kurokawa's Takara Beautilion, with a delicate prefabricated, modular, and expandable tubular lattice framing rounded-edge cubical capsules employed as showrooms for Takara's products for the beauty industry, with sumptuous interior spaces designed by Ekuan Kenji and his GK design firm (Plate 10).[37]

Elsewhere, the Metabolist biological metaphor of cellular growth, decay, and replacement was made explicit in a "Wall of Capsules" display in the Symbol Zone, curated by the Metabolist group, including photographs of cells and other biological forms, as well as a model of a fetus as a "capsule of life." Meanwhile, the connection between the capsule form and the spacecraft, space station, or space suits as paradigmatic "capsules" of the Space Age was made clear by the inclusion of a model of an Intelstat communications satellite plugged into Tange's space frame roof, as well as such forms as the "projector towers," whose cylindrical, visored capsule shapes evoked an astronaut's space suit, protruding above the underground hall connected to Kurokawa's Takara Beautilion.

Ultimately, in its atomized form, enclosure from the outside world, industrial fabrication or prefabrication, and capacity for "stacking" or "clustering," the "capsule" as seen throughout the expo environment could be seen as the logical extension of the thousands of condominium and apartment units for individuals and nuclear families being constructed nearby in Senri New Town. In retrospect, the expo's juxtaposition of ubiquitous form of "capsule" with a highly secularized and carefully managed space of "festival" seems to presage the dominant form of urban lifestyle of the post–High Growth Era, which was divided between highly atomized living spaces and the secular "festival" spaces of shopping centers and amusement parks.

"Managed" Utopia and Hidden Apocalypse

Many of the visions of the future offered by the expo pavilions were fundamentally utopian in nature, from the convenient ultramodern lifestyles promoted by the Sanyo and Takara pavilions to the promise of technological advancement offered by the electronics and communications displays. Perhaps the most clearly and conventionally utopian of these future visions was the Mitsubishi Future Pavilion described above, in which the power of nature would be tamed and every aspect of air, land, and sea would be peacefully developed under mankind's "management." The overall expo site design and Symbol Zone design, while more sophisticated and innovative, also offered a vision of the future city as a place of social management through a combination of spatial design and computerized systems that would monitor and manage the flow of people and promote carefully controlled interpersonal exchanges—a "science fiction" of the future city as a bureaucratically managed "information society."[38] As I will discuss in the next chapter, this vision of technological management was an immediate target for cultural critics of the expo. Moreover, even from within the displays and discourse generated by the expo site planners and designers themselves, darker possibilities for the future could not be completely suppressed from the expo site and its predominant vision of future "Progress and Harmony" through technological progress, urban planning, and technological management.[39]

For example, perhaps the most iconic element of the expo, Okamoto Tarō's Tower of the Sun, included among its four sun faces an enigmatic black sun facing the rear of the Festival Plaza space. In one newspaper interview, Okamoto stated that the multiple faces of his tower would "express anger at all the disharmony and contradictions in the world" and that the "Black Sun" in particular would "glare at the ceremonial space for receiving the prime ministers of all nations."[40] Several commentators, including Sawaragi Noi and Bert Winther-Tamaki, have linked Okamoto's Tower of the Sun, and particularly his "Black Sun," with the theme of "nuclear dread" expressed more explicitly in his concurrent mural in Mexico City, *Ashita no shinwa* (The myth of tomorrow, completed 1968–69), which was subtitled "Hiroshima and Nagasaki" and depicts skeletal figures in flames, as well as a representation of the Japanese sea trawler, the *Lucky Dragon #5*, which was irradiated by an American hydrogen bomb test in 1954.[41]

Elsewhere within the expo's Symbol Zone, Kawazoe Noboru, as subproducer of the "World of the Future" Aerial Exhibition, tried to address concerns about the dystopian possibilities for mankind's future through the inclusion of a "Wall of Contradictions," which sought to draw attention to the possibility of both the "instantaneous destruction" of nuclear war and the "gradual destruction" of environmental damage, as well as the lingering global "contradictions" of racial discrimination and other social ills through displays of photos and photomontages.[42]

Similarly, in the article "From Expo to Pollution: A New Stage for Future Studies," published soon after the closing of the fair, Komatsu Sakyō warned of the potential destruction of modern civilization by environmental imbalance and catastrophic climate change—a warning that the endless "progress" and development promised by the official expo thematic program might not be sustainable:

> If the "accumulation of heat and carbon gas" in the air and water resulting from the enormous energy consumption of our giant industrial society reaches a certain level, then the "thermal balance" of the atmosphere and oceans will naturally collapse. If this happens, the polar ice might melt and cause a great advance of the oceans, or cloud cover might increase, causing a "man-made ice age." This is not simply a science fiction fantasy. . . . In the near future—probably, nearer than we expect—our civilization may have to live much more modestly—more from the restrictions of "environmental balance" than from the [limitations] of natural resources. I have my doubts, however, about whether our hypertrophied "industrial civilization" can learn to "behave modestly" before it is visited with destruction.[43]

However, as Komatsu's article bitterly notes, elements of critique and warning regarding the "Progress and Harmony for Mankind" in the expo were actively suppressed by government officials. Most conspicuously, the Symbol Zone producers were compelled to remove from the "Wall of Contradictions" graphic documentary photographs of corpses and keloid scars of Hiroshima victims, intended to illustrate the horror of nuclear warfare, leaving a less gruesome, but still apocalyptic, photomontage of mushroom clouds and urban destruction in its place.[44]

It is fascinating to observe in the statements above a shared critical vocabulary employed by three of the principal collaborators on the Osaka Expo Symbol Zone through such key words as "disharmony," "contradictions," and "destruction." Both Okamoto and Kawazoe attempted to highlight contemporary society's "disharmony" and "contradictions" amid the prevailing utopian atmosphere of the expo, while Kawazoe and Komatsu even raised the specter of an apocalyptic environmental "destruction" alongside omnipresent threat of nuclear Armageddon—a specter of environmental disaster that, as articulated by Komatsu, could be visited on "industrial civilization" as a result of the disruption of the "thermal balance" of the atmosphere and oceans (similar to the scenario raised by Kawazoe's narrative "Dai-Tōkyō saigo no hi" [The last days of greater Tokyo] as early as 1961, discussed in chapter 1). These remarks highlight a shared critical consciousness underlying the articulation of the official expo theme of "Progress and Harmony for Mankind" and show the degree to which the expo was not only a physical meeting point for a network of artists, architects, writers, and academics but the scene of intellectual exchange and contention as well.

Postlude: Responses to the Osaka Expo in the English-Language Press

In addition to ubiquitous coverage in the Japanese press, which contributed to a national "Expo Fever" and the fair's record-setting 64 million visitors, the Osaka Expo received considerable attention from both the international popular press and the more specialized architectural press. Amid the English-language coverage of the fair, Columbia University architecture professor Ervin Galantay's report for *The Nation* stands out as a particularly thoughtful attempt to relate the design solutions offered by the architects of the expo to the urban planning and environmental challenges faced by Japan:

> The new Japan—pushing toward second place among industrial powers—is increasingly alarmed that it may end up as a world leader in environmental ugliness and pollution. As travelers quickly discover, the serenity of rural Japan is vanishing while the urban environment seems to deteriorate in direct relation to the rising national product. It is against this back-

> ground that the theme of the Osaka Expo '70, "Progress and Harmony," must be evaluated. A postwar emphasis on production, accelerated by the shortchanging of social obligations, has multiplied factories and jobs while congestion, smoke, smog, noise and pollution have been allowed to grow unchecked.[45]

In this context, Galantay notes the infusion of 2.3 billion dollars into greater Osaka's infrastructure and civic improvements; in response to the pollution crisis in Osaka, he mentions the establishment of a River Basin Joint Sewerage Project, a tree-planting campaign, the relocation of industrial plants from upriver sites to reclaimed harbor land, and the computer monitoring and regulation of air quality.[46] With regards to the expo site itself, Galantay enthuses that "as an example of public order combined with individual exuberance it is a lesson for planners everywhere."[47] Galantay cites Tange's carefully designed transportation infrastructure as a success and claims that "on less acreage than Montreal provided, but with twice as many daily visitors, the Osaka Expo supplies the large-scale experiment that psychologists have awaited—the test on human beings of Calhoun's experiment which proved that for rats optimal social behavior can be maintained under conditions of extreme crowding, if the physical environment is meaningfully structured."[48] However, despite the site's much-vaunted infrastructural planning and Galantay's positive appraisal, in fact numerous accidents due to overcrowding were reported on the monorails and moving sidewalks from the start of the fair, and as attendance spiked during holidays and peak summer months, traffic jams, stifling crowds, and long lines for pavilions and on-site transportation proliferated under the summer heat, leading to the expo's derisive nickname "zankokuhaku" (brutality fair) in place of "bankokuhaku" (world's fair).[49]

Within the architectural press, British critic Martin Pawley's review was noteworthy for its focus on the information systems, as well as the extensive use of video displays, sound, and lighting throughout the expo. Regardless of the exuberant physical architecture of the expo buildings and site, it was this shift from an emphasis on the physical environment to the media environment and information systems that led Kawazoe to refer to each pavilion of the expo as "a device to environmentalize various media" *(tashū no media o kankyōka suru tame no sōchi)* and, with reference to Isozaki Arata's concept of the "invisible city," to dub the Festival Plaza site as an "invisible theme pavilion."[50] Pawley picks up on this shift from physical environment to media environment in his analysis of the fair, which he frames in the article's title as "Architecture versus the Movies":

> The proliferation of multi-media displays, robot experiments and synchronous sensory stimulation in general . . . has had an astonishing effect upon the form and meaning of the pavilions constructed to house such magic. Expo '70 reveals the obsolescence of daring architectural design in a way which—until the development of media reached its present level—would have been impossible. . . . The problem posed by Expo '70 is this. If the environment of the future is to be created according to the principles governing perception rather than that of construction . . . then the design of that environment, with its accompanying software, is going to become the de facto province of systems and media men, electronics and computer experts, film directors and editors, photographers, and yes, shopfitters.[51]

In the popular press, as well, commentators such as American travel writer Myra Waldo, in her *Japan Expo '70 Guide*, pointed to the prominent role of technology in the fair:

> EXPO '70, the first world exhibition ever staged in Asia, is in many respects unlike any other world exhibition ever held before. But if you think this means that it is charmingly low-keyed and oriental you're wrong. More than any other exposition EXPO '70 points the way into a new century—the century when machines will relieve man of many of the drudgeries of life. . . . EXPO '70 makes machines, computers, automation and electronic devices lively and interesting. You'll watch with fascination as a towering robot controls lighting, sound effects and props of Festival Plaza's stages. You'll quickly accept the fact that moving sidewalks can be practical and comfortable aspects of world cities. You'll take for granted that a computer can help you find your lost child among tens of thousands of people.[52]

Waldo's remarks are indicative of a turning point, or at least the layering, of Western expectations from an "orientalist" expectation of a "charmingly low-keyed" Japan toward a "techno-orientalist" gaze in which Japan is figured as the "high-tech" utopian or dystopian world of the future. Press coverage of the expo in the United States tended to be combined with alternately excited and alarmed discussions of Japan's rise as a global economic and technological power. For example, one of *Time* magazine's reports on the fair, pointedly titled "Toward the Japanese Century," asserted that "no country has a stronger franchise on the future than Japan."[53] It is to this "techno-orientalist" image, generated from both within and without Japan, together with the evolving imagination of the "cyber city," to which I will turn in the next chapter.

5 Liquid Cities

The Technopolis from Expo to Cyberpunk

Throughout the late twentieth century, architects, critics, and fiction authors repeatedly imagined the dematerialization of the Japanese city effected by new media and information technologies. As has been discussed earlier, Isozaki Arata's seminal essay "Invisible City" (1967) describes an urban environment of increasing fluidity, flux, and media noise: "Constant movement, diffusion, rejection of fixed images, and infinite increases of advertising and noise are part of daily life in Tokyo and other cities," Isozaki wrote.[1] The influence of the Metabolist architects and theorists, their attention to process and change in architecture and urban life, as well as their attraction to organic metaphors to describe such change, can be seen in Isozaki's description of the urban environment in a "liquid state of constant organic reproduction and division."[2] Yet while the organic metaphors employed by the Metabolists typically referred to metamorphosis in the built, physical environment, in Isozaki's writings this organicism seems to apply not only to the physical environment but also to the underlying flows of energy and information. To comprehend and intervene in such a liquid city, Isozaki seized on the possibilities of information technology as well as cybernetic and systems theory. Spatial elements of the city would be "reduced to codes" and "reorganized as a system model"; such elements could then be subject to computer simulation as a new form of urban planning. The future city, newly understood and designed as a "cybernetics environment," would be a "man-machine system" possessing a "wide variety of movable equipment" and a "self-instructing feedback channel." For Isozaki, this is the newly emerging invisible city, a space of simulation and cybernetic interaction where "technology and planning overlap."[3]

In the following years, architects continued to use metaphors of dematerialization and liquification to describe the transformation of the Japanese city. While Isozaki imagined the city broken down into "codes" and "signs" by the cybernetically/semiotically oriented urban planner, subsequent critics described the city itself transforming into signs, codes, and floating images—information to be read, consumed, and remixed by the city's users.[4] For example, in the 1980s, architect Itō Toyoo described Tokyo as a "simulated city" where "our bodies float amid vast images and showers of sounds."[5] Similarly, architect and critic Yatsuka Hajime wrote that architecture had acquired the quality of "signs rather than substance"; Japanese cities were imbued with an "invisible and multi-layered network of information flow"; in the process, they had lost their characteristic "integrity" and "depth."[6]

While Norbert Wiener's writings on cybernetics and Marshall McLuhan's media theory were significant intertexts for Isozaki and his peers in the 1960s, by the 1980s and 1990s, the interpretation of the Japanese city by Japanese as well as foreign architects, critics, and novelists both influenced and was influenced by postmodern theoretical ideas, including Fredric Jameson's idea of "depthlessness" as a defining feature of postmodernism, posited as the cultural expression of multinational capitalism (1984); Baudrillard's "simulacrum," in which the contemporary experience of the "hyperreal" is produced from "miniaturized cells, matrices, memory banks, models of control" (1982); and Deleuze and Guattari's explorations of the rhizome, deterritorialization, and nomadism as figures for semiotic and social organization outside of conventional informational and political hierarchies (1980).[7]

As introduced in the previous chapter, at roughly the same time that Isozaki was envisioning the "invisible city" and exploring the possibilities of computer simulation, a wave of scholarly and journalistic writing in Japan introduced the concept of the "information society" *(jōhō shakai)* to the public. The idea that Japan was shifting from an industrial to a postindustrial economy based on the information and service sectors, and that new communications and information technology would transform social patterns of work and leisure, was embraced and promoted in such urban planning proposals as Tange Kenzō's Plan for Tokyo 1960 and his follow-up study *Nihon rettō no shōraizō* (The future image of the Japanese archipelago, 1966), as well as Kurokawa Kishō's "Metapolis—The Hishino Plan" ("Teijū tan'i keikaku no rinen to hōhō," 1967) and other writings. The "information society" discourse was also reflected in a series of governmental reports and initiatives whose very titles such as the "technopolis," "teletopia," and "new media communities" projects betray the optimistic premise that bureaucratic guidance and cooperation between public investment, private enterprise, and local communities and citizens would lead to a more prosperous society that was fulfilling for both the collective and the individual.

As these technocratic initiatives pushed to the fore, a counter-discourse emerged, exemplified by such critics as structural anthropologist Kitazawa Masakuni and sociologist Kurihara Akira, who warned of the overreach of the "managed society" *(kanri shakai)*. As Kitazawa summarizes, the "managed society" is a "society administered through highly sophisticated mechanisms for forecasting, planning, and control," based on "quantitative analysis of data and compilation of a set of optimum conditions for that society's well-being." In such a society, the "power elite" gently controls all aspects of life, including political discourse, and dangers spring from the "great difficulty of drawing a clear boundary between service and authoritarian control."[8] In terms of architecture and urban space, public plazas *(hiroba)*—including the Osaka Expo's Festival Plaza and the Shinjuku Station West Exit Plaza—emerged in the "managed society" critiques as key sites of contestation between ideals of direct communication, freedom of assembly, and political and artistic expression versus the repressive forces of surveillance and security. As I will explore below, even the emergence of a new type of consumer culture in 1970s Shibuya was initially critiqued through the lenses of the "plaza" and the "managed society."

Although they share some elements of the 1960s and 1970s Situationist critiques of media and urban space,[9] these critiques of the "information society" and the "managed society" can also be productively related to the discourse around "control societies" and "control space" by more recent authors working in European and American contexts such as Gilles Deleuze, Wendy Hui Kyong Chun, and Sze Tsung Leong. In his "Postscript on Control Societies" (1990), Deleuze proposes a shift between the "disciplinary societies" of the eighteenth, nineteenth, and early twentieth centuries as identified by Michel Foucault and "control societies" emerging in the late twentieth century. While disciplinary societies are broken into sites of confinement such as prisons, hospitals, factories, and schools, and subjects are organized into the categories of "individual" and "mass," in control societies "individuals become '*dividuals*' and masses become samples, data, markets, or '*banks*.'"[10] Authority in such control societies no longer converges in an owner such as the state or a private enterprise but is diffused into a "transmutable or transformable coded configuration, of a single business where the only people left are administrators."[11] The shift in structures of control identified by Deleuze is similar to what is described by the "managed society" critics, although the critics typically imagine such controls being distributed across State bureaucratic and security apparatuses in collusion with private capital, while for Deleuze the locus of power becomes even more diffuse—the world in this paranoid vision is transformed into a "single business" configured as an instrument of control.

In *Control and Freedom: Power and Paranoia in the Age of Fiber Optics* (2006), Wendy Hui Kyong Chun follows Deleuze's reading of control societies to examine "control" and "freedom" as key discursive categories in the internet age, not as opposite or complementary terms but each offering a myriad of contradictory pitfalls and possibilities. According to Chun, the paranoia found in Deleuze's vision is itself endemic to the control society, fulfilling the aims of control by "imaginatively ascribing to control power that it does not yet have and by erasing its failures"; moreover, such paranoia "drives the desire for technological objects and for control-freedom as a means of prevention."[12] Similarly, in his essay "Ulterior Spaces" (2001), Sze Tsung Leong updates the mechanisms of the control society by examining such millennial technologies as the global positioning system, computer-based geographic information systems, and electronically scannable universal product codes as systems for organizing urban space and tracking and planning the flows of products and consumers. Leong proposes the term *control space* to describe urban space that has been reduced through such technologies to a "receptacle for numeric quantification, a domain within which information is both extracted and deployed."[13] "Control space," he continues, "is the desire to make space simultaneous with the irrationalities and vicissitudes of the market." Under such conditions, "architecture grows increasingly flexible, increasingly ephemeral, increasingly targeted to changing needs and tastes, increasingly mutable"—a situation close to that described by Itō Toyoo twelve years earlier in his essay on Japanese architecture in the "sea of consumption," examined below.[14]

As indicated in Itō's essay, a major turning point in the evolution of the Japanese city occurred in the 1980s, when the economy recovered from the 1970s slump, real estate prices soared, brand-oriented consumerism flourished in the city's more prosperous nodes, and a new wave of demolition and construction further accelerated the metabolism of the Japanese cityscape. The "bubble economy" era also saw Japanese companies and real estate firms acquiring high-profile assets abroad and foreign as well as domestic architects increasingly using Tokyo as a canvas for showy postmodern architectural projects. This "bubble," however, proved fleeting, as another turning point arrived in 1991 with the bursting of the real estate and stock market price bubble, ushering in twenty or more years of economic retrenchment and increasing social anxieties and displacements. Nevertheless, the technological landscape of the Japanese city (including the built environment as well as the daily practices of urban dwellers) continued to evolve through the ensuing decades, with such developments as the rise of cell phones and mobile computing, the growth of 24-hour convenience stores as one-stop hubs for daily purchases and financial transactions, and the rise of a new center for virtual play in the "electric town" of Akihabara, originally known primarily as a site to purchase small electronic parts, which transformed into an international center for gaming and *otaku* fans of electronic games, manga, and anime.[15]

In this chapter, I will attempt to provide a historical perspective on the millennial "liquid city" of Tokyo, first by observing in more detail the technological visions realized and promoted by architects Isozaki Arata and Kurokawa Kishō at the 1970 Osaka Expo and the bureaucratic urban planning attempts to guide the evolution of the "information society" in the subsequent decades. I will examine criticism of expo architecture and technology as well as the role of the State and private enterprise in the molding of urban space and control of its uses—criticism that challenged the precepts of the "managed society." In addition, I will observe the role of architects and critics such as Itō Toyoo and Yatsuka Hajime in attempting to come to terms with the rapid transformation of the city amid the growth of information technology and the rise of the consumer society of the bubble economy and its aftermath. Finally, I will sketch the convergence of the urban and the technological in the rise of the Japanese city as a paradigmatic site for the "future" in cyberpunk narratives from the 1980s and 1990s, including Ridley Scott's *Blade Runner* (1982), William Gibson's *Neuromancer* (1984), and Masaki Gorō's *Venus City* (1991). Increasingly, from the 1980s onward, the "techno-orientalist" association between Japan/Asia, technology, and the future is generated both outside of and within Japan: a matrix of desire and fear toward both technology and the Other.

In examining both fictional and nonfictional writings about technology and the Japanese city from the 1960s through the 1990s, we can observe a shift from bureaucratic attempts to implement the "technopolis" through the planning process and economic guidance to a perception of the city itself transforming through new patterns of consumption and media and technology usage. While in the first phase the agent—and, to critics, the antagonist—of urban transformation was seen to be the technocratic State in collusion with the national business sector, in the second phase, the change was more often ascribed to the patterns and practices of consumers and the diffused enticements of consumer capitalism. Tellingly, the antagonist for cyberpunk narratives is typically not the totalitarian State, as in Orwell's *1984*, but rather diffuse multinational corporations and their doubles: the international crime syndicate and the terrorist organization—the shape-shifting representatives of the paranoid imagination of the "control society."

The 1970 Osaka Expo as Cybercity

As outlined in the previous chapter, the Osaka Expo's Festival Plaza was designed with a minimum of permanent displays. Rather, the space itself was designed as an "invisible monument" in which the exchanges of information between visitors to the expo were to occur. While Tange Kenzō oversaw the design of the physical environment of Festival Plaza and its massive space frame roof, Isozaki Arata was placed in charge of designing the plaza's event systems, in order to actualize communication in the form of stage events in the performance area of the plaza to the rear of the Tower of the Sun. Isozaki's work was concentrated not on creating any permanent architectural features but rather on the establishment of an interactive "environment" (*kankyō*).[16] Isozaki's design featured moveable lighting suspended from trolleys mounted in Tange's space frame roof, moveable stage and seating components, and two giant robots, nicknamed Deku and Deme, to assist with the staging. Deku was designed as a "sub-control station" or moving control tower for directing lights, sound, and photography; Deme, designed as a "performance robot," was equipped to emit light, sound, smoke, and scents to contribute to stage performances. Deme's anthropomorphic form included two arms for moving stage components, props, and even people, as well as two transparent spherical "eyes" that were actually control rooms for robot operators. While both robots included stations for human operators, they were also designed to respond automatically to environmental conditions on stage and among the crowd; the pattern of these responses, in the form of light and sound generated by the robots, was programmed in advance as a type of score.[17] Isozaki argued that the stage devices for his Festival Plaza "liquified architecture, which had been solid and spatial, into something momentary, experiential, and temporal."[18]

Similarly, Kurokawa Kishō argued that the extensive use of video and multiscreen environments throughout the Osaka Expo's pavilions transformed the fair site into a "training center" preparing visitors for a new experience of the highly mediated, information-based city. Like Isozaki, he suggested that the solid physicality of architecture was already in a process of dematerialization; for Kurokawa, physical architecture will enter a new state of "interpenetration" with intangible images and "spiritual" impulses. In an interview with architecture critic Martin Pawley, he explained:

> I think architecture is destined to become a very metaphysical thing. You know today architecture is still fundamentally walls, floors and windows, but there is already an imaginable state of affairs where all these elements could become somehow simply images—there is going to be an interpenetration between very spiritual, very visual things and the physical world that we now work with. It is pointless to suggest that people will not understand this—they live with it already, information overload is the norm for urban man. What we must do is to learn to select and discriminate. I see the multiscreen, mixed media pavilion as a training center for just that.[19]

Kurokawa also conceived of the capsule, which was an architectural form that he promoted throughout the expo, as a cybernetic "feedback mechanism" to help the occupant receive, filter, and transmit information. As he put it in his "Capsule Declaration," "just as an astronaut is protected by a perfect shelter from solar winds and cosmic rays, individuals should be protected by capsules in which they can reject information they do not need and in which they are sheltered from information they do not want, thereby allowing an individual to recover his subjectivity and independence."[20] The traditional "sheltering" function of the home would thereby be applied to the new era in which physical and intangible forces interpenetrate. Furthermore, Kurokawa suggested that the information economy will pass through two stages: the first in which information is purchased monetarily by the individual consumer in a primarily unidirectional flow and the second being a multidirectional age of "creative information" in which specific information possessed by or created by the individual will be bartered in exchange for information from the outside. During this latter phase, a capsule that can "transmit, receive and feed back information at any time" will be of high value.[21]

Isozaki's event systems presided over by the robots Deme and Deku, the cybernetic environment of the capsule as promoted by Kurokawa, and the pervasiveness of multiscreen and multimedia displays in the various individual pavilions, frequently controlled by computer systems, were some of the prominent elements contributing to the realization of the expo "city of the future" as a highly cybernetic, mediatized environment—which we might retroactively term a model or simulation of a "cybercity."[22] The expo site infrastructure further included numerous applications of information technology that were promoted in the press and in official expo publicity for their innovations. These included computer systems to track, compile, and display data on numbers and locations of expo visitors, the flow of automobiles in parking lots, and information on missing children and lost articles; searchable visitor guide information terminals located throughout the grounds and pavilions; and extensive electronic communications systems and infrastructural support systems.[23] Indeed, as explicated by Kawazoe Noboru, Tange and his collaborators conceived of the entire expo site, with its various transportation and information subsystems, as a "giant physical environmental system" or "device" *(kyōdai na butsuriteki kankyō no sōchi)* on "the scale of a city."[24]

However, this collaborative technical and social vision also became the target of critics from the left concerned about the development of the Japanese city along the technocratic and information-capitalist lines exposed by the expo. For such critics, the expo's utopian "city of the future" was in fact an urban dystopia heralding a coming "managed society" distinguished by electronic surveillance and bureaucratic control—a "techno-structure," in the words of art critic Haryū Ichirō, in which "information" itself became a fetish and the collusion of the State and corporate capital led to the repression of individual freedom and expression.[25] For example, artist Yoshimura Masanobu (himself a collaborator on Isozaki's plaza), in a piece for the *Asahi Shinbun* newspaper, referred to the Festival Plaza as a "managed plaza" *(kanri kōjō)* where authoritarian control and security took precedence over spontaneous human exchanges, while in the *Mainichi Shinbun* newspaper, Yoshida Mitsukuni, a science historian, similarly described the expo site as a space where visitors would be "constantly managed and monitored by computers and security guards, and hustled along."[26] Citing the example of security guards breaking up a spontaneous go-go line dance that formed in the Festival Plaza between regularly scheduled performances, Haryū Ichirō stated that "the plaza, which was supposed to liberate people from their everyday existence, has, on the contrary, become a symbol of Expo '70: a plaza built by power and imposed on the spectators."[27] Summarizing his critique of the expo, Haryū wrote, "In terms of economics, Expo '70 stands for the liberalization of capital, the reorganization and strengthening of industry in order to achieve economic domination over Asia; in terms of culture, under the banner of the information revolution, the expo represents the merger of science and art and the use of technology in order to consolidate and manage ideology within the system."[28]

Haryū also leveled an unsparing critique of Kurokawa Kishō's vision of capsule living promoted at the expo, in which consumers could freely choose and assemble their living spaces from a repertoire of prefabricated components. For Haryū, Kurokawa's vision, "based on the premise that in an information society the alienation of industrial society will vanish and that harmony between technology and humanity will naturally prevail," is delusional in that it "deliberately disregards how this stunning process of transformation and renewal is born not out of human desire, but provoked by the entreaties of capital."[29] In mass-producing components for living, different types of units would be manufactured to respond to different consumer desires. However, under this logic, Haryū warned, capital would be capable of manipulating and even manufacturing desire. "Computers will be capable of turning people's desires into numbers to be calculated, and in doing so, strengthen the manipulation and domination of the masses." Made-to-order production, he concludes, "does not necessarily bring individuality and collectivity into harmony. Rather, a situation emerges where individual desires are bypassed and wrapped in a false notion of the public, while capital supporting private enterprise monopolizes individuality and freedom of expression. The information society that Kurokawa paints with rosy colors is transformed into a tightly controlled society based on a *techno-structure*."[30]

Technocratic Utopias

Regardless of such critiques, the notion of a coming information society promoted in various forms at the Osaka Expo was broadly embraced in bureaucratic circles in the Japanese governmental ministries and economic think tanks and strongly informed the coming two decades of economic policy and urban planning proposals. As Tessa Morris-Suzuki describes in her critical analysis, *Beyond Computopia: Information, Automation, and Democracy in Japan* (1988), the "information society" concept was embraced in a series of influential bureaucratic reports, which outlined the transformation of the Japanese economic base from an industrial to a postindustrial economy founded on media and information technologies. These reports also speculated on the social outcomes of mediatization, including the increase of leisure time, self-cultivation, and human creativity, as well as the development of decentralized, flexible, and harmonious social interactions through new communication networks. Such discourses, in Morris-Suzuki's view, constitute a "technocrats' Utopia" in which "a world of material abundance and spiritual fulfillment will be achieved . . . through the spontaneous evolution of the existing system" under the "benign guidance of the ruling elite."[31]

In terms of urban planning, one aspect of the bureaucratic embrace of the "information society" was the governmental promotion of new urban or suburban developments and industrial parks oriented toward information technology, under the various banners of "wired cities" *(yūsen toshi)*, "technopolis" *(tekunoporisu/kōchō gijutsu shūseki toshi)*, "teletopia" *(teretopia)*, and "new media communities" *(nyū media komyūnitei)*. As introduced in chapter 1, by 1967 Kurokawa Kishō had already introduced his plan for Hishino New Town based on the concept of the metapolis, an intermediate urban unit between the size of a house and a metropolis, designed to function as a part of the developing global ecumenopolis through its information, communications, and transportation systems.[32] Kurokawa's vision of a networked city influenced the 1969/1970 National Comprehensive Development Plan produced by the Japanese government's Economic Planning Agency, and Kurokawa himself was appointed to the agency's Research Committee for Large-Scale Development Projects and Information Networks.[33]

In the following decade, two government ministries, the Ministry of International Trade and Industry (MITI) and the Ministry of Posts and Telecommunications (MPT), introduced rival "wired city" plans to outfit certain homes and public buildings in the existing New Towns in Tama (near Tokyo) and Higashi Ikoma (near Osaka) with advanced cable and fiber optic networks, as well as a battery of experimental communications equipment including two-way TV, facsimile devices, and home printers.[34] Despite the mixed success of these experiments in terms of successful integration of the trial technologies into the lives of residents in the model communities,[35] after completion of these two test projects the two rival ministries pressed on in the 1980s with more extensive plans to establish "teletopia" cities and "new media communities" throughout Japan.[36] Meanwhile, in 1983 MITI also launched an ambitious new "technopolis" program, aiming to establish new high-tech provincial towns with the aim of dispersing technological development throughout the country; twenty-six sites were chosen for "technopolis" development. These were to be towns of about 50,000 in population near a "mother city" of at least 150,000 people, with high-amenity residential areas, leading-edge communications infrastructure, and research and industrial facilities focusing on advanced technology.[37]

Within Tokyo, the most ambitious bureaucratic/techno-utopian plans were a series of proposals for establishing a "Tokyo Teleport Town" on Tokyo Bay—the same site, of course, as Tange Kenzō's epochal proposal for a megastructural development in his "Tokyo Plan 1960." By the 1980s, in response to the soaring real estate prices and construction boom of the bubble economy, a new wave of proposals emerged for Tokyo Bay focusing on traditional landfill-based development (rather than Tange's "linear city" megastructural vision), including new proposals by Tange and Kurokawa Kishō.[38] Following on the MPT's "teletopia" initiative from 1983, in 1985 Tokyo governor Suzuki Shun'ichi announced the plans for "Tokyo Teleport Town," a new Waterfront City Subcenter including landfill-based developments in the Aomi, Ariake, and Daiba areas, planned to house a residential population of over 60,000 and a working population of over 100,000: a model community for the information society featuring high-tech amenities and advanced communications infrastructure, as well as sports, recreational, and shopping facilities. The completion of the development was slated for 1996 and planned to coincide with a Tokyo Frontier Exposition held at a Tokyo Frontier Media Park to be designed by Itō Toyoo.[39]

However, because of the bursting of the real estate bubble in 1991 and subsequent recession, plans for the Tokyo Teleport Town were severely curtailed, including much of the housing and business center development; plans for the Frontier Exposition and Frontier Media Park were scratched. Nevertheless, much of what remained of the new bay development centered on the media industries and retained a techno-futurist, megastructural architectural orientation, including the Fuji Television Headquarters designed by Tange Kenzō (1996), the Tokyo Big Sight convention center (1996) featuring its Conference Tower of inverted titanium pyramids, the giant Tokyo Telecom Center (1996), and the National Museum of Emerging Science and Innovation (Nihon kagaku miraikan, 2001), threaded to the existing city across the bay by the new transportation infrastructure of Rainbow Bridge and the Yurikamome AGT (automated guideway transit) line. The shift in the project's orientation from an urban "subcenter" and model living community to primarily a shopping and entertainment district focused on the theme-park-like space of Odaiba symbolizes the gradual shift from the 1980s onward from technocratic, utopian urban planning driven by the national and metropolitan bureaucracies, to increasingly privatized economic development oriented toward a consumer society.

Over the decades that the government was staging the Osaka Expo and seeking to promote technological advancements in suburban New

Towns, peripheral areas, and the frontier of Tokyo Bay, the architecture and culture of the existing Tokyo cityscape continued to evolve through a combination of government initiatives, private industry, and popular practices. These include the redevelopment of two major commuter and commercial centers to the west of the city: Shinjuku in the 1960s and Shibuya in the 1970s. These large-scale projects bookended the 1970 Osaka Expo, and cultural and social critics often related their interpretation of each of these urban spaces, and both their official and popular uses, to the ideology and practices that were introduced at the expo.

The remaking of Shinjuku in the 1960s included the draining of the Yodobashi Water Purification Plant in order to build a new urban "subcenter" *(fukutoshin)* of skyscrapers to the west of Shinjuku station, the construction of new Odakyū and Keiō Department Stores at private rail line terminals, and the building of a new spiral-shaped Shinjuku Station West Exit Plaza designed by Le Corbusier disciple Sakakura Shunzō (1901–1969), which was intended to move commuters from the rail and subway lines to the new department stores and offices of the west Shinjuku subcenter. Meanwhile, the crowded streets of Kabukichō and vicinity to the north of the station had become the locus for the city's underground arts scene and leftist subcultures. For several months over the spring and summer of 1969, as war raged in Vietnam and the 1970 renewal of the U.S.–Japan Security Treaty loomed, musicians calling themselves "folk guerillas" gathered with students and activists on the West Exit Plaza to sing protest songs, debate issues, gather signatures and donations for political causes, and distribute or sell "mini-komi"—independent, small-scale publications. These gatherings were broken up by riot police after the official designation of the area was changed from "plaza" *(hiroba)* to "concourse" *(tsūrō)* and the young people who had gathered there were charged with obstructing pedestrian traffic.[40] Critics were quick to note the irony of the police crackdown on these spontaneous gatherings in the plaza of Shinjuku at the same time as the architects of the state-sponsored Osaka Expo were planning their Festival Plaza, ostensibly designed to encourage free exchanges of ideas and culture among people.[41] The context of the Shinjuku West Exit Plaza gatherings and their suppression is crucial to understanding the leftist critique of the expo's Festival Plaza as a managed plaza in which electronic surveillance aided an oppressive security regime.

In the 1970s, however, a new urban space with its own cultural zeitgeist emerged in Shibuya, another commuter center to the south of Shinjuku. This Shibuya culture centered on the newly renamed street Kōen dōri (Park Street), sloping upward from the vicinity of Shibuya station toward the NHK broadcasting center, Tange Kenzō's Olympic Stadium (Yoyogi National Gymnasium), and Yoyogi Park. Kōen dōri had its focal point in the Seibu Department Store group's new store Parco (opened in 1973) midway up the slope. Art critic Tōno Yoshiaki compared the scene at Kōen dōri to a street festival overflowing with crowds of young people and "bookshops, coffee shops, video arcades, record shops, boutiques, second-hand clothing stores, and crepe stands," punctuated by the "vertical fair" of Parco, filled with its own stalls and booths rented to tenant merchants, and capped by the cultural cachet of the Seibu Gekijō Theater.[42] Writing in 1976, in language inflected by Henri Lefebvre's *The Production of Space* (1974), architecture critic Makabe Toshiharu compared the "urban strategy" of the Seibu group's Parco to the transparently authoritarian functionalist "planning ideology" of the Shinjuku subcenter and what he judged to be the failed experiments of the Osaka Expo to generate a new image of the city. By contrast, Makabe argued, Parco's "Shibuya-ism"—which included its perspectival reinterpretation of the local urban amenities (coffee shops, theaters, Yoyogi Park, etc.), as well as its cosmopolitan, avant-garde advertising campaigns—succeeded in using the cityscape itself as a type of media to generate an "image" of urbanism that "pervades the city like a kind of mist" and "prevents contradictions [such as class and ideological conflicts] from becoming evident, or sometimes even incorporates these contradictions into its image-making."[43] Furthermore, Makabe argued, Parco avoided both the "plaza" and the monumental "temple" as architectural or urban forms, de-emphasizing the physical structure of the Parco store itself in favor of the eclectic "assemblage" of interior and surrounding street spaces, as well as the experiential "gestures" and "happenings" of Shibuya visitors.[44] As paraphrased by Tōno, the "Parco strategy" identified by Makabe was "the post-Expo establishment's way of realizing the false illusion of the 'plaza' that underlay Expo '70 in a soft, invisible form in Shibuya. In other words, the strategy was to establish an 'urban façade' or a zone of 'urban-ness' that would serve as a buffer between complete state control and the everyday life of the individual."[45]

In his essay from the following year, Tōno himself focused on the crowds of young people filling the streets of Shibuya. He contrasted the "relentless questioning" of the youth who participated in the folk rallies and sit-ins in Shinjuku with the "disorderly, elusive raw energy" of the youth of Shibuya. "To me," Tōno wrote, "it almost appears as though the people who built Parco at the middle of that hill—who conceived of this multidimensional festival space consisting of the horizontal Kōen-dōri and the vertical Parco building—were recreating the sit-in ideology of the '70s, transforming it and incorporating it ingeniously, or perhaps instinctively, as a kind of commercial strategy."[46] While Tōno admitted that the youth of Shibuya, operating within a strictly commercial context, exhibited only a "controlled freedom," he sought to move beyond the critique of state and corporate regulation of public spaces to appreciate the "human, innocent, compelling charming, rambling, and formless," quality of the late 1970s Shibuya crowds.[47]

This "street fair" atmosphere was further institutionalized in the same year (1977) by the metropolitan government's declaration of a "pedestrian paradise" *(hokōsha tengoku)*, closed to street traffic on Sundays and holidays, just north of Kōen dōri, from the edge of Yoyogi Park along the broad Omotesandō boulevard through the Harajuku neighborhood. This new form of public space was quickly appropriated by youth subcultures such as the *takenoko-zoku* street dance performers of the late 1970s (girls wearing flashy synthetic fashions such as could be purchased at the Takenoko Boutique in Harajuku and performing synchronized street dances to disco music) and the neo-rockabilly and '50s revival bands and dancers of the 1980s. However, tensions between public expression and state control played out in this arena just as they had in Shinjuku's West Exit Plaza; the "pedestrian paradise" was closed in the late 1990s because of concerns about noise and crime, including fears of drug dealing among Iranian immigrants who had also congregated in and around Yoyogi Park. In the twenty-first century, similar tensions over control of the public space erupted in Akihabara around concerns about the public propriety of cosplay and *otagei* ("otaku art") dance performances during the neighborhood's own weekly "pedestrian paradise"; these tensions intensified in 2008 after a mass killing incident during the street closure. This "Akihabara massacre" was linked in the press to purported antisocial and violent tendencies within the otaku subculture and led to suspension of the "pedestrian paradise" and strict regulation of public performances after the street closure resumed in 2010.[48] Thus, following the critics of the managed society, we could say that despite the appearance of ostensible buffer zones between explicit forms of state control and everyday life, we can trace a continuity in tensions between "unruly" popular appropriations of public space and the attempts of state and local authorities to control or suppress them, from Shinjuku's West Exit Plaza to the "pedestrian paradise" spaces of Yoyogi/Harajuku and Akihabara.

Itō Toyoo and the "Sea of Consumption"

In the 1980s, as the economy recovered from its downturn in the previous decade and the real estate market began to inflate, Tokyo entered its bubble economy period of real estate speculation and conspicuous consumption. Youth subcultures emerged based on the consumption of particular brands and consumer items, as well as insider knowledge of retail outlets, cafés, and restaurants, which were promoted by a highly developed media industry including television and fashion and lifestyle magazines. In the literary realm, this consumer lifestyle was captured by Tanaka Yasuo's 1980 novel *Nantonaku kurisutaru* (Somehow, crystal), which featured a female protagonist who was a college student and part-time model living in Tokyo and frequenting the shops, department stores, and eateries of Shibuya. The novel, which included an extensive set of footnotes with information on specific brand-name items mentioned in the main text, has been heralded as a paradigmatic example of postmodern literature, exhibiting contemporary culture as a series of empty signs (brands, products, fashions, etc.), consumed and displayed in a space of cultural play devoid of political consciousness or historical depth.[49]

Architect Itō Toyoo, who had apprenticed in Metabolist Kikutake Kiyonori's office in the 1960s and debuted in 1971 with his eccentrically hermetic capsule URBOT (Urban Robot), was a key interpreter of this new urban space in the 1980s and 1990s. As will be recalled from chapter 1, Itō personified his URBOT housing design as a robotic dwelling with "recessive heredity" who paradoxically rejected the incorporation of advanced technology that would "result in an integrated human-machine system."[50] Similarly, his earliest realized projects such as the White U house in Tokyo from 1976, featured minimalist, inward-oriented spaces that seemed to reject altogether the noise, commercialism, and "information overload" of the surrounding city. Nevertheless, Itō emerged during the 1980s and 1990s as a central commentator and practitioner in the consumerist and media/technology-saturated environment of bubble and postbubble Japan. Writing in 1989, Itō noted how architecture in the 1980s had become "constructed and consumed at a tremendous pace," with both domestic and visiting foreign architects featured prominently in magazines, newspapers, and TV on a daily basis. "This phenomenon of architecture becoming popular and flooding the streets," he wrote, "is directly analogous to its being treated no better than wastepaper, and becoming, essentially, an object of consumption." While some architects might have previously thought of their work in a separate category from consumer items because of its longer "service life" or its status as "an immobile presence rooted in the land," such thinking was no longer possible amid the "sudden circulation of capital" and the "sea of consumption" of bubble-era Japan: "Urban space itself underwent codification and superficialization so rapidly that there was no time even to speak out against it. For architects, the issue has now become a question of not whether we can reject consumer society and still survive, but of whether we understand how completely we must break free of the idea that architecture alone can exist outside of consumption."[51] Steeped as he was in the atmosphere of Metabolism as an apprentice to Kikutake, Itō must surely have recognized that the earlier movement had already rejected the idea of architecture as "an immobile presence rooted in the land" in favor of an architecture conceived in the beginning as open to change, growth, and deterioration; furthermore, Kurokawa's presentation of capsule architecture as a customizable personal product paved the way for an architecture for a consumer society.[52] Nevertheless, Itō perceived a new situation of acceleration and intensification in the 1980s, as well as an opening for responses from a fresh generation of architects.

As one response to the question of how architecture might be envisioned amid the 1980s "sea of consumption," Itō developed his

Pao, named after the Chinese term for Mongolian yurts. Itō's Pao was a dome-shaped, tentlike enclosure consisting of steel tubing and translucent textiles, unveiled in an exhibit at the Shibuya branch of Seibu Department Store in 1985.[53] Itō offered the portable and transient architecture of this postmodern yurt as a rest station for the "nomadic Tokyo women" *(Tōkyō yūboku shōjo)* who wandered among the commuter workplaces, retail outlets, galleries, cafés, and restaurants of Shibuya and other consumer centers. As art historian Jonathan Reynolds notes, Itō conceived of the Pao not only as a physical shelter but also as a media shelter, "a semipermeable membrane between its occupant and the media-saturated environment in which she lived," referring to Itō's dictum that architecture must be a "media suit" or "extension of our skin in relation to both nature and information."[54]

In its guise as a "media suit," Itō's Pao recalls Kurokawa Kishō's earlier conception of the capsule as "cyborg architecture" helping its occupant to receive, filter, and transmit information; in its function as a shelter for an "urban nomad," the Pao echoes Kurokawa's conception of the uprooted, mobile lifestyle of the capsule occupant defined as *Homo movens*. As discussed in chapter 1, Kurokawa's concepts were concretized in his Nakagin Capsule Tower, designed for the mobile life of frequently traveling or commuting white-collar workers. Nevertheless, while the affinity between Itō's Pao for urban nomads and Kurokawa's capsule for *Homo movens* is certainly striking, it is also important to note the differences as well as the similarities between these two architectural and ideological conceptions. First of all, as Reynolds notes, Kurokawa's capsules in the Nakagin Tower were constructed of harder and heavier materials than Itō's gauzy tents and were bolted into the tower's steel frame, in contrast to the more immediately portable Pao.[55] Moreover, the gender shift in the idealized occupants of each structure is significant: while Kurokawa's Nakagin capsules were marketed as a futuristic pied-à-terre for customers gendered as male businessmen *(sararīman)* commuting from distant suburbs or staying in Tokyo for brief periods,[56] Itō's Pao were presented as fashionable way stations for young females *(shōjo)*, who like Yuri, the protagonist of Tanaka's *Nantonaku kurisutaru* (Somehow, crystal), were positioned by male authors/architects as ideal representatives of the new consumerist lifestyle of 1980s Japan.

Itō addressed the interface of information technology and archi-

Plate 1. Kikutake Kiyonori, *Marine City* (1958, unbuilt), sketch. Copyright Kikutake Kiyonori. Courtesy of National Archives of Modern Architecture, Japan.

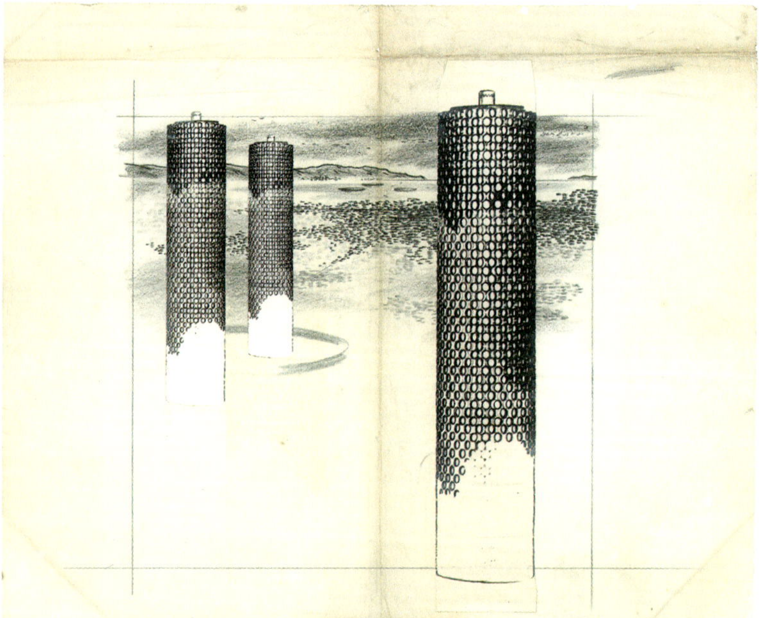

Plate 2. Kikutake Kiyonori, *Tower-Shaped Community* (1958, unbuilt), sketch. Copyright Kikutake Kiyonori. Courtesy of National Archives of Modern Architecture, Japan.

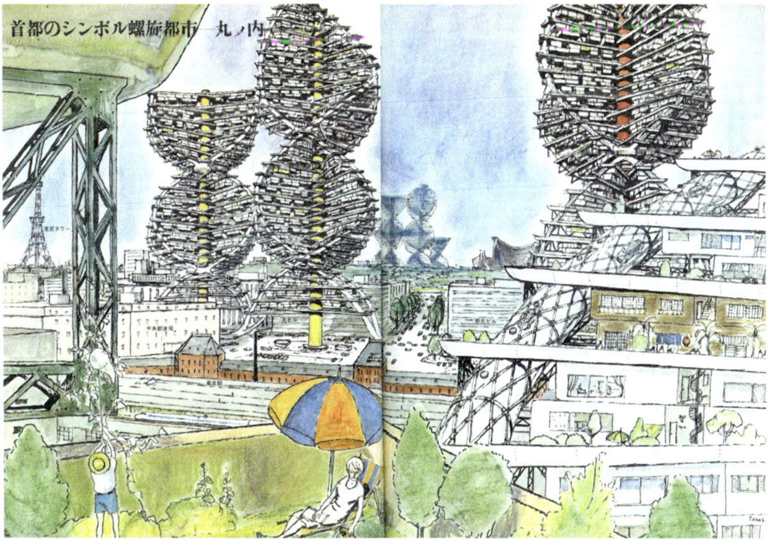

Plate 3. Terashima Ryūichi, *Spiral City, Symbol of the Capital: Marunouchi* (1966), sketch based on a design by Kurokawa Kishō. First published in *Taiyō* magazine, March 1966; reproduction permission courtesy of Sakurai Mari.

Plate 4. Terashima Ryūichi, *A Prefab Housing Complex with Plenty of Greenery: Tama* (1966), sketch based on a design by Kurokawa Kishō. First published in *Taiyō* magazine, March 1966; reproduction permission courtesy of Sakurai Mari.

Plate 5. Tange Kenzō, *Tokyo Bay Model, 1960* (Plan for Tokyo 1960). The Kenzō Tange Archive. Gift of Takako Tange, 2011. Courtesy of the Frances Loeb Library, Harvard University Graduate School of Design.

Plate 6. Tange Kenzō, *Tokyo Bay Model, 1960* (Plan for Tokyo 1960), detail. The Kenzō Tange Archive. Gift of Takako Tange, 2011. Courtesy of the Frances Loeb Library, Harvard University Graduate School of Design.

Plate 7. Isozaki Arata, *Hiroshima Ruined Again in the Future* (1968), photomontage. Copyright Isozaki Arata. Digital image copyright the Museum of Modern Art. Licensed by SCALA / Art Resource, NY.

Plate 8. Symbol Zone of the 1970 Osaka Expo, featuring Festival Plaza and space-frame roof designed by Tange Kenzō and Tower of the Sun monument designed by Okamoto Tarō. Photograph copyright Shinkenchikusha/DAAS.

Plate 9. Festival Plaza of the 1970 Osaka Expo, featuring stage devices, including the robot Deme, designed by Isozaki Arata, and the "Black Sun" face of the Tower of the Sun by Okamoto Tarō. Photograph copyright Shinkenchikusha/DAAS.

Plate 10. Kurokawa Kishō, Takara Beautilion, 1970 Osaka Expo. Photograph copyright Shinkenchikusha/DAAS.

Plate 11. Itō Toyoo, Sendai Mediatheque (2001). Photograph by author.

Plate 12. Ōtomo Katsuhiro, *Akira* (1988). A frame from the opening sequence of the anime shows an aerial view of Neo-Tokyo.

Plate 13. Oshii Mamoru, *Patlabor: The Movie* (1989). This scene shows dilapidated apartments lining a canal.

Plate 14. Oshii Mamoru, *Patlabor: The Movie* (1989). A "patlabor" mecha is visually allied with a cityscape of concrete, glass, and steel skyscrapers.

Plate 15. Yanobe Kenji, *Atom Suit Project/Osaka Expo* (1998), photo documentation. Wearing his Atom Suit, Yanobe walks toward Okamoto's Tower of the Sun, with Kikutake's Expo Tower visible in the distance. Copyright Yanobe Kenji. Photograph by Toyonaga Seiji. Courtesy of YAMAMOTO GENDAI.

Plate 16. Yanobe Kenji, *Tower of Life* (2003), photo documentation. Yanobe in his Atom Suit gazes at moss collected in the ruins of Kikutake's Expo Tower. Copyright Yanobe Kenji. Photograph by Toyonaga Seiji. Courtesy of YAMAMOTO GENDAI.

tecture more directly in several of his signature works of the 1980s and 1990s. For example, his Tower of Winds in Yokohama (1986) was a cylindrical tower outfitted with a translucent aluminum mesh "skin" covering composed of hundreds of computer-controlled light bulbs, neon rings, and floodlights that changed patterns in accordance with environmental noise and wind conditions—an interface with the "information" of the building's environment. His Egg of Winds (1991) was a rotating, oval-shaped object 16 meters wide, located at the gate of a housing project, which included projectors both within and outside of the "egg" to display multiple layers of information for residents, advertising, and video art—one idiosyncratic take on the ongoing spread of video screens and advertising across the urban landscape. In 1995, Itō won the competition to design what became one his signature buildings, the Sendai Mediatheque (2001), a large, six-story gallery, library, and media center with a translucent glass exterior "skin" (Plate 11). The plan also features minimum partition of interior spaces except for thirteen glass and steel "tube" elements penetrating all six floors of the building, designed as "spaces where information and different types of energy (light, air, water, sound, etc.) flow while facilitating vertical circulation" (Figure 4).[57] Itō's design seems to strive toward a utopian vision of transparency and public access, providing access to various types of information media (books, artworks, digital media) with a minimum of physical barriers and a range of sight lines and flows, both horizontally across the broad floors of the building, as well as vertically or diagonally through the interpenetrating glass tubes.[58]

However, the tendency of Itō's architecture itself to dematerialize into a flow of images and information was perhaps most pronounced in his installation entitled *Dreams* at the Victoria and Albert Museum in London in 1991, as part of the *Visions of Japan* exhibition curated by Isozaki Arata. Itō's instillation included forty-four projectors installed on the ceiling as well as beneath the transparent floor of the gallery, projecting a sea of "constantly changing images of Tokyo onto undulating aluminum and acrylic wall panels, wall hangings, and the acrylic floor."[59] Particularly in the context of an exhibit curated by Isozaki himself, Itō's project could be seen as a response to Isozaki's *Electric Labyrinth* (1968), which, like his essays such as "Invisible City" (1967), foreshadowed the possibility of cities dematerializing into chaotic

Figure 4. Itō Toyoo, interior of Sendai Mediatheque (2001), showing glass and steel tubes facilitating vertical circulation. Photograph by author.

systems of signs, information, and electronic simulation. However, while Isozaki's exhibit provocatively juxtaposed futuristic megastructural architecture (future) with the traumatic historical memory of Hiroshima and the Early Modern sign-systems of Edo (past), Itō's *Dreams* situated the present Tokyo as the already dematerialized, flattened, "informationized," and simulated city. Itō wrote that he felt that this exhibit space was "an accurate simulation of the reality of Tokyo, or perhaps it is more accurate to say that Tokyo is a simulated city. For instance, the experience of walking through the Kabuki-cho district at night closely resembles the experience of this imagistic space. In either space, our bodies float amid vast images and showers of sounds. When gazing into video-game screens, we are already on the other side of the screens."[60]

Writing in 1990, a year before Itō's *Dreams* exhibit, architect and critic Yatsuka Hajime seems to anticipate the insubstantial and undulating forms of this exhibit in his essay "An Architecture Floating on the Sea of Signs." Echoing Itō's description of architecture in the "sea of consumption," Yatsuka writes, "In the 'city of consumption,' architecture tends to become a flow of images rather than a stock of buildings." He goes on to connect consumerism and the dematerialization of architecture through their role in the "circuits of information and desire":

> Inasmuch as this consumerist process is related, both explicitly and implicitly, to the circuit of human desire, explicitly and implicitly, architecture necessarily symbolizes this desire in a profound way; it acquires the quality of signs rather than substance. Cities are now very complicated circuits of information and desire, which I call the "sea of signs," and through this invisible and multi-layered network of information flow they act as *loci* for consumption. If Japanese cities could be called "rhizomes," it would be because this system of information and desire is laid over and imbues the totality of architecture. Buildings today, more than ever, are an integral part of this invisible circuit. Although, no doubt, they still exist as real entities, they have already lost integrity, and lack the dimension of "depth," which, of course, is the common feature of the media. "Architecture as media," an axiom advocated as an assumptive theory some thirty years ago, now seems to be turned into reality without any reservation.[61]

This depthless architecture, overlaid by systems of information and desire, was realized in its most literal form in the ubiquity of giant video screens of building facade proportions—indeed often serving as the facade of buildings themselves—that proliferated in Japanese cities in the 1990s and onward.[62] Once again, Shibuya served as the epicenter for this nexus of "information and desire" with huge video screens on such buildings as Q-Front and 109–2 bordering the iconic "scramble crossing" in front of Shibuya Station.

Summarizing the postbubble trends in the Japanese cityscape for an international audience in 2011, architecture critic Igarashi Tarō noted the continuing proliferation of screens and the flattening of Tokyo architecture, asserting that building surfaces and their video advertising projections had become "more important than the shape and form of the buildings themselves." Meanwhile, in describing the penetration of information technology into the cityscape since the

1990s, he also pointed to the spread of mobile phones and the proliferation of "terminal" spaces pocketing the liminal spaces throughout Tokyo: convenience stores, automated loan machines, and karaoke boxes being a few such examples of "automated spaces where people can connect to networks via consoles and terminals."[63] These "terminal" spaces not only mark the portal spaces whereby individuals connect to electronic networks, but they also demonstrate the spread of what Sze Tsung Leong refers to as "control space" whereby the city is constantly remapped and reconfigured on the basis of "user data" and patterns of consumption—urban space as the "receptacle for numeric quantification."[64]

Finally, Igarashi's survey includes an almost obligatory reference to Ridley Scott's 1982 science fiction film *Blade Runner,* with its dystopian cityscape inundated by advertising video screens and neon signs (many of them in Japanese and Chinese). "Looking down on the area [in front of the station] from the second or third floor of Shibuya Station at night," Igarashi writes, "one has the impression that three giant television screens have been set down in the midst of the urban space. It is almost as though the futuristic predictions of the science fiction movie *Blade Runner* had become reality."[65]

While comparisons between *Blade Runner* and the contemporary city of Tokyo had become a cliché by the time of Igarashi's architectural survey in 2011, architect Itō Toyoo was an early interpreter and proponent of Scott's work from the 1980s. For example, in the essay "Burēdo rannā ni tsuite" (Concerning *Blade Runner,* 1990), Itō wrote that he always recalled Scott's film while walking amid the neon signs and crowds of Shinjuku's Kabukichō: the soaring skyscrapers of Scott's twenty-first-century Los Angeles, he continued, seemed to "suggest the future direction of Tokyo." Itō also noted the mixture of architectural anachronism and futuristic high tech in Scott's fictional Los Angeles, which is revealed in fragments as the film progresses from scene to scene, while a total picture or image of the city remains hard to construct.[66]

Itō's essay "What Is the Reality of Architecture in a Futuristic City?," from 1988, pursues his interest in Scott's work even further, while also responding to Ōtomo Katsuhiro's animated film *Akira,* which had just been released that year (discussed further in the next chapter). Itō gives four characteristics of a city "like present-day Tokyo" that are captured more effectively by science fiction films such as *Blade Runner* or *Akira* than by architectural drawings. These four characteristics are:

> 1. The relentless transformation into a labyrinth: The feeling of drifting through a complex space mounted on a futuristic vehicle. . . . 2. Spaces filled with noises produced by technology: The city atmosphere is suffused with a variety of sounds, colours, information and odours. These are not necessarily visualized but are mediated by technology and dispersed in the atmosphere, distributed in urban space with changing densities, like floating clouds or mist. In the movies, due to the appearance of humans with psychic abilities and androids, these atmospheric properties are discerned and recognized. . . . 3. An insubstantial world comprising only innumerable suspended symbols of consumption. . . . Up to ten years ago, the advertising signs in commercial spaces were no more than billboards or window displays, or at most affixed to the façades of buildings, but now they occupy entire interior spaces or even cover entire buildings. All urban spaces have now begun a cycle of incessantly changing signs of consumption. 4. Temporal cities created by the trails of bodies: Unreal spaces are produced through successions of events that are like fireworks set off throughout the city, which is sustained by a sense of distance completely different from the perspective and hierarchy of Western space.[67]

Itō's comments draw our attention to the effectiveness of these films in capturing the kinetic, visceral qualities of cities that architectural drawing cannot: by following the "spinner" flying cars of *Blade Runner* amid the skyscrapers of Los Angeles, or the futuristic motorcycles of *Akira* rushing at high speeds through Neo-Tokyo, the labyrinthine, kinetic, and visceral qualities of the city are uniquely manifest in these films. Furthermore, new relationships between human subjectivity and environment are revealed through the technologically enhanced senses of the characters, whether the detective scrutinizing a holographic record of a crime scene in *Blade Runner* or the anxious, violent telekinetic interactions between the Esper children and their urban surroundings in *Akira*. As Itō responds to these qualities in science fiction films, he struggles with the question of how his own architecture will function among the fluid "signs of consumption" and "changing densities" of information—or, as he put the dilemma himself, "how to make substantial architecture while substantial things are losing their meaning."[68]

Cyberspace and Techno-Orientalism

Itō's and Igarashi's citations of *Blade Runner* as a futuristic precursor to the contemporary experience of Tokyo point to the degree to which, from the 1980s onward, the Japanese cityscape has been viewed through an international lens of anxiety and desire associating Japan and its technology with global futurity—a structure of viewing that indelibly links together Japan and its cityscape with science fiction, particularly the postmodern, information technology–inflected form of SF known as cyberpunk.[69] In an influential chapter of their book *Spaces of Identity: Global Media, Electronic Landscapes, and Cultural Boundaries* (1995), David Morley and Kevin Robins employ the term *techno-orientalism* to describe this matrix of desire and anxiety related to a Japanese future. Media critic Ueno Toshiya expanded on the idea of "techno-orientalism" suggesting that it should not be seen only as an exotic vision of Japan originating in the West but also as a lens through which the Japanese had come to perceive or misperceive themselves.[70] In their essay, Morley and Robins discuss the "Japan Panic" in the West caused by Japan's growing economic dominance—symbolized by such incursions into the American economic sphere as the acquisition of New York's Rockefeller Center by Mitsubishi Real Estate in 1989 and Sony's purchase of CBS Records and Columbia Pictures in 1988 and 1989—as well as the increasing technological prowess of Japanese companies such as Sony and Matsushita. Morley and Robins trace the fears of Japanese "global hegemony" in American and European political and journalistic discourse and connect these preoccupations with the deep-seated Western fascination with, as well as fear of, the Asian or Oriental Other. In particular, they argue that Japan's recent rise has destabilized, in Western eyes, the correlation between the West and the modern, and the East and the premodern. "If the future is technological, and if technology has become 'Japanised,' then the syllogism would suggest that the future is now Japanese too. . . . Japan is the future, and it is a future that seems to be transcending and displacing Western modernity."[71] Within the cultural realm, key touchstones for this cultural construction are Ridley

Scott's film *Blade Runner* (1982, based on Philip K. Dick's novel *Do Androids Dream of Electric Sheep?*, 1968) and William Gibson's debut novel *Neuromancer* (1984), as well as his subsequent works such as the Bridge Trilogy of *Virtual Light* (1993), *Idoru* (1996), and *All Tomorrow's Parties* (1999).

Set in the year 2019, *Blade Runner* presents a dense cityscape representing a Los Angeles that has hypertrophied into a megalopolis covering the entire western U.S. seaboard and incorporating ziggurat-like megastructures taking up several city blocks and rising several hundred stories, towering above a Manhattan-like streetscape filled with fifty- or sixty-story skyscrapers.[72] Director Ridley Scott, working with production designers Syd Mead and Lawrence G. Paull, art director David Snyder, and special effects expert Douglas Trumbull, crafted a future Los Angeles with a dense, multilayered mise-en-scène (often composed of composites of up to twenty-seven separately filmed elements)[73] and informed by the concept of "retrofitting," in which the future cityscape, rather than being defined by the smooth lines of modernism and the sense of the "new," as presented in such earlier "futuristic" cinematic cities as William Cameron Menzies's *Things to Come* (1936),[74] would instead present a battered, improvised future in which newer technology has been layered haphazardly onto old—"upgrading old machinery or structures by slapping new add-ons to them."[75] Far from an idyllic future, the film presents a future city plagued by ills of pollution, climate change, overpopulation, and racial and class tensions, not to mention the struggle between biological humans and androids or "replicants."

In addition, the urban spaces of the film are packed with the visual information of countless neon signs in English, Chinese, and Japanese, as well as giant building-sized video screens and video advertisements and propaganda broadcast from vehicles floating above the streets. Writer William Gibson has said of the film's visual overload and media density: "Scott understood the importance of information density to perceptual overload. When *Blade Runner* works best, it induces a lyrical sort of information sickness, that quintessentially modern cocktail of ecstasy and dread."[76] Scott Bukatman argues that the dark and crowded mise-en-scène of Scott's film, as well as the exaggerated presence of visual media evoking "sensations of unreality and pervasive spectacle," anticipate the "dark city" of Gibson's own cyberpunk fiction, such as *Neuromancer,* in which "the density of the central, inner, city became an analogy for the dispersed matrices of information circulation and overload, while cyberspace itself [that is, the space experienced when connected to an electronic interface] presented an urbanism stripped to its kinetic and monumental essentials."[77]

Elements of the set for *Blade Runner* were inspired by the streetscapes of New York, Los Angeles, Hong Kong, Milan, Tokyo's Ginza district, and London's Piccadilly Circus; other visual inspirations for the film's set include Hollywood film noir, as well as the artwork of illustrator Jean Giraud, a.k.a. Moebius, and his colleagues drawing for the French SF and fantasy comics magazine *Métal Hurlant (Heavy Metal).*[78] Thus, while the visual sources for Ridley's film were eclectic, the elements of "Asian" influence play a particularly important role in the film's socioaesthetic construction of the "future city." As Giuliana Bruno describes: "The city is a large market; an intrigue of underground networks pervades all relations. The explosive Orient dominates, the Orient of yesterday incorporating the Orient of today. Overlooking the city is the 'Japanese simulacrum,' the huge advertisement which alternates a seductive Japanese face and a Coca Cola sign. In the postindustrial city the explosion of urbanization, melting the futuristic high-tech look into an intercultural scenario, recreates the Third World inside the first."[79] Even in Bruno's description, we can glean the presence of at least two overlapping types of "Asia" or "Orient" in the film: One is the Asian "hordes," including scores of nonwhite extras, which reflect white fears of a "Yellow Peril" immigrant population explosion inundating American cities (the "Third World inside the first"), as well as the underground "market" of shadowy transactions, crimes, and pleasures, all of which were staples of Hollywood film noir, as has been explored in Jane Chi Hyun Park's study *Yellow Future: Oriental Style in Hollywood Cinema* (2010).[80] A second is the "simulacrum" of the giant video advertisement in which a powdered "Asian" female face is seen popping pills and hawking Coca-Cola: a clearly gendered Asia/Japan as a signifier for postmodern technology, media, and transnational capitalism—in other words, a feminized Asia/Japan as the avatar of a consumerist techno-orientalism. Endowed with the power to explore this feminized, orientalized landscape is the protagonist and presumed subject of audience identification: the white, hypermasculine hard-boiled noir detective Deckard.

The opening chapters of Gibson's novel *Neuromancer* are set not in an Asian-inflected American city but rather in the imagined future Japan of Chiba City, across the bay from Tokyo. Just as the streets of Scott's *Blade Runner* are inundated with advertising and propaganda from huge screens and advertising blimps, so too Gibson's Chiba City and its tawdry black market/entertainment quarter of Ninsei are pocketed with the virtual images of holograms. Similarly, while the menace of Scott's Los Angeles is intensified by a polluted orange sky and torrential acid rains, Gibson's Chiba City lies under a "poisoned silver sky," "the color of television, tuned to a dead channel."[81] Furthermore, just as Scott's *Blade Runner* revolutionized cinematic visual culture with its dense, composited, multilevel, and "retrofitted" mise-en-scène, Gibson's *Neuromancer* challenged the norms of contemporary science fiction with its dense and imagistic prose style:

> Now he slept in the cheapest coffins, the ones nearest the port, beneath the quartz-halogen floods that lit the docks all night like vast stages; where you couldn't see the lights of Tokyo for the glare of the television sky, not even the towering hologram logo of the Fuji Electric Company, and Tokyo Bay was a black expanse where gulls wheeled above drifting shoals of white Styrofoam. Beneath the port lay the city, factory domes dominated by the vast cubes of corporate arcologies. Port and city were divided by a narrow borderland of older streets, an area with no official name. Night City, with Ninsei its heart. By day, the bars down Ninsei were shuttered and featureless, the neon dead, the holograms inert, waiting, under the poisoned silver sky.[82]

As Scott Bukatman explores in his study *Terminal Identity: The Virtual Subject in Post-Modern Science Fiction* (1993),[83] the physical cities of Chiba City/Ninsei, as well as the eastern U.S. megalopolis known as the Sprawl, already densely interpenetrated with information technologies, become analogies for the experience of Cyberspace, a second space or "paraspace" accessible through an electronic interface, which was famously defined in this novel as a "consensual hallucination" and "a graphic representation of data abstracted from the banks of every computer in the human system. . . . Lines of light ranged in the nonspace of the mind, clusters and constellations of data." Likewise, just as postmodern urban experience is likened to Cyberspace, so is

Cyberspace compared to the city: the visual impression of Cyberspace is described as being "like city lights, receding," set against "a gray disk, the color of Chiba sky."[84] Thus, the informationized, postmodern city is an analogue for Cyberspace, and vice versa; in Gibson's universe, both are strongly connected with the imagination of a high-tech, urban Japan, populated by both far-reaching multinational corporations and the criminal underworld of the yakuza. In parallel to *Blade Runner*'s Deckard, the protagonist of Gibson's novel is Case, a hard-boiled white male cyber-navigator who negotiates this orientalized data matrix.[85]

Kuroma Hisashi's Japanese translation of *Neuromancer* appeared in 1985, and, as Tatsumi Takayuki discusses, this translation helped to set off a boom in discussions of cyberpunk in Japanese magazines and journals in the late 1980s.[86] Meanwhile, Ōhara Mariko (born 1957) and Masaki Gorō (born 1957) emerged as leading voices of a new generation of Japanese SF writers who were often compared with the Anglo-American cyberpunks. Masaki, in particular, has been hailed by Tatsumi himself as the "first hardcore Japanese cyberpunk writer"[87] and was frequently compared with Gibson since his debut in 1986, although Masaki claims to have stopped reading Gibson's work and to have adopted a deliberately un-Gibsonesque writing style in response to the constant comparisons.[88]

Masaki's magnum opus, the novel *Viinasu shitei* (Venus city, 1992), presents a fascinating take on the future of Tokyo as well as the city's fictional twinned "paraspace" domain, the eponymous virtual reality world of Venus City. Despite the fact that the novel was published a year after the sharp decline in Japanese real estate and stock prices signaled the end of the 1980s bubble economy, *Venus City* portrays a twenty-first-century world of Japanese economic and cultural dominance and global Pax Nipponica, with heavy doses of triumphalist bubble-era Japanese nationalism and Nihonjin-ron discourse.[89] Simultaneously, however, the novel also provides a provocative take on subjectivity in "cyberspace"—in particular, the fluidity of gender and racial/national identity in virtual environments, as well as the market dynamics of self-styling in the virtual city. Thus, the novel provides one answer to media critic Scott Bukatman's question of how recent science fiction strives "to construct a new subject-position to interface with the global realms of data circulation"—constructions that Bukatman dubs "terminal identity."[90]

In near-future Tokyo, the novel's protagonist, Moriguchi Sakiko, is a white-collar worker for the ARC Corporation, whose offices are located in a new city center *(shin toshin)* built on Tokyo Bay. Her work as a "research navigator" involves retrieving information in global electronic archives through a full-body interface. By night, however, from her apartment in the old city center, Sakiko dons special goggles and a "data suit" and mounts a "3D magnetic stage" to appear as her avatar, Saki, in Venus City, a networked virtual reality system developed in Japan and marketed primarily to Japanese customers.

Midway through the novel, Sakiko, as narrator, comments on the relationship between Tokyo and Venus City:

> I exited the expressway at the Nishi-Ikebukuro exit. The streets were getting a little crowded. The transportation net here resembled a wriggling mass of roundworms. . . . More than 20 million people were living in every corner of this tangled maze. . . . And 3D magnetic stages were installed in a considerable percentage of those peoples' homes. Venus City was a second, imaginary city constructed on top of this tangled city's maze. The Japanese people in their narrow land had built a city so crowded, and yet, still not satisfied, they had layered an electronic city on top of it.[91]

The center of Venus City is a warren of bars and entertainment sites where VR participants interact with each other: Saki's primary hangout is a bar where (s)he banters and gambles with friends who sport similar "designer punk" avatar customization. The business model for the Venus City system is described in detail: customers can buy real estate, customize buildings, and even purchase licenses to operate businesses in Venus City. Ordinary users choose the gender (and gender pronouns) of their avatars and can choose their skin color, facial structure, body type, and clothing; more complex, unusual, or high-functioning body and clothing types cost more money. Saki has opted for an androgynous male body, translucent white skin, and the "designer punk" look of short-cropped hair, skintight long boots and gloves ornamented with chains, tight crimson pants and top, a leather belt riveted with bolts, and a loose gray half-coat belted with a chain.[92] Other Venus City denizens also self-segregate according to fashion protocols, such as lacy "décolleté style" or "rubber bondage" fetish style. Clearly, the subcultural logic and fashion economy of late twentieth-century Tokyo, exemplified in the consumer cultures/subcultures of such neighborhoods as Shibuya, Harajuku, and Akihabara, are mirrored in the business model of Venus City, in which both bodily and sartorial customization, including brand-name fashions or their simulation, can be had for a price. While users are given the freedom to explore second selves, the commodification of individual identity is raised to new heights. There are no "plazas" here for public interaction or civic discourse where the terms of the software in Venus City are debated. Rather, there are pedestrian-oriented streets where one's personal fashion can be displayed and others' appreciated, as well as warrens of bars and clubs where avatars congregate according to shared fashion/subcultural preferences.

Saki becomes involved in the rescue of Junko, a woman with a face "like a Japanese doll" pursued by a mysterious silver-skinned man. It turns out that Junko is actually the avatar of Jim, who is Sakiko's American boss at the ARC Corporation. The silver-skinned man is seemingly a criminal from a shadowy foreign organization trying to blackmail Jim/Junko into revealing secret research results with economic, geopolitical, and existential implications for Japan; this criminal may also be one of the rumored "Gods of the Net" *(netto no naka no kamigami)*, powerful beings who, unlike ordinary users, manage to live full time in the virtual world. Much of the dramatic and psychological tension (and occasional humor) of the novel derives from acts of trans-gender and trans-racial/-national passing between the "physical world" and Venus City: Sakiko, a xenophobe who dislikes her American boss Jim in her daytime life, ends up romantically involved with her boss's female "Japanese" avatar. Ironically, Jim, a Japanophile, is transformed into the "Japanese doll" avatar not by personal choice but out of force by the sadistic, mysterious foreign blackmailer, "outing" his Japanophilia in its most clichéd form against his will.

The seemingly contrastive user experiences of Sakiko/Saki and Jim/Junko aptly illustrate the dynamics of "control" and "freedom" explored by Wendy Hui Kyong Chun, as introduced at the outset of this chapter. On the one hand, within the predetermined software protocols of the Venus City system, Sakiko seems to have both "control" and "freedom" in controlling the appearance and guiding the behavior of her avatar Saki in the Venus City world. Jim, on the other hand, is, on a daily basis, sent the software protocols determining the appearance and functionality of his avatar Junko and forced to appear in Venus City through intimidation and blackmail. Junko, in turn, is frequently trapped in confined spaces and physically and sexually abused by the avatars of Jim's mysterious blackmailer and his henchmen. This paranoid vision of complete loss of freedom and control is the opposite side of the coin of illusory personal freedom and control offered to Sakiko through her participation in the virtual consumer society of Venus City.

Despite the city's expansion to a new "urban subcenter" over Tokyo Bay, the physical environment of Tokyo in the novel is rather prosaic; meanwhile, in the "paraspace" of Venus City the dematerialization of architecture becomes complete—realizing in fictional form Kurokawa's prediction from 1970 of a state of affairs where the "walls, floors, and windows" of the city become "simply images." In addition, the consumer customization of identity in Venus City re-creates the logic that Kurokawa attempted to establish with his idea of capsule dwellings individualized to order out of a catalog of possible components and that Haryū criticizes as a scheme in which "computers will be capable of turning people's desires into numbers to be calculated" and where "individuality and freedom of expression" would be predetermined by a capitalist "techno-structure."

Furthermore, as illustrated by the racial and gender passing performed by the customized avatars in the novel's paraspace world, the techno-orientalist elements of the cyberpunk genre are present in Masaki's text to the point of excess, complete with a satiric reversal: Sakiko masquerades as the white male cyberpunk hero, while Jim is forced into the role of the hypersexualized and fetishized Asian female. Thus, as Baryon Tensor Posadas argues, rather than celebrating the seemingly liberating capacity to inhabit other gender and racial identities in the virtual realm, Masaki's novel "calls attention to the racialized and gendered infrastructure of techno-Orientalism that often undergirds utopian valorizations of the virtual in cyberpunk."[93] Indeed, as Posadas suggests, Masaki's text seems to be not so much mapping a new imaginative territory of the future or virtual city and its inhabitants but illuminating the very limitations of the SF/cyberpunk imagination of such cities and subjectivities, dominated by the persistent tropes of techno-orientalism.[94]

While this chapter is only a rough sketch, I have attempted to trace various iterations of the "invisible city," "liquid city," "technopolis," or "cyber city" from the late 1960s through the 1990s, as they have intersected with debates over the "information society" and "managed society," hyperconsumption, postmodernism, cyberpunk, and techno-orientalism. Architects, critics, bureaucrats, filmmakers, and fiction authors have all been participants in this ongoing negotiation of the urban imaginary. In tracing their debates, I have sought not only to explore the history of the association between new media/technology and the "future" Japanese city but to underline the very historicity of this association as a contingent and contested cultural construction. The final chapter will continue this endeavor by examining the critical dimensions of the depiction of "future cities" by animators Ōtomo Katsuhiro and Oshii Mamoru and artist Yanobe Kenji.

6 Metabolist Echoes

Akira, Patlabor, and Yanobe Kenji

As I have examined thus far, the Metabolist architects largely belonged to the "Generation of Charred Ruins" born in the Shōwa single-digit years circa 1930, rose to cultural prominence during the height of the High Growth Era in the 1960s, and achieved an apogee of influence with the 1970 Osaka Expo. By the 1980s, 1990s, and beyond, however, other architects and architectural movements had risen to the fore, and the Metabolist architects increasingly looked abroad for hosts and sponsors of their most ambitious projects.[1] Nevertheless, I would contend that in the realm of narrative and visual arts, several prominent artists continued to engage with the ideas and legacy of Metabolism, demonstrating the continued cultural relevance of their works and ideas, even as they were interpreted through shifting historical perspectives. In this chapter, I will examine the echoes of Metabolist ideas and visual imagination in the *Akira* narratives of Ōtomo Katsuhiro (both the animated film from 1988 and the manga that was serialized from 1982 to 1990), Oshii Mamoru's two anime films *Patlabor: The Movie* (*Kidō keisatsu patoreibaa: The Movie*, 1989) and *Patlabor 2: The Movie* (*Kidō keisatsu patoreiba 2: The Movie*, 1993), and the sculptures and performance art of Yanobe Kenji, especially his Atom Suit Project of 1997–2003.

Ōtomo's highly influential film *Akira* was in production coextensively with the serialization of the manga, and foreshortens the story arc of the latter, but both works share the same basic setting of a near-future Neo-Tokyo, a city built over Tokyo Bay after a psychic explosion has destroyed the former metropolis. Both film and manga follow the members of a youth motorcycle gang whose friendship is torn apart when the government attempts to coopt Tetsuo, one of the gang members, in order to develop his psychic powers, which might eventually rival that of Akira, the child who caused the initial catastrophic explosion of Tokyo.

Oshii's *Patlabor* films are well-respected works within the director's extensive oeuvre but less well known internationally than his blockbuster cyberpunk film *Ghost in the Shell* (1995). The *Patlabor* films were part of a media franchise spanning televised anime, original video animation, films, manga, video games, and a light novel, which was developed by the artists' collective Headgear, including Oshii, manga artist Yūki Masami, mecha designer Izubuchi Yutaka, character designer Takada Akemi, and screenwriter Itō Kazunori. They feature a near-future story world in which mecha, or human-piloted robots, called "labors" in the story world, are used for construction work, and "patrol labors," or patlabors, are used for police and military work.

Yanobe Kenji (born 1965) is one of a number of artists who rose to international prominence in the 1990s whose works responded to Japan's burgeoning popular culture of manga and anime and their otaku fandom. These artists include Nara Yoshitomo (born 1959), Murakami Takashi (born 1962), and Mori Mariko (born 1967). Yanobe's works incorporate sculptural elements and are often designed as suits, vehicles, or "mecha" suit/vehicles to be worn or piloted by a human or animal user. Yanobe himself wore his radiation-resistant "Atom Suit" in performance projects in Chernobyl and Osaka that were documented through photographs and video.

The works discussed in this chapter share three major preoccupations with Metabolist architectural theory and design: the expansion over Tokyo Bay (in the cases of *Akira* and *Patlabor*); the "capsule" architectural form as it reappears in the guise of the "mecha" piloted robot, "metal suit," or "media suit" (in the cases of *Patlabor* and Yanobe's Atom Suit Project); and the motifs of apocalypse and ruins (in all three examples). In *Akira,* the motif of expansion over Tokyo Bay reveals one dimension of Ōtomo's cyclical view of history, reviving the Neo-Tokyo plan that was first proposed at the height of postwar reconstruction; for Oshii, this motif is the vehicle for a critique of the internalized imperialism of Japan's postwar construction state. In Oshii's work, the motif of Tokyo Bay expansion is also connected with the technics of the mecha, a piloted robot that, as discussed in the introduction, combines the three key elements of the "capsule" architectural form: mobility; enclosure, as a protective shell or membrane; and the function of a cybernetic node in an information network. This "mecha" or "media suit" form is revisited in Yanobe's work, which includes a literal return to the "ruins" of the 1970 Osaka Expo, where the Metabolists' capsule architecture had its most dramatic showcase. Yanobe's work in particular brings Metabolist works into the current century, connecting the Metabolists' circular conception of time with the anxieties, melancholy, and nostalgia of a generation coming to age after the expo's utopian moment had passed and finding itself at home in a "postapocalyptic" present.

Ōtomo Katsuhiro's Neo-Tokyo

The opening title sequence of Ōtomo Katsuhiro's film *Akira* is surely one of the most famous in all of anime. The first shot shows an aerial view of an elevated highway transecting a dense modern cityscape. The picture frame pans upward, following the highway toward its vanishing point, as more of the sprawling city is revealed. The date of 1988.7.16 (identifying the temporal setting of the shot, which was also the film's release date) and the location, Tokyo, appear in white titles at the center of the screen. Centered in the shot, we see a distant cluster of skyscrapers, which some viewers may recognize as the Shinjuku subcenter. The horizon, with distant mountains and blue sky, comes into view, and the camera stops its panning motion. Then, from the space between the skyscrapers and the horizon, we see the distant ripple of an explosion, which rapidly expands toward the viewer, engulfing the city in a massive fireball comparable only to that of a hydrogen bomb. After white screen and static, we are presented with a much more distant aerial view, zooming slowly in on a city that has metastasized to fill most of Tokyo Bay: titles identify this as Neo-Tokyo in the year 2019, thirty-one years after the Third World War (Plate 12).[2] The screen cuts to black, and the camera pans out, revealing a giant crater. The film's title, *Akira*, appears in bold red letters over the crater. This shocking and often-imitated title sequence prefigures a number of aspects of the film, in a powerful mixture of fiction and historical echoes.[3]

The first and most obvious historical echo, is, of course, the destruction of two Japanese cities by atomic bombs at the end of the

Second World War, a trauma that Ōtomo revisits unflinchingly in the opening seconds of the film. A second, less obvious historical echo, however, is the name Ōtomo gives for the city rebuilt after its fictional destruction in 1988 and expanded over Tokyo Bay: "Neo-Tokyo," which duplicates the name given to the 1959 proposal by the think tank Council for Industrial Planning at the height of the Tokyo's period of reconstruction from its own wartime destruction. As described in chapter 1, the never-executed "Neo-Tokyo" plan of 1959 proposed a partial infill of the bay utilizing earth loosened by the explosion of an atomic bomb; this plan stimulated the appearance of Tange Kenzō's own renowned, but unbuilt, Tokyo Bay expansion proposal, the Plan for Tokyo 1960.

In the fictional realm of the film's plot, in superimposing the title *Akira* over the crater from the explosion identified with World War III, Ōtomo prefigures what the viewer pieces together in more detail as the film progresses: that the explosion destroying Tokyo in 1988 was not the result of an atomic attack by a foreign power but was a psychic eruption caused by a child named Akira, whose psychic powers had been artificially stimulated through a secret government program (the chaos after this explosion apparently leading to a third world war, before Tokyo could be rebuilt as Neo-Tokyo). Further historical echoes are spread throughout the film: we see shadows of the student protests and street riots of the 1960s, millennial movements such as those that accompanied the fall of the Tokugawa *bakufu* in the nineteenth century, underground revolutionaries reminiscent of the 1930s or 1960s, conflicts between a corrupt, ineffectual civilian government and an activist military (represented by the Colonel) strongly recalling Japan's wartime regime, and finally a delinquent youth culture, represented by Kaneda's *bōsōzoku* motorcycle gang, reflecting the dissatisfied social undercurrents during the time of the film's own creation, the ostensibly prosperous 1980s.[4] We also see in the film preparations for a new Tokyo Olympics, echoing the spectacle of 1964 that transformed the map of postwar Tokyo, signaling Japan's reemergence after the Second World War, and featuring Tange Kenzō's renowned Olympic gymnasium as an architectural focal point. Indeed, the climactic confrontation between the film's would-be hero, Kaneda, and its resentful antihero, Tetsuo, occurs at the site of the (fictional) new Olympic stadium.

Film scholar Isolde Standish analyzes this mash-up of historical events as typical of the postmodern mode of pastiche—characteristic of the treatment of time identified by Fredric Jameson as the "perpetual present."[5] However, rather than merely a schizophrenic, depthless, or ahistorical view of time as described by Jameson, I would argue that Ōtomo's film and manga convey a definite historical consciousness: a cyclical view of time that is both dystopian and utopian. *Akira* is a rejoinder to those who would identify late 1980s Japan, at the height of the bubble years, as having achieved peace, prosperity, and stability. Like Olympic time—the recurrence of an international festival every four years—historical time in *Akira* is cyclical rather than linear. In a profoundly dystopian mode, however, the mistakes, tragedies, and traps of the past are never absent from time's cycle; they flicker in and out of phase like the cities and ruins of Isozaki's "Incubation Process." Apocalypse, as well, is not teleological but cyclical. The militarism, millennialism, revolutions, coups d'état, apocalyptic weapons, and destruction and reconstruction of cities of the past and future all exist in embryonic form in the present (just as Tetsuo's literal embryonic form and childhood experiences reappear at key moments throughout Ōtomo's manga upon which his film is based). In this sense, the film's echoes of the 1964 Tokyo Olympics are more than a reminder of the rebuilding and reconstruction of Tokyo after the destruction of World War Two. Rather, I would argue, they are a citation of the cyclical form of Olympic time, as well as the Metabolist ideas of cyclical growth and decay applied to the forms of the city.

The jumps in scale in Akira's world also have a utopian as well as an apocalyptic element. Just as Kawazoe's Metabolist manifesto posited human society as part of a continuum "from atom to nebula," or as Asada's scale calibrated the relationships between objects of exponentially varying sizes, Ōtomo's *Akira* probes the connections between the molecular and the cosmic: the potential for the energy in a child's mind to engender a city-engulfing explosion; and the recurrence, in the manga, of the visual motif of the helix across vastly differing scales, from the strands of DNA to the smoke traces of vast explosions; or, in the film's ending, the utopian suggestion that Testuo's cataclysmic psychic evolution has even created a new universe.

These cyclical historical recurrences and organic motifs, so closely aligned with the theories of Metabolism, have an even more prominent role in the manga version of *Akira*. In the manga, Neo-Tokyo is reduced to ruins and rubble yet again midway through the narrative, as Akira, whose bodily tissues had been kept by the government in a secret cold storage facility underneath the new Olympic site, has been reconstituted and unleashes yet another giant fireball to engulf the city. Amid the new ruins, Akira and the power-mad Tetsuo proclaim a Greater Tokyo Empire, opposed by both international/American forces (reminiscent of postwar Allied troops), on the one hand, and Kaneda and his allies, including the mysterious psychic Lady Miyako, on the other. In this version of the *Akira* tale, echoing ever more strongly Isozaki Arata's aphorism that "all future cities are ruins," Neo-Tokyo is indeed in ruins, and the ruins of the city become the "incubation mechanism" for whatever new civilization the children of *Akira* are able to create. Indeed, in the final scenes of the manga, after the climactic confrontations between the principal characters, the ruins seem to miraculously reconstitute themselves into a gleaming new city, as the surviving children ride motorcycles through the ruined streets, accompanied by the spirits of their fallen peers.

Oshii Mamoru's *Patlabor* films

While the *Akira* stories seem to incorporate into their narrative and visual DNA a number of elements of Metabolist architecture and theory discussed throughout this study, the two *Patlabor* films of Oshii Mamoru stand out even more dramatically as a critique of postwar architectural and urban planning developments. Like *Akira*, the fictional future world of *Patlabor* features an expansion of Tokyo over Tokyo Bay. In the former case, I would argue, Ōtomo's vision of Neo-Tokyo establishes historical resonances with Tokyo's post–World War II reconstruction even as it indicates the expansionist, hypermodern (and yet dystopian) trajectory of the story's post–World War II urban society. However, in the case of *Patlabor*, it is the very aesthetics of the transformation of Tokyo as the city expands across the bay—what is lost as well as what is gained—together with the methodology of this expansion, involving an intensified cybernetic relationship of humans and machines, that comes under Oshii's critical purview. Chief among the contrasts between Ōtomo's and Oshii's visions is their view of ruins: while the ruins of *Akira* are generative, offering the possibility of a millennial renewal or evolutionary advance of human society, the ruins of *Patlabor* are elegiac.

Set at the turn of the twenty-first century, the *Patlabor* films imagine a world in which Tokyo Bay is being transformed through the "Babylon Project," which includes the construction of a huge dike and beltway connecting Kisarazu in Chiba Prefecture east of the bay and Kawasaki in Kanagawa Prefecture west of the bay, thereby allowing the water level to be controlled through a series of sluices. According to the explanation offered within the first film, the draining of the bay waters enabled by this dike will open more than forty-five thousand hectares (nearly 175 square miles) to real estate development, effectively doubling the size of metropolitan Tokyo.[6] This giant construction project is made possible through the use of "labors"—bipedal, humanoid giant construction machines or robots piloted by a human occupant. In the *Patlabor* world, these labor devices, while highly effective in transforming the Japanese cityscape, are prone to sabotage, hijacking, hacking, or "going berserk." To respond to the threat of crime committed by errant labors, the Metropolitan Police have established a special section of "patrol labors" or patlabors, also piloted giant robots, as a police force. In both films, police officers and pilots of the patlabor police force act as detectives to try to find the human plotters behind the berserking labors and other threats to the Babylon Project.

One of the first scenes in the first *Patlabor* movie (1989) is of an errant labor crashing through an older residential neighborhood in Taito Ward (near Ueno). Sharalyn Orbaugh describes the scene in her article "Future City Tokyo: 1909 and 2009":

> The old-fashioned buildings are low—two story at most—made of wood covered by a stucco-like substance, with heavy ceramic roof tiles, occasionally patched on the outside with sheets of thin corrugated iron. This style of architecture was prevalent from the nineteenth century . . . to the 1960s, and still exists in pockets of Tokyo despite all the natural and man-made disasters the city has experienced. . . . By the time *Patlabor I* was made, this kind of neighborhood was giving way to high-rise apartment buildings, and would strike viewers as old-fashioned but also "homey." Most people—young people especially—may not want to live in such drafty, flimsy, low-tech housing any more, but it is a reminder of a community consciousness that is often now idealized.[7]

A patlabor is promptly dispatched to this neighborhood to disable the rampaging labor, whose electronic operating system—a newly installed, ultraefficient "Hyper Operating System" (HOS)—has been hacked. Ironically, however, the rampaging labor is actually carrying out the work—albeit in a rogue and unsafe fashion—that the entire force of labors was created to do: clearing "slums" and older neighborhoods to make way for the modern high-rise buildings that increasingly dominate the *Patlabor* skyline under the aegis of Project Babylon. Later, the patlabor detectives uncover the mastermind behind the hack of the labors: Hoba Ei'ichi, a biblically obsessed chief programmer for the labors' Hyper Operating System. As the detectives trace Hoba's steps during the period of HOS development, they find that he has moved from place to place, living in twenty-six "boro apaato" or old, dilapidated apartments, similar to the ones destroyed by the rampaging labor in the scene described above (Plate 13). Tellingly, each of the old apartments has a view of the new steel, glass, and concrete skyscrapers built as part of Project Babylon; each is in a neighborhood that has been abandoned or is slated for demolition as part of the project. After recognizing their suspect's conspicuous pattern of *dérive* (drifting) movement from one old apartment to another, Matsui and Gōtō, two detectives assigned to trace Hoba's movements, discuss the pattern as follows:

> MATSUI: As I tracked down his past, it felt like time was passing me by. Places I used to know were just rotting away, or had become empty ruins. Look away for a moment, and it's all gone. And it happens before I can even consider what it all means. I guess the past is worthless in this city.
>
> GŌTŌ: This spot was part of the ocean until recently. And in a few years, a huge city will rise up from the sea in front of us. But before you know it, that will become yesterday's junk, too. It's like sitting through a sick joke. Maybe that's what Hoba wanted us to see.[8]

The reality of an ever-changing city, built, destroyed, and built again, was identified as a basic urban diagnosis by the Metabolist architects from the 1960s. However, these architects sought to embrace the ephemerality of the city and to design its processes of change so as to reduce the elements of chaos and benefit the city's residents. For

Oshii's characters, however, this constant change of the urban environment is merely bewildering. This sentiment can be seen as a reaction to the 1980s acceleration in the "metabolism" of Tokyo's change due to the bubble economy real estate and construction boom, with its "scrap and build" approach to urban development, as well as the continuation of state infrastructure projects that by the 1980s had become ends in themselves as part of a pervasive system of patronage, bid-rigging, and kickbacks between the ruling Liberal Democratic Party and large construction companies—a system that became known to critics as the *doken kokka* or "construction state."[9] Oshii reflects the contemporary critique of "scrap and build" and the "construction state" with his depiction of Hoba's resistance to the massive Babylon Project, but his critique was not unique.

A similar expression of regret at the sheer speed of historical change in the Japanese landscape can be seen, for example, in the photography and writing of Miyamoto Ryūji (born 1947), who had worked as an editor for the architecture magazines *Toshi jūtaku* and *Jūtaku kenchiku* before attracting notice for his richly detailed black-and-white photographs of scenes of urban buildings undergoing demolition in Tokyo and Hong Kong, which were collected in the books *Kyūryū jōsai* (Kowloon walled city, 1988) and *Kenchiku no mokujiroku* (Apocalypse of architecture, 1988).[10] In his essay from 1986, "Temporary Ruins," which comments upon his photographs of the demolition of cities, Miyamoto describes the pace of change besetting Tokyo in the 1980s as follows:

> This kind of change occurred at the time of the Tokyo Olympics [in 1964], but it seemed that the process was accelerated in the 1980's. The harbor was completely occupied; the highways ran aboveground; the newly developed city center bristled with skyscrapers. At the same time, old buildings with extensions and many different façades, a large number of brick buildings downtown, erected at the beginning of the Showa period, and the sheet-copper-sided homes and apartment buildings were all torn up by their roots. Everywhere, the streets were different, made new, everything was subordinated to efficiency, and perverted into a colorless space. Inconvenient old buildings were replaced with astounding speed; there was no time for them even to fall into decay. Ruins were not left around for long.[11]

As Jordan Sand discusses in his study *Tokyo Vernacular: Common Spaces, Local Histories, Found Objects* (2013), the disappearing cityscape of cheap, seemingly dispensable architecture, meticulously depicted in Oshii's film and described by Miyamoto as "old buildings with extensions and many different façades . . . and . . . sheet-copper-sided homes," was "discovered" and championed by the members of the Street Observation Studies group (Rojō kansatsu gakkai, founded in 1986), including artist Akasegawa Genpei and architecture historian Fujimori Terunobu, who found unexpected charms in the street-level neighborhoods that, while neither ancient nor up-to-date, nevertheless reflected the passage of history and harbored the sometimes quizzical residue of years of everyday life.[12] Indeed, according to critic Nagase Tadashi, architectural documentation from works associated with the Street Observation Studies group, such as Fujimori's book with photographer Masuda Akihisa, *Toshi no janarizumu: Kanban kenchiku* (City journalism: Signboard architecture, 1988), is directly "quoted" in the design of several residences occupied by Hoba or destroyed by rampaging labors in Oshii's *Patlabor*.[13] Nevertheless, it should be noted that the viewpoint of Hoba, who resists the relentless redevelopment and expansion of Tokyo with his acts of electronic sabotage, is nevertheless framed as a minority, even "criminal" viewpoint, while the ostensible "heroes" of the story, the "allies of justice" *(seigi no katagi)*, are the patlabor pilots, whose sleek cybernetic mounts are allied visually in the film with the modern, efficient, steel, concrete, and glass skyscrapers rising under the aegis of Project Babylon (Plate 14).[14]

The connections between the patlabor cyborg technology and the nature of (post)modern life are probed further in the film's sequel, *Patlabor 2* (1993). The focus of this film shifts from the transformation of the urban landscape under Project Babylon to the geopolitical situation of postwar Japan and the relationships between media, technology, and modern warfare. The film begins with a prologue depicting an international U.N. peacekeeping force in Southeast Asia under attack: the peacekeepers, manning patlabors (both bipedal versions and a six-legged, spider-like tank vehicle), are besieged by guerilla forces, who approach in a tank as well as on foot with portable rocket launchers. Throughout the scene, there is a strong emphasis on the apparatus covering the pilots' eyes, affording them vision of the heat signatures of both allied patlabors and attacking forces, as well as digital informational displays. While the apparatus ostensibly gives the pilots enhanced visual and informational capabilities, there is also noticeable and sometimes confusing flicker in the visual presence of the heat-signature elements. The scene ends with the patlabors destroyed by the enemy ambush.

This scene's video "flicker" continues during the opening credits, in which we follow a patlabor on a test run in a simulated environment of a city street. Compared with the confusing and panicked scene of guerilla warfare that opens the film, in which the patlabor pilots are effectively ambushed by the guerillas and not given permission to return fire, the credit sequence is much more upbeat in tone: the successful tests are accompanied by lively music and shots of young, competent-looking technicians and pilots putting the patlabor through its paces—walking, grasping with its mechanical hands, etc. We also see the visual elements put together. Echoing the visual "flicker" of the prologue, the elements of the simulated street scene flash separately into view: buildings, sky, pedestrians, a cat crossing the road—each visual element appears separately, emphasizing the mediated quality of the pilot's visual field and highlighting the difficulty of distinguishing between simulation and reality in a world increasingly dominated by cyborg technology. As Christopher Bolton writes in his study of the film, "the motif of an enhanced vision that has its own blind spots is made to reflect the trade-offs between technological amplification of bodily experience and a progressive alienation from our original bodies, threatening dehumanization."[15]

These opening scenes foreshadow the central plot points in the film: a series of attacks on key Tokyo-area transportation and communications infrastructure by a terrorist who is revealed to be a missing officer from the failed U.N. peacekeeping mission depicted in the opening scene. The motive behind the rogue officer's attacks appears to be to question the very nature of Japan's postwar and post–Cold War peace, which is interrogated in the film as a false peace that ignores Japan's role in supporting and profiting from distant international conflicts (including the fictional U.N. peacekeeping mission in the opening scene): the terrorist's actions will thus bring "a taste of war" back to a corrupt and complacent Japan. Moreover, the terrorist's modes of attack interrogate the very nature of modern warfare, which is heavily mediated by visual media, computer simulation, and technological prostheses to the human body. A central sequence in the film, for example, features an attack by a squad of American fighter jets from the Misawa joint Japanese–American air base in northern Japan. As Japanese Self Defense Force planes are scrambled to respond to the attack, they discover that in fact there are no airborne U.S. jets but that the attack is an elaborate simulation appearing only on radar screens and other electronic surveillance and imaging equipment.

This critique of the mediation of modern warfare thus leads us to a new perspective on the seemingly benevolent labor and patlabor mecha robot/vehicles, which, with their human pilots, are cybernetic agents of both the "construction state" and the police and military security apparatus. Indeed, taking the two *Patlabor* films together, we can see the link between the internalized imperialism of the "construction state"—in which the legacy of prewar and World War II–era expansionist imperialist urban projects has, as architecture critic Yatsuka Hajime argues, been transferred onto postwar architecture and urban planning's ambitious colonization of the sea and sky—and the neo-imperialism of a Japanese postwar "peace and prosperity" founded and sustained on hidden geopolitical violence (beginning with Japan's profiting as a supplier and staging base for the Korean and Vietnam Wars). The patlabor mecha can be seen as a type of "capsule" or "media suit" that is embedded into the networks of neo-imperial international warfare and exploitation and yet is also emblematic of the medial filtering processes both conveying and hiding this very participation in a system of violence: as Bolton puts it, an "enhanced vision" with its own "blind spots."

In his groundbreaking study of anime *Kurenai no metaru sūtsu: anime to iu senjō* (Scarlet metalsuits: The battlefield called anime, 1998), Ueno Toshiya comments on the homology between the mecha or "media suit" and the "invisible city," or experience of (post)modern urban life that has been imbricated in cybernetic systems: "Isn't the invisible city of today," Ueno writes, "approaching the state of a type of suit or machine? To the extent that the city is a suit for the people who live in it, and a type of media which makes communication (im)possible, it is already undoubtedly a 'media suit.' An expansion of territory is hidden here."[16] Thus, as Ueno reads the twin critiques of Oshii's *Patlabor* films, the experience of inhabiting a "media suit" with its dangerous blind spots is not limited to the pilots of the patlabor mecha devices but is shared by all of the inhabitants of Tokyo and other highly mediated "invisible cities."

Ueno's reading of Oshii resonates with the recent writings of Dutch art historian and media/urban theorist Lieven De Cauter, who has revived the notion of the "capsule" as originally conceived by 1960s architects including Kurokawa Kishō. Drawing on Kurokawa's cybernetic theory of the capsule, De Cauter expands or "redefines" the notion of capsules to include "virtual capsules" such as the mobile phone, the Walkman, and television or computer screens that situate the viewer in a "closed mental, virtual space that is far away from the actual spaces where you sit."[17] Furthermore, he conceptualizes much of modern technology as a combination of the capsule and the network:

> All networks, from the train network, to the motorcar network, to the air transport network, to the telephone network and the world wide web—all networks function with capsules. So from the perspective of the network I can refine or even redefine the concept of the capsule: I propose capsule here as the most general concept for every closed-off and plugged-in entity, which as a sum makes the networks what they are.[18]

The mecha or "media suit" functioning within the cybernetic "invisible city" as discussed in Ueno's reading of Oshii is analogous to the closed-off and plugged-in "capsule" functioning as part of a "network" as proposed by De Cauter. Furthermore, De Cauter issues a similar critique to Oshii and Ueno regarding the role of capsules in modern society in shielding the occupant from hidden long-range violence and rendering both visible and invisible, separate and linked, the spaces of safety or socioeconomic privilege and violence or precarity. The First World, De Cauter writes, can be seen as "an archipelago of fortresses, capsules and heterotopias within an expansive territory of chaos, exclusion, and poverty":

> The capsular society is the sum of the network space, the phantasmagoric space of consumption and the fortress: the armoured enclave against the hostile world outside in a global society increasingly characterized by the duality of rich and poor, inside and outside. The capsule is the device that makes the rigid distinction between inside and outside possible. Perhaps the rise of the capsule marks, in Foucaultian-Deleuzian terms, the

> transition from the disciplinary society to the control society: no longer internalized, order externalizes itself in (often invisible) technology.[19]

From this perspective, just as the goal of the hacker antagonist of the first *Patlabor* was to make visible the personal and communal losses perpetrated by the construction state, the goal of the hacker antagonist of the second film seems to be to pierce the membrane of the capsule separating the "inside" of a complacent peacetime Japan from the "outside" of geopolitical violence being carried out to sustain it.

Yanobe Kenji's Atom Suit Project

Oshii and Ōtomo, born in 1951 and 1954, respectively, represent a generation who grew up at the height of the postwar High Growth Era and began to produce their important works during the bubble economy years of the 1980s. Thus, while a later generation from the Metabolist architects or writers such as Komatsu Sakyō who had direct experience of the Second World War, they remixed or critiqued Metabolist urban ideas from the standpoint of artists nurtured under the same postwar conditions of economic expansion and ascendant national power. Artist Yanobe Kenji, born in 1965, produced work in the 1990s and 2000s that engaged with Metabolist ideas not only from a greater generational remove but from the perspective of an artist operating under changed economic and social conditions following the collapse of the 1980s bubble economy. As such, his work gives us a further opportunity to probe the relevance of the Metabolist movement in the twenty-first century.

Despite his generational remove, Yanobe had a special personal relationship to the work of the Metabolist architects: born in Osaka, when he was six years old his family moved to Ibaraki, a suburb of Osaka near the site of the Metabolists' showcase, the 1970 Japan World Exposition (Osaka Expo). In interviews, he describes the formative experience of playing on the expo site amid the ruins of the buildings that were in the process of being demolished after the expo was complete:

> We moved near the Osaka Expo site around 1971, just before I entered elementary school. So, the Expo had already ended,

> and most of the site was an empty lot with only the Tower of the Sun, Great Roof, Japan Pavilion, and Steel Pavilion remaining. Those ruins were the perfect place for me and my friends to go exploring. I remember playing in the empty expanse under the Great Roof when no one was there, watching the Japan Pavilion be demolished by an iron wrecking ball. It was just like virtual time travel to a world where the City of the Future had been destroyed and mankind had perished. That was my Expo experience.[20]

As further inspiration for his future artistic works, Yanobe also cites his experience of glimpsing Isozaki Arata's famous piloted giant robot Deme, which was employed to assist in staging events on the Festival Plaza, through a fence at the expo site, before the robot was destroyed along with the other expo artifacts.[21]

In retrospect, we can see the influence of Metabolist ideas and forms starting with Yanobe's debut work, *Tanking Machine* (1990), which was a type of isolation tank or meditation capsule raised on four legs, filled with a body-temperature saline solution, and capped with an enigmatic British World War II gas mask that the artist had collected while studying in the United Kingdom. Visitors to the exhibit were encouraged to enter the tank in bathing suits and attempt to achieve a meditative state inside. Even in this early work, Yanobe's creation seems to tease at the idea of the manga/anime mecha with its vaguely anthropomorphic or robotic form implied by its four legs, gas-mask head, and human inhabitant temporarily embedded within its saline, womb-like interior. Yanobe's subsequent works further experimented with variations on the pod (or capsule), mecha, and "media suit" forms, such as his Weapons for Conquest series begun in 1991, incorporating references to popular culture including Godzilla, Disney, and anime, as well as topical references to the Gulf War. Soon after an accident struck the atomic power plant in Mihama, Fukui Prefecture, in 1991, Yanobe constructed his Yellow Suit, a wearable radiation protection suit covered with lead and steel plates.[22]

Yanobe next combined the radiation suit form with a reference to manga and anime pioneer Tezuka Osamu with his Atom Suit series, named for Tezuka's famous fictional robot Tetsuwan Atomu (Mighty Atom, a.k.a. Astro Boy, created in 1952), a nuclear-powered robotic boy who symbolized the peaceful application of nuclear energy. In addition to the "Atom" name, Yanobe's Atom Suit series incorporated protuberances on the helmet evoking Testuwan Atomu's signature spiky tufts of hair, together with Geiger counters placed next to sensitive or vulnerable areas of the body, such as the eyes, viscera, and genitals, with a digital screen displaying radiation levels at the center of the suit at the chest or belly. The suits, vehicles, and pods for Yanobe's Weapons for Conquest and Atom Suit series and related works incorporated the shared aspects of the Metabolist "capsule" as well as the "mecha" featured in Japanese anime: enclosure/protection; mobility; and cybernetics/network/node (particularly the Geiger counters that electronically register the user's position within a "network" of radiation).[23]

Yanobe deepened his engagement with Metabolism in 1997–2003 when he took his Atom Suit series out of the gallery space, and, wearing a comparatively lightweight version of the suit himself, created a series of site-specific performance and documentary photography works entitled the Atom Suit Project. The first of Yanobe's site-specific works was a visit to the nuclear reactor at Chernobyl and abandoned city of Pripyat that was within the contaminated Exclusion Zone evacuated after the world's worst nuclear power plant disaster in April of 1986. Accompanied by a photographer, Yanobe in his bright yellow Atom Suit posed in front of the power plant, in such locations as an abandoned school, movie theater, amusement park, and military facility, and interacted with workers who still maintained an active power-producing reactor at the Chernobyl site at the time of Yanobe's visit in 1997, as well as a small number of residents who had remained in or returned to the zone despite the evacuation orders.[24]

The second major location for Yanobe's Atom Suit Project was the site of the 1970 Osaka Expo itself, the very grounds where he had played among the semidemolished buildings as a boy in 1971 (Plate 15).[25] Thus he brought his work full circle to his initial formative experience of "virtual time travel to a world where the City of the Future had been destroyed and mankind had perished." By the time Yanobe first revisited the expo site in his Atom Suit in 1998, the grounds had been reclaimed as the Expo Commemorative Park, and only a few landmarks from the expo remained, including an amusement park, Kikutake Kiyonari's Expo Tower, and the Expo Museum of Fine Arts, which had been remade into the Osaka National Museum of

Art. In addition, Okamoto Tarō's famous Tower of the Sun now presided over the verdant landscaped park as its focal point, no longer surrounded by Tange Kenzō's giant space-frame roof or the countless national and corporate pavilions of the expo. Moreover, Yanobe was actually able to participate in events surrounding the demolition of two of these remaining landmarks: the artist was allowed to visit Expo Tower before it was dismantled in 2002, and he held a solo show, entitled *Megalomania*, in the Osaka Museum of Art in 2003—the last exhibit in this space before it was also demolished, after the museum's collection had been transferred to a new facility in downtown Osaka. Finally, as a culminating performance of his solo exhibit and entire Atom Suit Project, Yanobe donned his Atom Suit and climbed to the top of the Tower of the Sun to occupy the eyeball that had been illegally occupied or "eye-jacked" by a protester during the 1970 expo.[26]

In interviews and exhibition texts surrounding the Atom Suit Project, Yanobe referred to both Pripyat/Chernobyl and the Osaka Expo as "Ruins of the Future" *(mirai no haikyo)*, echoing architect Isozaki Arata's words in his poem "Incubation Process" that "future cities are themselves ruins."[27] Indeed, for their resonance with Isozaki's words, the photographs of Yanobe entering the soon-to-be-demolished Expo Tower are especially poignant. As described in chapter 4, Kikutake's expo observation tower incorporated a Metabolist superstructure-and-capsule form through its combination of a vertical space frame and a set of spherical polyhedron capsules, with circular windows affixed to each triangular polyhedron face, fastened at a point roughly two-thirds up the vertical frame. Photographs and video documentation for the Atom Suit Project show Yanobe in his yellow radiation suit and helmet—resembling an astronaut or deep-sea diver—a lone traveler to the abandoned futuristic interior, which is now dilapidated and covered with moss and other plants. Indeed, the moss-covered floor of the capsule has now literalized the metaphor central to Isozaki's poem "Incubation Process": the degraded metal floor of this ruined building from the City of the Future has "incubated" a lush growth of moss. Responding to the environment of "new life forms" proliferating in this ruined future city, Yanobe took plant samples from the tower floor and incorporated them as "fruit of the future" into his sculptural works *New Deme* (2002) and *Tower of Life* (2003, Plate 16).[28]

While Isozaki's words in the 1962 poem "Incubation Process" that "Future cities are themselves ruins" were a kind of prophecy from the height of the High Growth Era, Yanobe occupied a very different position in 2002. In his yellow "Atom Suit," he performed the role of a time traveler from the literal "future" from the perspective of the Metabolist heyday, yet from a contemporary perspective he was visiting the ruins of a lost "bright future"—a world, in the expo slogan, of "Progress and Harmony for Mankind" that was never fully realized, or was perhaps a false promise or premise to begin with. In between the 1970 Osaka Expo and Yanobe's performances at the turn of the millennium lie the Oil Shock of 1973, the swelling and bursting of the 1980s bubble economy, the collapse of the Soviet Union and its alternative communist utopia, and the Chernobyl nuclear disaster, as well as alarming accidents at nuclear facilities in Japan at Mihama in 1991 and Tokaimura in 1999, the traumatic events of the Kobe earthquake of January 1995 and the Tokyo subway sarin gas attack of March in the same year, and the descent into Japan's "lost decades" of economic malaise and social anxiety.

Key to understanding the valences of Yanobe's work is the fact that the first site in his Atom Suit Project was not the expo grounds but the Chernobyl nuclear power plant and the city of Pripyat constructed to house the plant's workers. Founded in the Osaka Expo year of 1970, Pripyat in particular is a fascinating ideological twin of the expo's "City of the Future": a planned city of modernist buildings built in a radial pattern around the city center, Pripyat boasted a medical complex, an amusement park, and numerous sports and cultural facilities, including a Palace of Culture, a riverfront café, a cinema, four libraries, and an art school with a concert hall. In keeping with the utopian tone of the city plans, the city's first streets were named "Enthusiasts" and "Friendship of the Peoples."[29] Such a "model city" construction can be seen as a manifestation of the promotion of the positive value of nuclear power—an "atoms for peace" ideology that was embraced by both antagonists in the nuclear Cold War, as well as by America's Cold War ally Japan, as exemplified in the nuclear-powered manga and anime hero Tetsuwan Atomu.[30] Pripyat's ideology of the "Peaceful Atom" and the "Friendship of the Peoples" was mirrored in the Osaka Expo's official slogan of "Progress and Harmony for Mankind": the notion that scientific "progress" and the peaceful development of human "harmony" could go hand in hand, despite the recent historical evidence to the contrary provided by the Holocaust, Japanese atrocities of the Second World War, the atomic bombings of Hiroshima and Nagasaki, and the ongoing Cold War.

In visiting Chernobyl as well as the Osaka Expo site in his Atom Suit, then, Yanobe bore witness to the collapse of both Pripyat and the expo's utopian visions. As Yanobe himself stated in an interview: "Atomic power was formerly seen as the symbol of hope for the future, as was the Osaka Expo. That idea was destroyed with Chernobyl. We have lived in the crevice between prosperity and decay."[31] The design of Yanobe's Atom Suit further clarifies his artistic stance and subjective relationship to the Chernobyl and expo sites: Its incorporation of Tetsuwan Atomu iconography signals the artist's indebtedness to postwar popular culture and his desire to appropriate or inhabit the optimistic, spunky persona of the *shōnen* (boy) robot and hero. Yet, the location of Geiger counter sensors on the most vulnerable parts of the suit-wearer's body—eyes, viscera, and genitalia—emphasizes the precariousness of the millennial subject: it is a protective suit for an intrepid but vulnerable individual, traversing a pair of melancholy yet strangely beautiful postapocalyptic landscapes.

"The Crevice between Prosperity and Decay"

Yanobe's work seems prophetic indeed in the light of the disaster at the Fukushima Daiichi Nuclear Power Plant following the deadly earthquake and tsunami that struck the Tohoku (northeastern Japan) region on March 11, 2011—the world's second largest nuclear power plant disaster after the Chernobyl reactor whose ruins Yanobe visited in 1997.[32] To many in Japan, the Fukushima disaster decisively revealed the limitations of the "atoms for peace" ideology and the myth of safe nuclear power symbolized by Tetsuwan Atomu and further brought into question the "progress and harmony" supposedly ensured by the public works of the construction state, which included the protective concrete seawalls that were overwhelmed by tsunami in many coastal towns, as well as the Fukushima Daiichi Power Plant itself. In the words of the Reconstruction Design Council's report to the Prime Minister's Office, the disaster not only punctured the "myth of safety" provided by the "benefits of post-war peace," but in broader terms, "in the face of the threat from nature and the hubris of human arrogance, this disaster revealed in one fell swoop the inherent vulnerability of modern civilization."[33] Indeed, the vast scale of the March 2011 disaster and its cascading effects, from earthquake to tsunami to nuclear disaster and beyond, brought to mind for many public commentators Komatsu Sakyō's narrative *Japan Sinks*, which had warned of cascading disasters whose effects reach beyond the normal calculations of probable risk and had dared to imagine the Japanese people as a nation of refugees.[34]

In linking the Testuwan Atomu character, the 1970 Osaka Expo site proclaiming "Progress and Harmony for Mankind," and the Chernobyl/Pripyat nuclear disaster sites through his performances in his Atom Suit, Yanobe Kenji had embodied the precarity of subjectivity in millennial Japan, at the "crevice between prosperity and decay." This precarious position was to be realized all the more explicitly by the thousands of refugees from the nuclear plant evacuation zone and the millions of lives affected by the radiation releases following the meltdown of three nuclear reactors, after tsunami waves flooded the plant's seawalls and disabled the emergency generators used to cool the reactors and spent fuel pools. The radiation detection equipment worn by Yanobe in his Atom Suit performances became part of daily life for many in the disaster zone, including tens of thousands of schoolchildren remaining in Fukushima Prefecture who were issued individual portable radiation dosimeters.[35]

Indeed, even before the March 2011 disaster, "precarity" had become a watchword of postbubble, millennial Japan, particularly with regard to the lives of young people financially insecure after the collapse of the postwar "lifetime employment system." Symbolic of such precarity in the popular press of the late 2000s were the young, unemployed or underemployed "net café refugees" or "cyber homeless," who spent their nights in the cubicles of internet and manga cafés that had adapted to provide vending points for basic necessities including shelter, food and drink, a limited degree of privacy, and showers, as well as internet access.[36] Were not such mobile, plugged-in, cocooned, yet vulnerable "net café refugees" inhabiting their own type of cybernetic capsule in the cubicle of an internet café, the ultimate, bathetical expression of Kurokawa's *Homo movens*?

The social and economic situation of current-day Japan (and the world beyond) thus necessitates a complex and ambivalent reckoning with the ongoing legacy of Metabolism and the futurity of late twentieth-century science fiction. The megastructural solutions offered in the most exuberant era of Metabolist architectural proposals, and celebrated in Komatsu Sakyō's *Kūchū toshi 008* (City in the air 008), while incorporating their own ecological logic, nevertheless seem ill-suited to today's era of limited resources and suspicion of architectural egoism and large state projects—a suspicion renewed for many in the post–March 2011 era witnessing the revival of the top-down, concrete-pouring construction state in the form of a controversial archipelago-scaled system of seawalls in the Tohoku tsunami disaster area, many built to a height of over 12 meters (41 feet), which by March 2018 had already reached 395 km (245 miles) at a cost of 1.35 trillion yen (nearly $13 billion).[37]

Meanwhile, despite the resurgent popularity of "capsule hotels" among a new wave of international tourists in Japan,[38] the frame-and-capsule construction of Kurokawa Kishō's famed Nakagin Capsule Tower in Tokyo appears to have been an architectural dead end, and, at the time of this writing, Kurokawa's tower is currently dilapidated and endangered, another "ruin of the future" like the expo buildings visited by Yanobe Kenji at the turn of the millennium. Yet as the films of Oshii and the writings of Ueno and De Cauter suggest, the cybernetic environment of the capsule and network, where communication and vision are both augmented and occluded, as well as the plugged-in yet atomized subjectivity such environments engender, is indeed the prevailing situation for much of the industrialized and postindustrial world, and coming to terms with such environments and subject positions is an ever more pressing task.

With another Tokyo Olympiad approaching, the cyclical temporal vision of Ōtomo, where the scenarios and character types of the past are constantly reseeded into the present and where new cycles of catastrophe and millennial salvation are always looming, seems especially foreboding. However, in addition to such apocalyptic scenarios, the works examined in this study also point to systems of discernment connecting the microscopic to the macroscopic, the organic to the inorganic, that can have constructive as well as destructive applications.[39] In contemplating our own futures, we might still be inspired by such Metabolist legacies as Kurokawa's methodology of designing through time using both temporal and spatial modules of exponentially varying scales, or by Kawazoe's example, in "Dai-Tōkyō saigo no hi" (The last days of greater Tokyo) of imagining how the "metabolism" of built environments will interact with the evolving "metabolism" of the natural environment, including natural disasters and anthropogenic climate change. For, as the works of Yanobe Kenji underscore, we are all now dwelling in city of the future, and its ruins.

Notes

Introduction

1. The references are to Komatsu Sakyō's novel *Kūchū toshi 008* (City in the air 008, 1969), which incorporates elements of Kurokawa Kishō's Helix City Plan for Tokyo 1961 (Tōkyō keikaku 1961—helix keikaku) first published in Kurokawa, "Propositions d'urbanisme au Japon" (Propositions for urbanism in Japan), 86–87; Kikutake Kiyonori's Ocean City (Kaiyō toshi, 1960), with quote from Kikutake, "Ocean City," 27; Kurokawa Kishō's "Capsule Declaration" (Kapuseru sengen, 1969; included in Kurokawa, *Metabolism in Architecture*, 75–85); Isozaki Arata's "Invisible City" (Mienai toshi, 1967) and other texts discussed in chapter 5; Masaki Gorō's *Viinasu shitei* (Venus city, 1992); Kawazoe Noboru's "Dai-Tōkyō saigo no hi: Tōkyō no metsubō—gaisetsu" (The last days of greater Tokyo: An outline of Tokyo's destruction, 1961); Komatsu Sakyō's *Japan Sinks* (Nihon chinbotsu, 1973), *Shuto shōshitsu* (The capital vanishes, 1985), and *Virus: The Day of Resurrection* (*Fukkatsu no hi*, 1964); Isozaki's "City Demolition Industry, Inc." (Toshi hakaigyō, KK, 1962); Komatsu's *Nihon apacchi zoku* (The Japan Apache tribe, 1964); Isozaki's *Hiroshima Ruined Again in the Future* (Futatabi haikyō ni natta Hiroshima, 1968); and Itō Toyoo's "The Logic of Uselessness" (Muyō no ronri, 1971 (included in Itō, *Tarzans in the Media Forest*, 22–32).

2. In her 1966 essay "What Do You Mean: Science? Fiction?," SF author and editor Judith Merril defined "speculative fiction" as "stories whose objective is to explore, to discover, to *learn*, by means of projection, extrapolation, analogue, hypothesis-and-paper-experimentation, something about the nature of the universe, of man, of 'reality.' . . . I use the term 'speculative fiction' here specifically to describe the mode which makes use of the traditional 'scientific method' (observation, hypothesis, experimentation) to examine some postulated approximation of reality, by introducing a set of changes—imaginary or inventive—into the common background of 'known facts,' creating an environment in which the responses and perceptions of the characters will reveal something about the inventions, the characters, or both." Merril, "What Do You Mean," 35–36. I will discuss Suvin's related concept of the "novum" in chapter 1. Following Merril, "speculative fiction" became an alternate moniker of "science fiction," and either or both terms can be implied by the semantically ambiguous "SF," which is favored in Japan.

3. Kikutake Kiyonori, one of the key members of the Metabolist group, had experience in wood-frame construction and pursued his own "system of

replacement" using a combination of traditional materials, as well as new materials such as reinforced concrete, in early projects such as the Ishibashi Cultural Center (1956), the Eifukuji Kindergarten (1956), and his own influential personal home, the Sky House (1958). See Oshima, "Introduction," 13, 16–18; and Thompson, "Learning from Kikutake," 51–54.

4. Sadler, "New Babylon versus Plug-in City," 59. Conrads and Sperlich's book was translated and adapted in an English-language edition as *The Architecture of Fantasy: Utopian Building and Planning in Modern Times.*

5. On links between the space program and Archigram design, see Sadler, *Archigram*, 38, 100; and Banham, *Megastructure*, 17, 22. For an overview of the "space-age architecture" of the 1960s avant-garde, see Hautajärvi, "Plastic Bubbles and Capsule Homes," and Home, "Alternative Futures."

6. On Isozaki and the U.S. National Aeronautics and Space Administration's (NASA) Mission Control Center, see Furuhata, "Multimedia Environments and Security Operations," 65–66. I will explore Kurokawa's capsule architecture in chapters 1 and 5. For discussions of the cybernetic influence on Archigram and other 1960s avant-garde architectural movements, see Schrijver, *Radical Games*, 95–146, and Sadler, *Archigram*, 90–139.

7. The 1970 World Expo followed a decade of steady growth of science fiction as a publishing genre and fan culture in Japan. The first SF coterie magazine, *Uchūjin* (Space dust) was founded in 1957, while the commercial *SF Magajin* (SF magazine), founded by Hayakawa Publishing in 1959, featured extensive translations of international science fiction authors as well as stories by Japanese authors. The institutional growth of science fiction continued throughout the 1960s, with the first Japanese SF convention in 1962 (Nihon SF Taikai), the founding of the Japan SF Writers Association (Nihon SF Sakka Kurabu) in 1963, and the creation of the Seiun Award for Science Fiction in 1970. By 1970, such major authors as Hoshi Shin'ichi, Tsutsui Yasutaka, and Komatsu Sakyō had established themselves at the forefront of the domestic SF scene. See chapter 4 regarding the founding of future studies in Japan.

8. On Satō Haruo's story, see Yiu, "New Map of Hell"; for a translation of the work, see Yiu, *Three Dimensional Reading*, 211–39. For a comparison of Lang's *Metropolis* with the versions by Tezuka and Ōtomo/Rintarō, see Bird, "States of Emergency."

9. For a discussion of Le Corbusier's architecture and urban planning as a form of utopian social engineering, see Fishman, *Urban Utopias of the Twentieth Century*, 163–264.

10. See Schrijver, *Radical Games*, 41–94, for a discussion of the Situationist critique of CIAM's functionalism.

11. For a discussion of Metabolism in relationship to CIAM and Le Corbusier's influence, see Lin, *Kenzo Tange and the Metabolist Movement*, 1–9, 76–79.

12. Banham, *Megastructure*, 8, 70.

13. Maki, *Investigations in Collective Form*, 8.

14. Maki, 9. While Maki refers to cycles of change in architecture and city design, he avoids the term *metabolism,* maintaining a distance between the proponents of this term (chiefly Kawazoe, Kikutake, and Kurokawa) and his own ideas "collective form" or "group form," proposed together with Otaka Masato as a separate subsection in the original Metabolist manifesto. In his book *Investigations in Collective Form,* Maki writes of striving toward an ideal of "master form which can move into ever new states of equilibrium and yet maintain visual consistency and a sense of continuing order in the long run." Therefore, for Maki, a megastructure "composed of several independent systems that can expand or contract with the least disturbance to others would be more preferable to the one of a rigid hierarchical system." Maki, 12.

15. Dates refer to original publication of the designs. See Mori Bijutsukan, *Metaborizumu no mirai toshi* (The future city of Metabolism), 48, 95–97.

16. Kikutake, "Ocean City," 21–27. Kikutake's plans for Tower-Shaped Community and Marine City were first unveiled in *Kokusai kenchiku* (International architecture) in January and February 1959 (26, nos. 1 and 2) and are collected in Kikutake, *Between Land and Sea,* 92–99. The two proposals were later revised and expanded in *Metabolism 1960,* with the addition of a new, related proposal, Ocean City or Unabara. It should be noted that while Kikutake employed the inorganic metaphor of crystallization to describe the growth of his Ocean City in *Metabolism 1960,* the detailed descriptions of growth and propagation of Ocean City are developed through an extended analogy to the organic process of cell division. See Nyilas, *Beyond Utopia,* 54–63.

17. Lin, *Kenzo Tange and the Metabolist Movement,* 131.

18. Tange's Plan for Tokyo 1960 and Suzuki's Tokyo Teleport Town will be discussed further in chapters 1 and 5, respectively. Most recently, the Tokyo Bay front has been the site of renewed development in the construction of high-rise residential towers as well as facilities for the upcoming 2020 Olympics: the Venue Plan concept outlined by Tokyo City divides the venue sites into the Tokyo Bay Zone and the Heritage Zone incorporating venues used at the 1964 Olympics, including Tange's Yoyogi National Gymnasium. See "About Heritage Zone and Tokyo Bay Zone," Bureau of Olympic and Paralympic Games Tokyo 2020 Preparation, accessed January 20, 2019, https://www.2020games.metro.tokyo.jp/eng/taikaijyunbi/taikai/map/heritage-tokyobay/index.html.

19. Schnellbächer, "Has the Empire Sunk Yet?"

20. Yatsuka, "'Metaborizumu nekusasu' to iu 'kindai no chōkoku'" (The "overcoming modernity" known as the "Metabolism nexus"), 11–12. See also Furuhata, "Architecture as Atmospheric Media," 57–59, and the section "Senchū kara sengo fukkō e" (From wartime to postwar recovery) in Mori Bijutsukan, *Metaborizumu no mirai toshi,* 19–23, which features unbuilt designs for settlements in Manchukuo, as well as the unrealized International Exposition of Japan 1940, in addition to Tange's Greater East Asia Co-prosperity Sphere Monument, as a prehistory to Metabolism.

21. Rem Koolhaas and Hans Ulrich Obrist's book *Project Japan: Metabolism Talks* highlights the role of Tange Lab graduate and lifelong bureaucrat Shimokōbe Atsushi (1923–2016) as a connector between the Japanese State and the Metabolist architects. From 1952 through 1979, Shimokōbe was an official in the Economic Planning Agency and later the National Land Agency and contributed to the Comprehensive National Development Plans in 1969 and 1977; he appointed Kurokawa Kishō and other architects associated with Metabolism to numerous study groups informing the Economic Planning Agency and National Land Agency projects and reports. See Koolhaus and Obrist, *Project Japan*, 638–57, 661–95.

22. See Hanes, "From Megalopolis to Megaroporisu," 69–70, 75–80.

23. Quoted in Igarashi and Iso, *Bokura ga yume mita mirai toshi*, 28. A similar critique is presented in Asada and Isozaki, "From Molar Metabolism to Molecular Metabolism," 65.

24. In his essay from 1969, "Kapuseru de wa ōsama de aru" (In the capsule, one is king), Maki Fumihiko offers "informational function," "defensive function," "self-regulating function," "metabolic exchange function," and "gathering/assembling function" as the paradigmatic functions a capsule should have (46).

25. *OED Online*, s.v. "capsule," accessed May 24, 2016, https://www.oed.com/view/Entry/27609.

26. GK, "Kono tenimuhō na kotai no sahō," 54. Kurokawa's discussion of the capsule as "cyborg architecture," in his "Capsule Declaration" points toward a similar conception. GK's article was published in a special issue of *SD (Space Design)* magazine from March 1969 entitled "Kapseru gainen no kakuchō" (Extension of the capsule concept), which featured Kurokawa Kishō's "Capsule Declaration" and Kawazoe Noboru's "Han-kachi to shite no kapuseru" (Capsule as an anti-value), discussed below. The issue also includes a graphic essay by Awazu Kiyoshi, the essay by Maki Fumihiko cited above, and a discussion of Archigram's view of the capsule written by Nakamura Toshio. It should be noted that although Kurokawa's contribution to this volume, "Oh! Saibōgu no okite" ("Oh! The laws of the cyborg"), subtitled "Kapuseru sengen 1969" ("Caspule Declaration 1969"), is cited as the source for the English-language essay "Capsule Declaration," collected in *Metabolism in Architecture*, it is a much abbreviated version, conveying Kurokawa's main points in a single page, which were expanded upon in the later English version, as well as in Kurokawa's Japanese-language book *Homo mobensu: toshi to ningen no mirai* (*Homo movens*: The future of cities and humans, 1969).

27. Colomina, "Unbreathed Air 1956," 47, 50. For further discussion on the connections between postwar modernist architecture, the military/defense industry, and American Cold War popular culture, see Colomina, *Domesticity at War*.

28. As Metabolist theorist Kawazoe Noboru put it, "The development of information culture makes large organizations unnecessary; inevitably, these large

organizations will dissolve into smaller groups and form a [new] organization through networks. . . . The society of the future will likely be composed of autonomous individuals and small groups. We think of the capsule as something that will envelop such individuals and small groups such as the nuclear family." Kawazoe, "Han-kachi to shite no kapuseru" (The capsule as an anti-value), 38.

29. Kurokawa, "Capsule Declaration," in *Metabolism in Architecture,* 82–83. In his article "Kurokawa's Metabolic Space," Tobias Cheung discusses the intellectual matrix of Kurokawa's writings and particularly his theory of *Homo movens,* the nomadic inhabitant of emergent cybernetic capsule environments. Cheung describes Kurokawa's *Homo movens* as "a biomated agent [that is, a synthesis of technology and bioorganism], a hybrid of the technic space in which he moves. . . . Kurokawa's life-worlds are based on a double process of inside-outside movements that change, through stimuli and systemic reactions, both sides of the exchange, the inner and the outer world. Existential desires and structured space coexist for Kurokawa in a dynamic field of mutual interactions, and the field of meaningful signs is not fixed" (141).

30. Kawazoe, "Han-kachi to shite no kapuseru," 41–42. The quotations in English are taken from an English abstract of the article in the unpaginated English table of contents.

31. Kurokawa, *Metabolism in Architecture,* 79–82. Similarly, in his essay, "Kapuseru de wa ōsama de aru," Maki Fumihiko cites "neighboring space" *(kaiwai kūkan),* as a necessary complement to "capsule space" (46).

32. Kawazoe, "Han-kachi to shite no kapuseru," 45.

33. Schrijver, *Radical Games,* 117, 114.

34. In tracing the cultural history of capsules, it is also noteworthy that one year after the debut of *Mazinger Z* and Kurokawa's Nakagin Capsule Tower, Abe Kōbō published his novel *The Box Man* (*Hako otoko,* 1973) narrated by an eccentric protagonist who has fashioned a mobile home out of a cardboard box. *The Box Man* protagonist could be considered a low-tech cyborg, whose cardboard home both serves as protection against a hostile environment and functions as a kind of camera, as discussed by Christopher Bolton in his study *Sublime Voices: The Fictional Science and Science Fiction of Abe Kōbō,* 198–204.

35. William M. Tsutsui, "Oh No, There Goes Tokyo," 104.

36. Yatsuka, "Godzilla versus the Metabolist Mega-Monuments," 353.

37. William M. Tsutsui, "Oh No! There Goes Tokyo," 112.

38. On the alternation of creation and destruction in *Godzilla* and *Ultra Q* series, see also Tatsumi Takayuki, *Full Metal Apache,* 12–15.

39. Tanaka, *Apocalypse in Contemporary Japanese Science Fiction,* 15–18.

40. In his essay "The Philosophy of Metabolism" interpreting the Metabolist group to a Western audience, Kurokawa Kishō explicitly connected the Metabolists' architecture principles with the cyclical Buddhist concept of *samsara* (wandering or transmigration): "The acknowledgement by the Metabolist group in its 1960 book that society is part of a greater circle of life coincides with this

doctrine *[samsara]*. The principle that architecture should change with time, the principle of replaceability and interchangeability, and the principle of the metabolic cycle, as well as the belief that architecture, cities, and humanity itself are ephemeral, are all in accord with the doctrines of *samsara* and *laksana-alaksanatas*." In Kurokawa, *Metabolism in Architecture*, 35.

41. Tellingly, Komatsu was one of the first critics to hail Godzilla's importance as a "symbol of the primal fear that has been revived in the present era by the advancement of science." Komatsu, "Haikei Iwan Efurēmofu sama: 'Shakai shugiteki SF ron' ni tai suru hanron" (Dear Ivan Efremov: A counter-argument to 'A socialist theory of SF,'" 1963), in *Komatsu Sakyō zenshū kanzenban* (Komatsu Sakyō collected works complete edition), 28:247.

42. Fortin, *Architecture and Science-Fiction Film*, 60.

43. Such intermedial relationships and aesthetics, with a focus on late twentieth-century American entertainment media, are brilliantly explored in Angela Ndalianis's *Neo-Baroque Aesthetics and Contemporary Entertainment*. While it does not focus on architecture or cityscape, Marc Steinberg's *Anime's Media Mix: Franchising Toys and Characters in Japan*, provides a fascinating look at transmedial aspects of Japanese animation.

44. Gleiniger and Vrachliotis, "Editorial," in *Simulation*, 9.

45. In Abe's *Inter Ice Age 4*, computer simulations reveal the likelihood that Tokyo will be flooded because of the rapid melting of polar ice caps, spurring the development of a research program into a race of humans that can live under water. See chapter 2 for a discussion of Isozaki's essay. For a discussion of the history of simulation as a concept and computer simulation as an architectural method, see the essays in Gleiniger and Vrachliotis's *Simulation: Presentation Technique and Cognitive Method*.

1. City Visions

1. Dower, *Embracing Defeat*, 45–46.

2. See Ishida, "Japanese Cities and Planning in the Reconstruction Period"; Ichikawa, "Reconstructing Tokyo"; and Sorensen, *Making of Urban Japan*, 158–68.

3. Karacas, "Occupied City," 195–97. According to Karacas, Washington Heights consisted of several hundred housing units, while Grant Heights had over a thousand. The land containing Washington Heights was returned to Japan in 1964, with some of the units converted to housing for Olympic athletes, before being torn down to create Yoyogi Park. Grant Heights was not returned to Japan until 1974, when it was redeveloped as the massive Hikarigaoka housing complex.

4. Karacas, 197.

5. The census statistics cited by Harris show an increase in the urban population of Japan of 56.7 percent from 1945 to 1950, 61.1 percent in 1950–55, and 18.1 percent in 1955–60, for a total urban population increase of nearly 60 million, or 63.3 percent of the total population, by 1960. However, these numbers

are skewed somewhat by the expanded definition of urban areas after many villages were incorporated into cities in the Amalgamation Act of 1953. See Harris, "Urban and Industrial Transformation of Japan," 52–54; and Sorensen, *Making of Urban Japan*, 171–73.

6. Hanes, "From Megalopolis to Megaroporisu," 65.

7. Harris, "Urban and Industrial Transformation of Japan," 50.

8. Sorensen, *Making of Urban Japan*, 182.

9. Sorensen, 185–88. Several important postwar writers, including Abe Kōbō, Gotō Meisei, and Takahashi Takako, explored the new physical and psychological space of the *danchi* in their works. See Maeda, *Toshi kūkan no naka no bungaku* (The literature of urban space), 555–633; Karube, *Abe Kōbō no toshi* (Abe Kōbō's city); Prichard, *Ruined Maps*; Sakaki, "'There's No Such Place as Home'"; and Tillack, "Concrete Abstractions."

10. Sorensen, *Making of Urban Japan*, 191–92.

11. Tange, *Kenzo Tange 1946–1996*, 40–41, 108–19.

12. On the protest movement, see Packard, *Protest in Tokyo*; Apter and Sawa, *Against the State*; Avenell, *Making Japanese Citizens*; and Kapur, *Japan at the Crossroads*.

13. See, for example, Hidaka and Satō, *Nippon shindan* (Japan diagnosis). See also the chapter "From the Anti-security Treaty Movement to the Tokyo Olympics: Transforming the Body, the Metropolis, and Memory," in Igarashi Yoshikuni, *Bodies of Memory*, 131–63.

14. The World Design Conference was held on May 11–16, 1960. Foreign designers and architects participating in the conference included Herbert Bayer, B. V. Doshi, Ralph Erskine, Louis Kahn, Jean Prouvé, Paul Rudolph, Alison and Peter Smithson, and Raphael Soriano. For a record of the World Design Conference, see World Design Conference Organization, *World Design Conference 1960*. See also Koolhaus and Obrist, *Project Japan*, 174–204.

15. Kawazoe Noboru, quoted in Lin, *Kenzo Tange and the Metabolist Movement*, 20.

16. For example, Kurokawa and Kikutake were invited to participate in the exhibition *Visionary Architecture* at the Museum of Modern Art in New York the following year. Lin, 24.

17. The discussion below focuses primarily on the architectural theories of Kawazoe, Kikutake, and Kurokawa. Ōtaka and Maki distanced themselves somewhat from the conceptions of Metabolism as outlined by Kawazoe and put forth a separate theory of Group Form. For a record of the World Design Conference, see World Design Conference Organization, *World Design Conference 1960*. On the origins of the Metabolist group, see Wendelken, "Putting Metabolism Back in Place," 279–93; Lin, *Kenzo Tange and the Metabolist Movement*, 16–62; and Koolhaus and Obrist, *Project Japan*, 174–221.

18. Itō's "The Logic of Uselessness," as translated by Thomas Daniell, is included in the collection *Tarzans in the Media Forest*, 22–32. The original essay

was first published in the November 1971 issue of the journal *Toshi jūtaku* (City housing) and is collected in Itō Toyoo, *Kaze no henyōtai: kenchiku kuronikuru* (The wind's shape-changer: Architecture chronicles), 15–27.

19. Kawazoe, "City of the Future," 99, 100, 110.

20. As mentioned in the introduction, other architects and designers of the time were also experimenting with the concept of fixed framing or superstructural elements and detachable modules, such as Hungarian-French architect Yona Friedman's plans for Mobile Architecture and Paris Spatial (1959–61) and British architect Peter Cook's Plug-in City (1962–64). See Schaik and Máčel, *Exit Utopia*.

21. Kikutake, "Tower-Shape Community," in Kawazoe, *Metabolism 1960*, 28–39.

22. Kikutake, "Tower-Shape Community," in Kawazoe, *Metabolism 1960*, 15–19.

23. Kurokawa, *Metabolism in Architecture*, 105–9. Kurokawa's Nakagin Capsule Tower should not be confused with the vernacular form of the capsule hotel, which has become an internationally famous element of the Japanese cityscape, and which features small independent "capsules" for hotel guests within the confines of a conventional "box" building structure. In fact, in 1979 Kurokawa himself participated as a consultant in the creation of the first such "capsule hotel," the still-operating Capsule Inn Osaka.

24. Kurokawa, 76. For an elaboration of Kurokawa's theory of *Homo movens*, see Kurokawa, *Homo mobensu*; see also Cheung, "Kurokawa's Metabolic Space."

25. Kurokawa, *Metabolism in Architecture*, 75.

26. Kurokawa, 79.

27. Kurokawa, 83. In his essay "The City of the Future," Kawazoe imagines individuals usurping many of the current functions of architects and freely assembling their own dwellings, as they currently assemble their own outfits of clothing. Kawazoe, "City of the Future," 107, 110.

28. Kurokawa, *Metabolism in Architecture*, 80.

29. Kurokawa, 75.

30. Mori Bijutsukan, *Metaborizumu no mirai toshi*, 41. In its exploration of exponential increases in size from the subatomic to the galactic, Asada's scale anticipates designers and filmmakers Charles and Ray Eames's film *Powers of Ten* (1968), which was based on Kees Boeke's book *The Universe in Forty Jumps* (1957). See Colomina, "Enclosed by Images," 328.

31. Kawazoe, *Metabolism 1960*, 5.

32. Mori Bijutsukan, *Metaborizumu no mirai toshi*, 41.

33. It is interesting to compare the Metabolists' view of scale with mathematician Benoit Mandelbrot's theory of "fractal" geometry or "self-similar" shapes appearing in nature across vastly different scales, first introduced in 1967. See the discussion of fractal geometry and Komatsu Sakyō's novel *Japan Sinks* in chapter 3.

34. Kurokawa's article was originally published as "Teijū tan'i keikaku no rinen to hōhō" (Concept and methodology of fixed units for planning), in *Kenchiku bunka* magazine in June 1967. It was translated and included in Kurokawa, *Metabolism in Architecture*, 67–74.

35. Kurokawa, *Metabolism in Architecture*, 71–74.

36. Kurokawa, 84.

37. Gottmann, "Megalopolis or the Urbanization of the Northeastern Seaboard," 200. On the reception of Gottmann's thesis in Japan, see Hanes, "From Megalopolis to Megaroporisu."

38. Doxiadis and Papaioannou, *Ecumenopolis*, 436.

39. Tange, *Nihon rettō no shōraizō*, 62. See also the discussion of Tange's work in Hanes, "From Megalopolis to Megaroporisu," 69–70, as well as Koolhaus and Obrist, *Project Japan*, 678–81.

40. Zhongjie Lin points out that the word *megastructure* was itself coined by Maki Fumihiko, an architect affiliated with the Metabolist group, and later popularized through Reyner Banham's book *Megastructure: Urban Futures of the Recent Past*. See Lin, *Kenzo Tange and the Metabolist Movement*, 9–10.

41. See Lin, 72–73.

42. Kikutake, "Tower-Shape Community," in Kawazoe, *Metabolism 1960*, 10, 13. Translations of Kikutake's articles on Marine City and Tower-Shaped Community, originally published in *Kokusai kenchiku* (International Architecture) in February 1959, are included in Kikutake, *Between Land and Sea*, 92–99.

43. Kikutake, "Tower-Shape Community," in Kawazoe, *Metabolism 1960*, 15.

44. Kikutake proposed numerous versions of the Marine City, Ocean City, or similar floating megastructures throughout his career, beginning with Marine City in 1958, and continuing with Ocean City or Unabara (ocean field) proposed in the 1960 Metabolist manifesto, both of which are the basis of the above description. One of Kikutake's later designs for a floating megastructure was realized in the form of the Aquapolis built for the Okinawa Ocean Expo of 1975: a structure the size of a city block buoyed by four giant floats. See Kikutake, *Between Land and Sea*, 93–96; Koolhaus and Obrist, *Project Japan*, 354–59; and Nyilas, *Beyond Utopia*, 50–67.

45. Kawazoe, "City of the Future," 104–5.

46. Lin, *Kenzo Tange and the Metabolist Movement*, 72.

47. Tange et al., "Mirai toshi Tôkyô" (Future City Tokyo); and Kawazoe, "Tōkyō no henshin" (The transformation of Tokyo).

48. Sorensen, *Making of Urban Japan*, 188–91.

49. See Koolhaus and Obrist, *Project Japan*, 266–93, for a catalog of Tokyo Bay proposals. For a discussion of the Tokyo Bay proposals focusing on Kikutake's contributions, see Kuan, "Visions of Tokyo Bay."

50. In addition to bringing his proposal directly to the Japanese people through his January 1961 New Year's Broadcast on NHK, Tange published versions of his plan in *Shinkenchiku* (March 1961) and *Japan Architect* (April 1961)

and in extended book form as *Tōkyō keikaku—1960: sono kōzō kaikaku no teian* (A plan for Tokyo—1960: Toward a structural reorganization). An abbreviated English version is included in Ockman, *Architecture Culture 1943–1968*. See also Lin, *Kenzo Tange and the Metabolist Movement*, 133–71.

51. Tange, "Plan for Tokyo, 1960," 327.

52. Tange, *Tōkyō keikaku—1960*, 29.

53. Banham, *Megastructure*, 49, 54.

54. Smithson, "Reflections on Kenzo Tange's Tokyo Bay Plan," 479. See also Lin, *Kenzo Tange and the Metabolist Movement*, 157–65, for a discussion of the critical reception of Tange's proposal.

55. Kawazoe, "City of the Future," 99.

56. Isozaki, "Invisible City," 406.

57. Suvin, *Metamorphoses of Science Fiction*, 64.

58. See chapter 2 for a discussion of "Fuka katei" (Incubation Process).

59. Komatsu, *Kūchū toshi 008* (City in the air 008), 24.

60. Igarashi and Iso, *Bokura ga yume mita mirai toshi*, 17–44.

61. Kawazoe's description of the "signalization" *(shigunaru-ka)* and "symbolization" *(shinboru-ka)* of Tokyo's urban systems during this period resonates with Isozaki Arata's description of the coming "symbolic" or "semiotic" stage in urban design, which he proposes in his essay "Invisible City," 406–7.

62. Kawazoe, "Dai-Tōkyō saigo no hi" (The last days of greater Tokyo), 12.

63. Kawazoe's story precedes by ten years Ursula K. Le Guin's *The Lathe of Heaven* (1971), which is cited by Adam Trexler as the "first novel directly concerned with anthropogenic greenhouse effect" in his study of primarily English-language fiction, *Anthropocene Fictions: The Novel in a Time of Climate Change* (8). For more discussion of climate change in Japanese fiction and nonfiction, see chapter 5.

64. Isozaki, "City Demolition Industry, Inc.," 857. The original text is included in *Kūkan e* (Toward space), 1–10.

65. Isozaki, "City Demolition Industry, Inc.," 855.

66. Isozaki, 855. The prospectus' third category of "Destruction of Images" *(imēji no hakai)* may be a reference to Kevin Lynch's influential work *The Image of the City*, published in 1960.

67. Isozaki, 858.

68. Forty years later, Isozaki commented on his earlier story and the subsequent developments in his career and Japanese architecture, in a follow-up story, "Rumor City" ("Ryūgen toshi," 2001), which has also been translated into English.

69. Daniell, "Fugitive," 4.

70. Kurokawa, *Metabolism in Architecture*, 75, 83.

71. Itō Toyoo, *Tarzans in the Media Forest*, 22.

72. Itō, 22–23.

73. Lem, *Invincible*.

74. Itō, 24.
75. Itō, 31.

2. Ruined Cities

1. Written roughly fifteen years after the first Metabolist manifesto, Kurokawa's essay "The Philosophy of Metabolism" was an attempt to consolidate the architect's work and the theory of Metabolism for an international audience, prefacing the volume *Metabolism in Architecture*, the first major single-volume presentation of Kurokawa's work in English. Isozaki's influential essay "Invisible City" was first published in the journal *Tenbō* (Outlook) in November 1967 and was anthologized in his book *Kūkan e* (Toward space) in 1971, with the essay dated to 1966. A partial translation in English, from which this excerpt is taken, was published in Joan Ockman's *Architecture Culture 1943–1968: A Documentary Anthology*, which also dates the essay to 1966. This chapter will focus on the image of ruins in Isozaki's and Komatsu's work; however, the significance of ruined landscapes for Kurokawa's work and writing is discussed in Igarashi Tarō, "Kisho Kurokawa: Buddhism and Metabolism."

2. From Komatsu's 1968 essay "Haikyo no kanata" (Beyond the ruins), in Komatsu, *Komatsu Sakyō zenshū kanzenban* (Komatsu Sakyō collected works complete edition), 15:184–85.

3. The term Nosaka initially used was the "Burnt-Out Ruins and Black Market School" *(Yakeato yami-ichi ha)*, in the essay "Yakeato yami-ichi ha no ben: Naokishō o jūshō shite" (Burnt-out ruins and black market school speech: Receiving the Naoki Prize). Nosaka, 187–90.

4. Nosaka Akiyuki defined this "school" or generation as those born in the years 1929 through 1931 (Rosenbaum, "'Generation of the Burnt-out Ruins,'" 281). Other chronological definitions expand this to the "Showa single digit" generation, i.e., 1926–1934 (Rosenbaum, 284), or to those born in the 1930s (Claremont, "Yakeato Poet," 92). Rosenbaum defines the "Generation of the Burnt-out Ruins" more loosely as "the cohort of Japanese who were born during the war, grew up amidst it and came of age at its end" (Rosenbaum, "'Generation of the Burnt-out Ruins,'" 283). Perhaps because his works are considered outside of "pure literature" *(jun bungaku)*, Komatsu is infrequently mentioned as a writer associated with the Burnt-out Ruins School, although critic Ishikawa Takashi points out both Komatsu's membership in the *yakeato* generation and the importance of ruins in his work (Ishikawa, "Komatsu Sakyō," 413).

5. In his essay "The Ruin," German sociologist and critic Georg Simmel (1858–1918) describes the tension between human spirit and nature represented by the ruin as the moment at which "the balance between nature and spirit, which the building manifested, shifts in favor of nature." Simmel, "Two Essays," 379. For a classic study of the history of European ruin gazing, see Macaulay, *Pleasure of Ruins*.

6. Komatsu, *Komatsu Sakyō zenshū kanzenban*, 28:177.

7. Isozaki, "Invisible City," 403.

8. The title of the special issue in Japanese was "Genbakuka no sengo 10 nen: Nihonjin no kenchiku to kenchikuka," *Shinkenchiku* 30, no. 8 (August 1955). This special issue included discussion of nuclear power, as well as the atomic bomb, and included a discussion entitled "Genbaku jidai to kenchiku" (The nuclear age and architecture) between Asada and nuclear physicist Taketani Mitsuo, who is said to have had a strong theoretical influence on Metabolist thinkers including Kawazoe and Kikutake. See Koolhaus and Obrist, *Project Japan*, 145, 229; and Sawaragi, *Sensō to banpaku*, 26–27.

9. Kawazoe, *Metabolism 1960*, 48.

10. Kawazoe, 49.

11. Koolhaus and Obrist, *Project Japan*, 42.

12. Isozaki, *Japan-ness in Architecture*, 88.

13. Isozaki, 87–88. The original essay, "Fuka-katei," was first published in *Bijutsu techō* in April 1962; collected in Isozaki, *Kūkan e*, 40.

14. Isozaki, *Japan-ness in Architecture*, 88.

15. Isozaki, "Mienai toshi," in *Kūkan e*, 384. My translation; this section is not included in Ockman's collection.

16. Isozaki, "Invisible City," 403. Isozaki also elaborated on these ideas in the essays "Porusesu puranningu ron" (A theory of process planning, 1962) and "Toshi dezain no hōhō" (The method of urban design, 1962), both included in the anthology *Kūkan e*.

17. Isozaki, "Purosesu puranningu ron," in *Kūkan e*, 66–69.

18. From a statement circulated at the *Electric Labyrinth* exhibit at the Milan Triennial '68, quoted in Morikawa, "Denkiteki meikyū no foto korāji" (The photo collages of *Electric Labyrinth*), 14.

19. Isozaki, *Island Nation Aesthetic*, 29.

20. Komatsu, "Haikyo no kūkan bunmei," 173–74. Isozaki also writes of the experience of Japan's surrender, in connection with the theme of ruins, in similar terms: "The destructions of houses and buildings that we had considered mainstays of our way of life; the established belief of the national state with the Emperor at its head; and the social system that controlled even the smallest daily activities, had collapsed and vanished, leaving behind only the void of the blue sky overhead." Isozaki, 28.

21. Komatsu, "Haikyo no kūkan bunmei," 174. In a later essay on "Ruins," Isozaki similarly refers to the moment of surrender as "the end of history": "There was not a cloud in that sky over the Japanese archipelago on the day Japan surrendered. . . . There was a marvelous silence; the passage of time halted; more, it was the end of history." Isozaki, "Ruins," 11.

22. Komatsu, 177–78.

23. Komatsu, 179–80.

24. Komatsu, 180.

25. Komatsu, *Nihon appachi zoku*, 3.

26. Komatsu, 3.

27. It is estimated that a population of around eight hundred—primarily ethnic Koreans mixed with some ethnic Japanese and Okinawans—lived in shantytown dwellings and scavenged the extensive bombing site, where over thirty thousand machine relics are said to have remained as late as 1952 (Tatsumi, *Full Metal Apache*, 158). The term *Apache* seems to have emerged from press reports describing the scrap thieves, drawing an analogy of the outlaw status and ethnic otherness of the Apache tribe, whose fierce resistance to white American domination of their territory was familiar to Japanese popular culture through such Western movies as the John Ford/John Wayne Western *Fort Apache* from 1948.

28. Komatsu, *Nihon appachi zoku*, 4.

29. Komatsu, 5.

30. Komatsu, *SF e no yuigon*, 121.

31. Kojève, *Introduction to the Reading of Hegel*, 158–62. Kojève himself excepted Japan from the posthistorical "Animality" represented by postwar American culture, asserting that the "snobbishness" of the Japanese distinguished them from the Animal. ("Snobbishness," it should be noted, is definitely not a characteristic of the Apache in Komatsu's tale.) In more recent times, Hiroki Azuma has examined postmodern Japanese society through the lens of Kojèvian "Animalization" (Azuma, *Otaku*), while Georgio Agamben has examined the possibilities of reclaiming the "Animal" in the posthistorical era (Agamben, *Open*).

32. Park Yu-ha, "Kyōbō suru hyōgen"; and Tatsumi, *Full Metal Apache*, 157–64.

3. Planetary Cities

1. The three works referred to here are *Shuto shōshitsu* (The capital vanishes, 1985), *Japan Sinks* (*Nihon chinbotsu*, 1973), and *Virus: The Day of Resurrection* (*Fukkatsu no hi*, 1964).

2. In discourses of globalization, "deterritorialization" is most often used to refer to the process whereby goods and cultural forms become detached from their roots in local or national geographies and cultures. However, in reference to Komatsu's novels, we can also think of "deterritorialization" in conjunction with the more literal process of separation of people and their culture from a geographic home territory. See Appadurai, *Modernity at Large*; Papastergiadis, *Turbulence of Migration*, 100–21; Tomlinson, *Globalization and Culture*, 106–49; and Heise, *Sense of Place and Sense of Planet*, 51–58.

3. In the introduction to their edited volume *The Planetary Turn: Relationality and Geoaesthetics in the Twenty-First Century*, Amy J. Elias and Christian Moraru define the planetary consciousness that they see emerging in contemporary fiction and criticism as follows: "In this emerging worldview and critical theory, the planet as a living organism, as a shared ecology, and as an incrementally integrated system both embracing and rechanneling the currents of modernity is the axial dimension in which writers and artists perceive themselves,

their histories, and their aesthetic practices" (xii). As I will explore in this chapter, however, while Komatsu's writings could be seen as one early articulation of such a planetary vision, they also highlight the geopolitical tensions, ambiguities, failures, and gaps underlying such an "incrementally integrated" planetary "system," from the standpoints of both global ecologies and the idea of "cosmopolitan" cultural identity.

4. Heise, *Sense of Place and Sense of Planet*, 55.

5. Heise, 205.

6. Komatsu, *Fukkatsu no hi*, 281–90, 326–31; and Komatsu, *Virus*, 203–10, 235–37.

7. This is a prominent, elegaic appearance of the motif of ruins explored in chapter 2. A similar elegiac scene occurs in *Japan Sinks: Part Two* when the submerged landscapes and cityscapes of Japan are surveyed from an underwater camera that broadcasts the images to Japanese refugee communities around the world on the twenty-fifth anniversary of the sinking of the archipelago. Komatsu and Tani, *Nihon chinbotsu dainibu*, 1:85–93.

8. See, for example, Anthony Giddens's definition of *globalization* as "the intensification of worldwide social relations which link distant localities in such a way that local happenings are shaped by events occurring many miles away and vice versa." Giddens, *Consequences of Modernity*, 64.

9. Komatsu, *Virus*, 62–63.

10. Komatsu, 63.

11. Komatsu, 63.

12. Komatsu, 62.

13. Heise, *Sense of Place and Sense of Planet*, 63.

14. Komatsu, "Banpaku kara kōgai e" (From expo to pollution), 50.

15. As outlined in Spencer R. Weart's history, the early 1970s were a threshold in public awareness of climate change, with the hypothesis of global cooling, as well as global warming, receiving attention. Komatsu's 1970 warning on climate change preceded by one year the first international conference on the subject, "Study of Man's Impact on Climate," held in Stockholm in 1971. Between Komatsu's 1970 article and his 1974 study *Ijō kishō*, a steady stream of new research emerged: *Science* magazine, for example, featured articles by S. I. Rasool and S. H. Schneider, "Atmospheric Carbon Dioxide and Aerosols: Effects of Large Increases on the Global Climate," *Science* 173 (1971); G. J. Kulka and R. K. Matthews, "When Will the Present Interglacial End?," *Science* 178 (1972); and R. Bryson, "A Perspective on Climate Change," *Science* 184 (1974). The year 1974 also saw attention to this issue in the popular press, with such articles as "Ominous Changes in the World's Weather?," *Fortune*, February 1974, and "Another Ice Age?," *Time*, June 26, 1974, followed by "The Cooling World," *Newsweek*, April 28, 1975. Komatsu's book-length study, however, preceded by two years popular book-length works on this issue in the United States, such as Lowell Ponte's *The Cooling* and Stephen H. Schneider and Lynn E. Mesirow's

The Genesis Strategy: Climate and Global Survival. See Weart, *Discovery of Global Warming*, 63–113, 216–19; and Black and Weisel, *Global Warming*, 38–48.

16. Komatsu, *Komatsu Sakyō zenshū kanzenban*, 35:186–206. Leading up to this work, Komatsu also published two interdisciplinary nonfiction books on the subject of planetary studies, composed of discussions with geologists, biologists, anthropologists, and other experts: *Jinrui wa horobiru ka* (Will human beings perish?, 1970) and *Chikyū o kangaeru* (Thinking about the earth, 1972). See Komatsu, *Komatsu Sakyō zenshū kanzenban*, vol. 30.

17. Rachel Carson's *Silent Spring* was published in the United States in 1962 and was first published in Japanese translation in 1964. Komatsu's story "Seijaku no tsūrô" (Silent corridor) was included in the short story collection *Adamu no sue* (The descendants of Adam). See Colligan-Taylor, *Emergence of Environmental Literature in Japan*, 211; and Thornber, *Ecoambiguity*, 70–71.

18. Tanaka, *Apocalypse in Contemporary Japanese Science Fiction*, 143.

19. The phrases in quotations are references to the "Wall of Contradictions" in the World of the Future section of the 1970 Osaka Expo, curated by Kawazoe Noboru and colleagues, as discussed in chapter 4.

20. Lorenz expressed such concerns in the opening address to a meeting of climate scientists in Boulder, Colorado, in 1965, as well as in published articles in 1963 and 1967. See Weart, *Discovery of Global Warming*, 58–60.

21. Heise, *Sense of Place and Sense of Planet*, 121, 124–36.

22. Komatsu, *Virus*, 95.

23. This appears to be a reference to the Goldsboro, North Carolina, B-52 crash that occurred in January 1961, not 1957.

24. Perrow, *Normal Accidents*, 5, 23.

25. Komatsu, *Nihon chinbotsu*, 1:38.

26. The *Oxford English Dictionary* defines *fractal* as "a mathematically conceived curve such that any small part of it, enlarged, has the same statistical character as the original." The term *fractal* was coined by Benoit Mandelbrot in 1975, two years after the Japanese publication of *Japan Sinks*. However, Mandelbrot's initial work on "self-similar" shapes appearing in nature across different scales had been introduced to the public in the article "How Long Is the Coast of Britain?" in the journal *Science* in 1967. See Mandelbrot, *Fractals*; and Batty, "Fractals."

27. The phenomenon that came to be referred to as the "butterfly effect" was identified by mathematician and meteorologist Edward Lorenz circa 1963. See Gleik, *Chaos*, for an influential popular account of these developing sciences of chaos theory and dynamical systems.

28. In the discussion of cosmopolitanism and nationalism below, I am indebted to M. M. Bakhtin's concepts of dialogism and heteroglossia, particularly as summarized in the essay "Discourse in the Novel" included in *The Dialogic Imagination*.

29. According to the categorization of *chōhen*, or long works and collections

of *tanpen*, or short works, in the list of Komatsu's publications in Itō Yasushi, *Tsuitō*, 214–21.

30. Komatsu, *Shuto shōshitsu*, 1:69–70.

31. Komatsu, 2:310.

32. Komatsu and Tani, *Nihon chinbotsu dainibu*, 2:244–55. Coauthor Tani Kōshū discusses the tension between cosmopolitanism and nationalism in a roundtable discussion with Kotani Mari, Morishita Katsuhito, and Ishiwa Yoshiyuki (Kasai and Tatsumi, *3.11 no mirai*, 147–58). In his review of *Japan Sinks: Part Two*, critic Katō Kōichi attributes the conflict between cosmopolitanism and nationalism to the contradictory coexistence within Komatsu of nationalism and the ethos of "postwar democracy." Katō Kōichi, review of *Nihon chinbotsu dainibu*, by Komatsu Sakyō and Tani Kōshū, *Kinokuniya shohyō kūken booklog* (blog), September 26, 2006, https://booklog.kinokuniya.co.jp/kato/archives/2006/09/post_33.html.

33. Komatsu, *SF damashi*, 129–30. Yamamoto/Ben-Dasan's theories are discussed in Befu, *Hegemony of Homogeneity*, 105–11. There are striking echoes of Yamamoto's idea of Nihonkyō (Japaneseness as a "civil religion") as discussed by Befu and the theories of Japanese "common sense" *(jōshiki)* as a quasi-religious source of identity offered by Torikai. Komatsu, *Shuto shōshitsu*, 2:248–56.

34. See Schnellbächer, "Has the Empire Sunk Yet," 38–42; and Langer, *Postcolonialism and Science Fiction*, 75–80.

35. Napier, "Panic Sites," 331–36.

36. Komatsu and Tani, *Nihon chinbotsu dainibu*, 1:129–212.

37. For prototypes of such tales Csicsery-Ronay cites *Robinson Crusoe* and *King Solomon's Mines*. Csicsery-Ronay, *Seven Beauties of Science Fiction*, 225–29.

38. Csicsery-Ronay, 227–28.

39. Indeed, as Csicsery-Ronay points out, the failure of the Handy Man to develop or maintain control of the fertile corpse is a theme of what Csicsery-Ronay terms "critical sf," as opposed to the original adventure story formulation where the conversion of the corpse is successful. Examples of "critical sf" discussed by Csicsery-Ronay include Lem's *Solaris* and the Strugatskys' *Roadside Picnic*, while more ambivalent tales of the tension between Handy Man and fertile corpse include Herbert's *Dune* and Robinson's *Red Mars*. Csicsery-Ronay, 249–52.

40. As Spencer Weart details, the team at the U.S. Weather Bureau led by Joseph Smagorinsky and Syukuro (Shukurō) Manabe, as well as the team of Yale Mintz and Akio Arakawa at UCLA, produced the earliest computerized climate simulation models working from the late 1950s through the mid-1960s. (Both Manabe and Arakawa were born in Japan and received their doctorates in physics at the University of Tokyo.) In pioneering studies of anthropogenic climate change, Manabe and collaborator Robert Wetherall produced a study in 1967 predicting a temperature rise of 2°C based on an assumption of the doubling of carbon dioxide in the atmosphere, followed by a more technically

refined study in 1975 predicting a rise of 3.5°C. See Spencer Weart, "General Circulation Models of Climate," The Discovery of Global Warming, accessed August 10, 2018, https://history.aip.org/climate/GCM.htm.

4. Future City

1. The four-screen color film *Ichinichi nihyaku jonjū jikan* (240 hours in one day). The scenario for this film can be found in Abe, *Abe Kōbō zenshū 23* (Abe Kōbō collected works, vol 23), 63–84.

2. *Nihon bankoku hakurankai kōshiki kiroku* (Japan World Exposition official record), 444–45.

3. Komatsu, *SF damashi* (SF soul), 120. As with the expo, Komatsu played a key behind-the-scenes role in helping to organize this event. The symposium is also discussed in Brian W. Aldiss's autobiography *The Twinkling of an Eye: My Life as an Englishman*, 283–85.

4. "Shinya no bankokuhaku" was first collected in Tsutsui's short story collection *Bōshizō* (Portrait of mother and child), while "Jinrui no daifuchōwa" was first collected in the short story collection *Uma wa doyō ni aozameru* (The horse turns pale on Saturday). They are collected in Tsutsui Yasutaka, *Tsutsui Yasutaka zenshū* (Tsutsui Yasutaka collected works), 169–83, 184–91.

5. On the protest movement against the expo, see KuroDalaiJee, "Performance Art and/as Activism"; Lockyer, "Logic of Spectacle"; and Nakamori, "Criticism of Expo '70 in Print."

6. The three initial Thinking the Expo members were soon joined by anthropologist Kawakita Jirō, critic and French scholar Tada Michitarō, and economist Kamakura Noboru.

7. These articles were later collected in the volumes *Chizu no shisō* (The philosophy of maps) and *Tanken no shisō* (The philosophy of exploration).

8. This institute was a lively center of interdisciplinary research throughout the postwar era. Founded in 1939, in the postwar it was divided into a Japanese Department, Oriental Department, and Western Department, with French professor Kuwahara Takeo heading the last of these.

9. One continuing legacy of this ideological focus on multipolar humanism, as well as its underlying social network, was the establishment of the National Museum of Ethnology (Kokuritsu minzokugaku hakubutsukan, or Minpaku) on the grounds of the Expo '70 [Osaka Expo] Commemorative Park following the expo. Still open today as a museum and research facility, the Minpaku was founded in 1974 and headed by first director general Umesao Tadao in a building designed by Kurokawa Kishō.

10. Itō Yōichi, "Birth of Jōhō Shakai," 3–6. Umesao's article was republished in *Chūo kōron* three months later. Umesao, "Jōhō sangyō ron" (Theory of the information industries).

11. Komatsu, "Bankokuhaku wa mō hajimatte iru" (The world exposition

has already begun, 1966), in *Komatsu Sakyō zenshū kanzenban* (Komatsu Sakyō collected works complete edition), 28:261–71.

12. The thirty-six participants in the conference included core Thinking the Expo study group members Komatsu and Katō (Umesao was absent because of illness), as well as invited guests including artist Okamoto Tarō (who had not yet been tapped as an artist-producer for the expo), architects Yoshizaka Takamasa and Mizutani Eisuke, architectural critic Hamaguchi Ryūichi, historian Hagiwara Nobutoshi, illustrator Manabe Hiroshi, and science fiction author Hoshi Shin'ichi. According to Komatsu's account, the conference was at best a mixed success in terms of public relations, as the study group members had difficulty making their position understood to the press as an unofficial academic study group seeking to offer constructive criticism. Komatsu, "Nippon—70 nendai zenya" (Japan—on the eve of the 1970s), 246. This article is collected in Komatsu, *Kyōdai purojectuo ugoku* (Moving a giant project), 151–261. Komatsu also discusses the Thinking the Expo group and his experiences with the expo in *SF damashi*, 75–85, 102–14.

13. Author's translation of the Japanese version of the subthemes, as listed in *Nihon bankoku hakurankai kōshiki kiroku*, 62. On Ikeda's income-doubling plan, see Hein, "Growth versus Success," 114.

14. Author's translation of the Japanese version of the theme statement. "Nihon bankokuhaku no kihon rinen to tēma" (Fundamental principles and themes of the Japan World Exposition), in *Nihon bankoku hakurankai kōshiki kiroku*, 57.

15. "Nihon bankokuhaku no kihon rinen to tēma" in *Nihon bankoku hakurankai kōshiki kiroku*, 57.

16. See also Yoshimi, *Banpaku gensō* (Expo fantasy), 45–53, for a discussion of the debate over the expo's theme.

17. Komatsu, "Nippon—70 nendai zenya," 261.

18. Hayashi, *Nijūnengo no Nihon* (Japan twenty years hence).

19. The proceedings of this conference are compiled in Japan Society of Futurology, *Challenges from the Future*, including a complete list of participants in volume four. The Kyoto conference of 1970 followed the first International Futures Research Conference, which was held in Oslo in 1967. See "WFSF History," World Futures Studies Federation, accessed March 6, 2011, http://www.wfsf.org/index.php?option=com_content&view=article&id=46&Itemid=60.

20. See Bell, *Foundations of Futures Studies*.

21. In the United States, futurology would soon be popularized through such works as Alvin Toffler's *Future Shock* (1970) and Daniel Bell's *The Coming of Post-Industrial Society: A Venture in Social Forecasting* (1973). In Japan, the activities of the Future Studies Research Group helped to stimulate a media boom in interest in the topic in the late 1960s, a few years prior to the similar wave in the United States. Core publications of the members of the Future Studies Group in Japan include *Miraigaku no teishō* (Proposals for future studies),

coauthored by Umesao Tadao, Katō Hidetoshi, Kawazoe Noboru, Komatsu Sakyō, and Hayashi Yūjirō; *Shinpojiamu mirai keikaku* (Symposium: Future planning), edited by Komatsu Sakyō, with Kawazoe Noboru, Kawakita Jirō, and Katō Hideyoshi; Komatsu Sakyō, *Mirai no shisō: bunmei no shinka to jinrui* (The philosophy of the future: Human beings and the evolution of civilization); and Komatsu Sakyō with Kurokawa Kishō, *Nihon taimu toraberu* (Japan time travel). See also Hayashi, "Futures Research in Japan."

22. Kawazoe, "Bankokuhaku no bijon" (The expo's vision), in *Kawazoe Noboru hyōronshū* (Collected critical writings of Kawazoe Noboru), 201. Originally appeared as an article for *Yomiuri shinbun,* November 14, 1967.

23. Nishiyama, "Bankokuhaku kaijō keikaku," 197.

24. Nishiyama, 197–98. According to Kasahara Kazuto, Nishiyama was responsible for the first two drafts of the site plan and Tange for drafts three and four. Kasahara, "'Omatsuri hiroba' no tanjō" (The birth of the "Festival Plaza"). For further discussion of Nishiyama's plan, see Yoshimi, *Hakurankai no seijigaku,* 235.

25. For more on Nishiyama's conception of the "urban core" in his Osaka Expo site design, see Urushima, "Genesis and Culmination of Uzō Nishiyama's Proposal."

26. Cho, "Expo '70," 61.

27. Tange with Kawazoe, "Nihon bankokuhakurankai no motarasu mono" (What the Japan World Exposition will bring), 147. Author's translation.

28. Tange, "Bankokuhaku kaijō keikaku" (The expo site plan: From project to plan), 203.

29. Quoted in Yoshimi, *Banpaku gensô,* 58.

30. The figure of the mandala was often employed to describe the spatiotemporal layout of the Theme Pavilion. See *Nihon bankoku hakurankai kōshiki kiroku,* 476.

31. The vast timescale of this display is reminiscent of Komatsu's major SF novel *Hateshi naki nagare no hate ni* (At the end of the endless flow) from 1966, the year before he began work as subproducer for the Theme Pavilion.

32. On the expo media environments, see Kawazoe, "Bankokuhaku no kenchiku" (The expo and architecture); Kawazoe, "Bankokuhaku wa kankaku no kakumei" (The expo is a revolution of the senses) (originally published in *Yomiuri Shinbun,* February 28, 1969), in *Kawazoe Noboru hyōronshū,* 203–7; Pawley, "Architecture versus the Movies"; and Furuhata, "Multimedia Environments and Security Operations."

33. Among the extensive literature on the ideological content of world's fairs and expos, see, for example, Greenhalgh, *Fair World;* National Building Museum, *Designing Tomorrow;* Roche, *Mega-events and Modernity;* Rydell, *World of Fairs;* and Wesemael, *Architecture of Instruction and Delight.*

34. The Hitachi Group Pavilion featured a flight simulator, while the IBM Pavilion (IBM Japan) included a moon landing simulator. The wireless telephone

developed by NTT was one of the first public demonstrations of this now-ubiquitous technology.

35. Ekuan's "street furniture" included street lighting and PA systems, clocks, mailboxes, phone booths, and signage, all with a unified design aesthetic overseen by Ekuan's GK (Group Koike) design collective. See Koolhaus and Obrist, *Project Japan*, 488–89.

36. Other international contributions to the "space frame" display were by Hans Hollein (Austria), Alexei Gutnov (Soviet Union), Giancarlo De Carlo (Italy), and Christopher Alexander (UK/USA). See Koolhaus and Obrist, 516–21.

37. Because of the prefabrication of units, the Takara Beautilion was assembled in a mere seven days. Further artistic collaboration on the Beautilion included graphic design by Awazu Kiyoshi and sound design by composer Ichiyanagi Toshi.

38. On the expo as harbinger of a "managed society," see Funakoshi, "Nihon bankoku hakurankai" (The Japan World Exposition), 15.

39. In his study *Sensō to banpaku* (Wars and expos), Sawaragi Noi discusses the apocalyptic undercurrent to the expo, referring to the association of Kawazoe, Komatsu, and Asada Takashi as "a sort of apocalyptic theory coalition." Sawaragi, *Sensō to banpaku*, 34–35.

40. Winter-Tamaki, "To Put on a Big Face," 96.

41. See Winter-Tamaki, 91–98; Sawaragi, *Kuroi taiyō to akai kani* (Black sun and red crab), 237–48.

42. Graphic designer Kimura Tsunehisa coordinated the photomontage. According to the text of the planning document cited by photographer Tamai Mizuo, who assisted Kimura, the montage was created in order to show the possibility of "gradual" as well as "instantaneous" threats to the "continuation of human life," which is an issue "of concern throughout the world" that "cannot be omitted from the Expo." Tamai, "Posutarization ni yoru Ōsaka banpaku" (The Osaka Expo created by posterization). Some images from the "Wall of Contradictions" photomontages can be seen in the official documentary film of the expo, *Kōshiki chōhen kiroku eiga*, minutes 32:00 through 33:02.

43. Komatsu, "Banpaku kara kōgai e" (From Expo to pollution), 50.

44. For coverage of this issue, see "Hiroshima no utae kiesō" (Hiroshima's appeal seems about to disappear), *Chūgoku Shinbun*, February 6, 1970; "Genbaku tenji usumeta mama" (Atomic bomb exhibit carried out in weakened form), *Chūgoku Shinbun*, March 14, 1970; and "Kage ga usui 'genbaku' tenji" (Atomic bomb exhibit lacking impact), *Asahi shinbun*, evening edition, March 14, 1970, 10.

45. Galantay, "Osaka Expo," 134.

46. Galantay, 135.

47. Galantay, 136.

48. Galantay, 134. Galantay refers to ethologist John B. Calhoun's experiments in which extreme overcrowding in the rodent environment led to multiple behavioral problems, which became a popular analogy for concerns of human overpopulation. See John B. Calhoun, "Population Density and Social Pathol-

ogy," *Scientific American* 206, no. 3 (February 1, 1962): 139–48; and Ramsden and Adams, "Escaping the Laboratory."

49. For coverage of expo accidents see, for example, "Ugoku hodō de shōgitaoshi: dantai no 30 nin jūkeishō" (Domino effect on the moving sidewalks: 30 group sightseers sustain light and heavy injuries), *Asahi shinbun*, evening edition, March 26, 1970. On the "brutality fair," see, for example, "Panku shita 'zankokuhaku': kaijō e teku teku daikōshin" (A "brutality fair," with a flat tire: Crawling procession to the expo site), *Asahi shinbun*, September 7, 1970, 3.

50. Kawazoe, "Bankokuhaku no kenchiku," 211, 210.

51. Pawley, "Architecture versus the Movies," 289, 292. Pawley continued to write on the theme of architecture and the information age throughout his career in such works as *Theory and Design in the Second Machine Age*.

52. Waldo, *Japan Expo '70 Guide*, 11.

53. "Toward the Japanese Century," *Time*, March 2, 1970, 20.

5. Liquid Cities

1. Isozaki, "Invisible City," 403.

2. Isozaki, 403.

3. Isozaki, 404–5, 407.

4. It is striking that early utopian visions of "cyberspace" also introduced the ideal of "liquid architecture." For example, in 1991 Markus Novak wrote, "Cyberspace is liquid. Liquid cyberspace, liquid architecture, liquid cities. . . . Liquid architecture is an architecture that breathes, pulses, leaps as one form and lands as another. Liquid architecture is an architecture whose form is contingent on the interest of the beholder; it as an architecture that opens to welcome me and closes to defend me; it is an architecture with doors or hallways, where the next room is always where I need it to be and what I need it to be." Novak, "Liquid Architecture in Cyberspace," 250. See also Heuser, *Virtual Geographies*, 66–79, for a discussion of "liquid architecture" and the "poetics of cyberspace," as well as the chapter "Liquid Cities" in McQuire, *Media City*, 87–110.

5. From Itō's essay "Architecture for the Simulated City" ("Shimyureitedo shitei no kenchiku," 1991), in *Tarzans in the Media Forest*, 83.

6. Yatsuka, "Architecture Floating on the Sea of Signs," 40.

7. The dates given refer to the original publication of Jameson's essay "Postmodernism, or the Cultural Logic of Late Capitalism," Baudrillard's *Simulacres et simulation*, translated as *Simulacra and Simulation* in 1994, and Deleuze and Guattari's *Mille Plateaux*, translated as *A Thousand Plateaus: Capitalism and Schizophrenia* in 1987. The quotes from Baudrillard are from *Simulacra and Simulation*, 2. Yuriko Furuhata argues that the "cybernetic turn in Japanese architecture [of the 1960s] paved the way for the subsequent, separate reception of French critical theory—in particular, structural semiotics that brought attention to the systematic understanding of signs and codes—in the 1970s and 1980s," and singles out Isozaki Arata as a key figure bridging these discourses

through his participation with the noted postmodern theorist (and nephew of architect Asada Takashi) Asada Akira in the international ANY conference series. Furuhata, "Architecture as Atmospheric Media," 72.

8. Kitazawa, "Militarism in the Management Society," 201, 202. See also Kurihara, *Kanri shakai to minshū risei* (The managed society and popular reason); and Ivy, "Formations of Mass Culture."

9. On the Situationist critiques of urban space and media and their relationship to architectural trends of the 1960s, see Schrijver, *Radical Games*, 41–94.

10. Deleuze, "Postscript on Control Societies," 319.

11. Deleuze, 320.

12. Chun, *Control and Freedom*, 9, 250.

13. Leong, "Ulterior Spaces," 769.

14. Leong, 773. See below for Itō's writings on architecture "in the sea of consumption."

15. On mobile phones, see Itō Mizuko, *Personal, Portable, Pedestrian*; on convenience stores, see Hosoya and Schaefer, "Tokyo Metabolism"; on the architecture and culture of Akihabara, see Morikawa, *Shuto no tanjō: Moeru toshi Akihabara* (The birth of a city of taste: The moe city Akihabara); for an analysis of the changing international media configurations of otaku and Akihabara, as well as tensions over street culture and public space in the neighborhood, see Galbraith, "Akihabara."

16. On the significance of the term *kankyō* (environment) to Isozaki and related artists who were experimenting with electronic and intermedia art at this time, see Chō, "Expo '70," 65–66; Yoshimoto, "From Space to Environment"; and Sawaragi, *Sensō to banpaku* (Wars and expos), 67–100.

17. The sound design and programming was created in collaboration with the composer Matsudaira Yoriaki. See Yatsuka, "Gendai kenchiku ni okeru nōtēshon no bōken" (The adventure of notation in contemporary architecture), 20. See also Furuhata, "Multimedia Environments and Security Operations," 65–67, for a discussion of the Festival Plaza and Isozaki's interpretation of cybernetics.

18. Mori Bijutsukan, *Metaborizumu no mirai toshi* (The future city of Metabolism), 192–93.

19. Pawley, "Architecture versus the Movies," 290.

20. Kurokawa, *Metabolism in Architecture*, 82.

21. Kurokawa, 83.

22. On the theory and case studies of cybercities, see Graham, *Cybercities Reader*.

23. Tsukio, "Jōhō shisutemu" (Information systems), 282. See also Furuhata, "Multimedia Environments and Security Operations," 67–71, on the use of technologies including computer systems, closed circuit television, and multiscreen control centers at the Osaka Expo.

24. Kawazoe, "Bankokuhaku no kenchiku" (The expo and architecture), 209.

25. Haryū, "Expo '70 as the Ruins of Culture," 51. See Cho, "Expo '70," 66,

and Funakoshi, "Nihon bankoku hakurankai" (The Japan World Exposition), 15, for discussions of this critique of the expo as a harbinger of the "managed society."

26. Yoshimura Masanobu, "Omatsuri hiroba ka kanri hiroba ka: kanryôteki henshitsu no gisei" (Festival Plaza or managed plaza? The sacrifices of bureaucratization), *Asahi Shinbun*, August 11, 1970, quoted in Cho, "Expo '70," 66; Yoshida Mitsukuni, "Senri o fututabi midori ni" (Making Senri green again), *Mainichi Shinbun*, September 13, 1970, quoted in Funakoshi, "Nihon bankoku hakurankai," 15.

27. Haryū, "Expo '70 as the Ruins of Culture (1970)," 48–49.

28. Haryū, 46.

29. Haryū, 51.

30. Haryū, 51.

31. Morris-Suzuki, *Beyond Computopia*, 22. As a key interpreter of the "information society" concept influencing bureaucratic policy, in addition to Hayashi Yūjirō (discussed in chapter 3), Morris-Suzuki cites Masuda Yoneji, who employed the term *computopia* in his volume *Konpyūtopia: Konpyūta ga tsukuru shinjidai* (Computopia: The new age created by computers, 1967). Masuda's work has been introduced in English with the volume *The Information Society as Post-Industrial Society*.

32. Kurokawa, *Metabolism in Architecture*, 57, 67–74.

33. Kurokawa, 67; and Koolhaus and Obrist, *Project Japan*, 682–83.

34. Komatsuzaki, "Telecommunications Policy in Japan," 161.

35. In their study of the social outcomes of these experiments, Itō Yōichi and Yutaka Oishi conclude that "these experiments found that people seem to prefer conventional, over-the-air, channels for education and entertainment programs, that they also seem to prefer conventional local print media for local 'living information,' and that very few people are interested in participating in two-way, interactive television programs." Itō and Oishi, "Social Impacts of the New Utopias," 203.

36. "Teletopia" projects involved the promotion of various technology initiatives in as many as seventy local areas by 1990. The initiative was expanded to include the establishment of "telecom plaza" information centers, "telecom ports" employing satellites and fiber-optic cable networks for international communications, and "telecom research parks." Akhavan-Majid, "Telecommunications Policymaking in Japan," 4.

37. Sorensen, *Making of Urban Japan*, 262. See also Tatsuno, *Technopolis Strategy*; and Castells and Hall, *Technopoles of the World*, 112–43.

38. On Tange's and Kurokawa's second-wave Tokyo Bay development plans, see Koolhaus and Obrist, *Project Japan*, 292.

39. See Bognár, *Tokyo*, 71, 352.

40. See Sand, *Tokyo Vernacular*, 33–53, for an extensive and nuanced discussion of the Shinjuku West Exit Plaza gatherings and the debate of the meaning of *hiroba* (plaza) in the context of both Shinjuku and the Osaka Expo.

41. See Tōno, "Artists Participating in the World Expo, Speak Out!" for an example of the critique linking Shinjuku Plaza and the expo's Festival Plaza.

42. Tōno, "Vertical Fair That Changed Shibuya," 316. For an overview of the history and functionality of Japanese department stores, as well as the relationship between department store commerce and the development of the Shibuya neighborhood, see Matsushita, "Depato." For more on the Parko and Seibu department stores and the transformation of Shibuya, see Havens, *Architects of Affluence*, 98–107. For a discussion of the cultural shift from 1960s Shinjuku to 1970s Shibuya, see Yoshimi, *Toshi no doramatourugii* (Dramatology of the city), 263–328.

43. Makabe, "Paruko no toshi senryaku," 34–35.

44. Makabe, 40, 45.

45. Tōno, "Vertical Fair That Changed Shibuya," 317.

46. Tōno, 317.

47. Tōno, 317.

48. See Galbraith, "Akihabara," 222–26.

49. On the postmodern aspects of Tanaka's novel, see Field, "Somehow."

50. Itō Toyoo, *Tarzans in the Media Forest*, 25, 22.

51. Itō Toyoo, "New Architecture Is Possible Only in the Sea of Consumption," 357.

52. Among Metabolism's avant-garde architectural peers, the pop-oriented Archigram movement in Great Britain tied architecture most closely to the "throwaway" consumer society: Archigram journal number three (August 1963) was devoted to the idea of "expendability" and architecture as a consumer artifact. See Sadler, *Archigram*, 35–36; and Schrijver, *Radical Games*, 128–34.

53. Itō expanded on this Pao project with an exhibit entitled "Pao II" at the Europalia exhibit in Brussels in 1989. The forms and materials of Itō's Pao exhibit were also echoed in his design for the Nomad Restaurant in Roppongi—designed from the outset as a temporary structure and demolished after two and a half years of operation. Itō described the restaurant as "taking the form of an enormous tent" and stated that it was intended to serve as "an oasis for travelers in the urban 'desert' of Tokyo." Itō Toyoo, *Toyo Ito*, 64. In his book *Allegories of Time and Space: Japanese Identity in Photography and Architecture*, Jonathan Reynolds provides a fascinating account of the trope of the "female urban nomad" in 1980s advertising and architecture, including Itō's work. See Reynolds, *Allegories of Time and Space*, 189–233.

54. Reynolds, *Allegories of Time and Space*, 213. For Itō's discussion of architecture as "media suit," see the essay "Tarzans in the Media Forest," in *Tarzans in the Media Forest*, 123–24.

55. Reynolds, *Allegories of Time and Space*, 222.

56. Kurokawa himself was frequently featured in the media as a male fashion icon: his own media-promoted, suave masculinity and jet-setting lifestyle as an avatar of the coming *Homo movens* was inexorably linked to his architectural

creations, especially the Nakagin Capsule Tower and his pavilions for Expo '70. See, for example, the photo layout in the Japanese *Playboy* magazine of February 12, 1974, which features photos of this "Prince of Architecture" together with his personal items, including eight sets of keys from various cars and dwellings, reproduced in Koolhaus and Obrist, *Project Japan*, 463–65.

57. Itō Toyoo, *Toyo Ito*, 134.

58. In "The Lessones [sic] of Sendai Médiathèque," Itō writes that the local government had introduced the concept of "barrier-free" meaning accessible to people with disabilities but that he also took "barrier-free" to mean free of administrative constraints and that he hoped that the tubes in his design would "restore vitality and joy to the spaces of public facilities." Itō Toyoo, "Lessones of Sendai Médiathèque," 7.

59. Reynolds, *Allegories of Time and Space*, 218.

60. From the essay "Architecture for the Simulated City" (Shimyureitedo shitei no kenchiku, 1991), in Itō Toyoo, *Tarzans in the Media Forest*, 83. For a discussion of Itō's work for the Visions of Japan exhibition, see Chaplin, "Cyberspace." Chaplin positively evaluates Itō's work as an example of Wendy Kellogg's conception of "augmented reality" as well as her own ideal of a "threshold" space that allows "mutual enhancement to take place between reality and cyberspace," creating a "complementary situation, somewhere between fact and fiction, visceral and virtual" (35).

61. Yatsuka, "Architecture Floating on the Sea of Signs," 40.

62. Such "TV screens of building façade proportions" were a distinguishing feature of Tokyo for American-based architect and scholar Vladimir Krstic, writing in 1997, in "Liquid Constructions," 38.

63. In their article "Tokyo Metabolism," architects Hosoya Hiromi (who has worked in Itō Toyoo's office) and Markus Schaefer examine the commercial practices that have evolved in millennial Tokyo, including "information and brand management" as exemplified by the 24-hour convenience store, which constitute a network of information, goods, and services "constantly fine-tuning itself to the metabolism of the city." Such information-based commercial practices, they argue, have realized the "Metabolists' dream" (as ascribed by the authors) of the harmonious coexistence of individual and collective, technology and man, within a flexible and ever-changing urban form. Hosoya and Schaefer, "Tokyo Metabolism," 762.

64. Leong, "Ulterior Spaces," 773.

65. Igarashi Tarō, "Post-Bubble City and Japan's New International Design."

66. Itō Toyoo, "Burēdo rannā ni tsuite" (Concerning *Blade Runner*), in *Tōsō suru kenchiku* (Penetrating-layer architecture), 113–14.

67. Itō Toyoo, "What Is the Reality of Architecture in a Futuristic City?" (1988), in *Tarzans in the Media Forest*, 64–66. The original essay, "Mirai toshi ni okeru kenchiku no riaritei to wa nani ka" is included in *Tōsō suru kenchiku*, 16–25.

68. From the essay "Architecture for the Simulated City" (Shimyureitedo shitei no kenchiku, 1991), in Itō Toyoo, *Tarzans in the Media Forest,* 90.

69. For a survey of Japanesque imagery in Anglo-American science fiction, see La Bare, "Future."

70. Ueno, "Japanimation and Techno-orientalism," 229.

71. Morley and Robins, *Spaces of Identity,* 168.

72. As described by special effects supervisor Douglas Trumbull, quoted in Webb, "'Like Today, Only More So,'" 46.

73. Webb, 46.

74. Menzies's film, based on a screenplay by H. G. Wells, featured sets designed by Vincent Korda with input from former Bauhaus designer and photographer László Moholy-Nagy. See Neumann, *Film Architecture,* 118–21.

75. Production designer Syd Mead, quoted in Sammon, *Future Noir,* 79.

76. Quoted in Webb, "'Like Today, Only More So,'" 45.

77. Bukatman, *Blade Runner,* 59, 56.

78. Sammon, *Future Noir,* 101, 74. Many critics have connected the temporal and visual eclecticism of *Blade Runner,* as well as its attention to the role of simulacra and simulation, with the aesthetics and philosophy of postmodernism: Giuliana Bruno, for example, relates the film to the qualities of "schizophrenic temporality" and "special pastiche" as discussed in Fredric Jameson's seminal essay "Postmodernism, or the Cultural Logic of Late Capitalism." Bruno, "Ramble City," 184.

79. Bruno, "Ramble City," 186.

80. Particularly in the chapter "American Anxiety and the Oriental City," focusing on *Blade Runner.* Park Jane Chi Hyun, *Yellow Future,* 51–81.

81. Gibson, *Neuromancer,* 7, 3.

82. Gibson, 6–7.

83. Bukatman, *Terminal Identity,* 146–54. Bukatman borrows the term *paraspace* from Samuel Delany, who defines its operation in science fiction as "an alternate space, sometimes largely mental, but always materially manifested, that sits beside the real world, and in which language is raised to an extraordinarily lyric level" and in which "conflicts that begin in ordinary space are resolved." Delany quoted in Bukatman, *Terminal Identity,* 157.

84. Gibson, *Neuromancer,* 51, 52.

85. For a discussion of Japanese motifs in Gibson's work, see Paulk, "Post-National Cool." For a critical reading of Gibson's vision of cyberspace and its gendered relationship to Orientalism, see Chun, *Control and Freedom,* 171–96.

86. Tatsumi, "Japanese Reflection of Mirrorshades," 368–70. For further discussion of the reception of American cyberpunk in Japan and the development of Japanese cyberpunk, see Kumiko Sato, "How Information Technology Has (Not) Changed Feminism and Japanism."

87. Tatsumi, "Japanese Reflection of Mirrorshades," 371.

88. Gregory and McCaffery, "Not Just a Gibson Clone," 78.

89. In the above-mentioned article "How Information Technology Has (Not)

Changed Feminism and Japanism," Kumiko Sato discusses the nationalistic tendencies in Japanese cyberpunk, which took upon itself the role to "write and rediscover Japan" (347), and focuses in particular on the figure of the female cyborg in Japanese cyberpunk, which she asserts has replaced the male "cyberspace cowboy" hero of American cyberpunk. Sato's analysis centers on Kambayashi Chōhei's *Battle Fairy Yukikaze* (*Sentō yosei Yukikaze*, 1984) and Noa Azusa's *The Flower of Babble* (*Baberu no kaori*, 1991). She also briefly discusses Masaki's *Venus City*. Sato, "How Information Technology Has (Not) Changed Feminism and Japanism," 348.

90. Bukatman, *Terminal Identity*, 8. Cyberpunk author Ōhara Mariko, mentioned above, offered another potent reconfiguration of identity and data through the processes of sampling and simulation, while highlighting gender fluidity and presenting fictional worlds that challenged patriarchal and heteronormative constructs, in such works as "Mentaru fimēru" (The mental female) from 1985 and *Haiburiddo chairudo (Hybrid Child)* from 1990. See Kotani, "Alien Spaces and Alien Bodies," 60–61; and Harada, "Gender Panic through Cyborgs: Simulated Sex/Gender and Excessive Maternal Performance in Ôhara Mariko's texts," in *Japanese Women's Science Fiction*, 127–89.

91. Masaki, *Vīnasu shitei*, 140.

92. Masaki, 15–19.

93. Posadas, "Virtual Worlds and Identity Tourism in Japanese Cyberpunk," 151.

94. Posadas, 154–56.

6. Metabolist Echoes

1. See Mori Bijutsukan, *Metaborizumu no mirai toshi* (The future city of Metabolism), 209–24, on the Metabolists' international projects.

2. The chronology for Ōtomo's manga is slightly different: Tokyo is destroyed in 1992 and the manga is set in Neo-Tokyo in the year 2030.

3. Christopher Bolton discusses the nuclear "origins" of the film, as well as the motif of ruins in the film and especially the manga, in his essay "From Ground Zero to Degree Zero: *Akira* from Origin to Oblivion."

4. See Standish, "*Akira*, Postmodernism, and Resistance," for a discussion of the youth subcultures reflected in the film, as well as its historical echoes.

5. Standish, 62.

6. A beltway connecting Kawasaki and Kisarazu has been a fixture of Tokyo Bay development plans since the 1959 Council for Industrial Planning proposal for Neo-Tokyo. While not accompanied by a complete bay infill development or serving as a dam as in *Patlabor*, the Tokyo Bay Aqua Line, a combination of bridge and tunnel connecting Kawasaki and Kisarazu, did in fact open in 1997.

7. Orbaugh, "Future City Tokyo," 96. Orbaugh's insightful reading of the city as "character" in *Patlabor I*, as well as in Ōtomo's *Rōujin Z* (1991), provides an exemplary study of architecture and urbanism in anime, concluding that "these films, like many other Japanese anime, attempt to imagine a world in which

the city environment undergoes constant change, and to imagine this world not as a tragic dystopia, but as a reality that may be acceptable" (100). While I agree with Orbaugh that there is a "celebratory" or at least nontragic tone in the scene of destruction of the old neighborhood by the rampaging labor in Oshii's *Patlabor I* (similar to the exhilaration one feels in watching Godzilla rampage through Tokyo), I would like to focus here on the critical aspects of the "nostalgia and sense of loss" (100) that Orbaugh also identifies in the film's view of an ever-ruined and rebuilt Tokyo, which I see as being in contrast to the positive view of ruins offered in Ōtomo's *Akira*.

8. Translation as provided in the subtitles of the DVD released by Bandai Visual in 2004. My use of the term *dérive* refers to the practice of the Situationist International in Europe, glossed by Lara Schrijver as "literally a 'drifting' through the city, a practice intentionally construed to investigate aspects of the city repressed by functionalism." Schrijver, *Radical Games*, 53. See also Sand, *Tokyo Vernacular*, 98, for a comparison of the urban tactics of the Situationists and the Japanese Street Observation Studies (rojō kansatsugaku) group.

9. See Gavin McCormack, *Emptiness of Japanese Affluence*, 25–77, for a historical overview and critical analysis of the *doken kokka* (construction state) system.

10. It is noteworthy that Miyamoto's book *Kenchiku no mokujiroku* (Apocalypse of architecture) includes as a preface an essay on ruins by architect Isozaki Arata.

11. Miyamoto, "Temporary Ruins," 51.

12. See Sand, *Tokyo Vernacular*, 88–109. In his article "Transpacific Cyberpunk: Transgeneric Interactions between Prose, Cinema, and Manga," Tatsumi Takayuki notes that William Gibson's 1990s Bridge Trilogy, and particularly the first volume in the trilogy, *Virtual Light* (1993), featuring a homeless community occupying the San Francisco Bay Bridge following a near-future Bay Area earthquake, was partly inspired by Miyamoto Ryūji's photography book *Kyūryū jōsai* (*Kowloon Walled City*, 1988), as well as artist Akasegawa Genpei's project of "Thomasson" Neo-Dada urban photography, which is closely connected to Akasegawa's participation in the Street Observation Studies Group (Tatsumi, "Transpacific Cyberpunk," 3–8). Tatsumi's article thus suggests a continuing genealogy of the aesthetic of "ruins" connecting Isozaki, Komatsu, Ōtomo, Miyamoto, Akasegawa, Oshii, and Gibson.

13. Nagase, "Fushoku suru kioku no Tōkyō," 205–6. In an interview, Oshii states that his position or view of Tokyo in his works set in the city is based on his own upbringing in the Ōmori neighborhood of Ōta Ward, in the industrial waterfront area south of Shinagawa. He suggests that the *Patlabor* films express the resentment the residents of such peripheral industrial and waterfront neighborhoods—which he describes as the true or "indigenous" Tokyoites—feel toward the more recent urban immigrants living urbane lifestyles in the city center. Hayamizu, *Tōkyō bēta* (Tokyo beta), 193–94.

14. As when the newly deployed Patlabor rises against a backdrop of skyscrapers to do battle with the berserking labor in the scene described above.

15. Bolton, "Mecha's Blind Spot," 124.

16. Yatsuka, "'Metaborizumu nekusasu' to iu 'kindai no chōkoku'" (The "overcoming modernity" known as "the Metabolism nexus"), 11–12; and Ueno, *Kurenai no metaru sūtsu* (Scarlet metalsuits), 38.

17. De Cauter, "Capsule and the Network," 95.

18. De Cauter, 96.

19. De Cauter, *Capsular Civilization*, 69.

20. Quoted in Sawaragi, *Sensō to banpaku* (Wars and expos), 152.

21. Yanobe, *Kenji Yanobe*, 92. Many of Yanobe's works are archived on the Kenji Yanobe Archive Project website, http://www.yanobe.com/artworks/index.html. Accessed August 1, 2018.

22. The Mihama plant, commissioned in the expo year 1970, was the first nuclear power plant to generate electricity commercially. An accident in February 1991 led to an emergency shutdown of a plant generator and triggered the emergency cooling system as well release of radiation to the outside.

23. See Yanobe, *Kenji Yanobe*, 3–39.

24. See Yanobe, 41–56, 64–65.

25. For a discussion of Yanobe's expo-related works, see Borggreen, "Ruins of the Future."

26. On the "eye-jacking" or "Eyeball Man" protest, see Lockyer, "Logic of Spectacle."

27. See chapter 2.

28. See Yanobe, *Kenji Yanobe*, 82–83, 90–93, 98.

29. "The Pripyat City History," Chernobyl, Pripyat, Chernobyl Nuclear Power Plant and Exclusion Zone, accessed June 30, 2017, http://chornobyl.in.ua/en/the-pripyat-city-history.html.

30. On the history and ideology of the Soviet nuclear energy programs, see Josephson, *Red Atom*. For one look at the role of "Atoms for Peace" in American propaganda, see Krige, "Techno-Utopian Dreams."

31. Yanobe, *Kenji Yanobe*, 67.

32. One of Yanobe's recent attempts to respond to the Fukushima disaster directly engendered a noted controversy. His *Sun Child* statue, which was initially displayed at the Expo Commemorative Park in October 2011, was donated by the artist to Fukushima City after a national tour and installed in front of the Com-Com Children's Creative Learning Center, with an unveiling ceremony on August 3, 2018. The statue depicts a bruised child in a yellow radiation protective suit who has just removed his helmet and looks hopefully up toward the sky; a Geiger counter on his chest reads zero, while he holds a sun emblem in his right hand, representing new sources of energy and hope for the future, according to a statement by the artist. However, the statue was criticized by local residents on social media and other venues, with some asserting the statue was insensitive

to residents or that it would lead to misunderstandings about the continued danger of radiation in the city. The statue was removed on September 18, 2018, and Yanobe issued an apology to city residents. Artist Statements of August 10 and August 28, Kenji Yanobe Archive Project, accessed January 19, 2019, http://www.yanobe.com/20180810_KenjiYanobe_Statement.pdf,http://www.yanobe.com/20180828_KenjiYanobe_Statement.pdf.

33. Reconstruction Design Council, "Towards Reconstruction," 11, 7.

34. For further discussion of Metabolism and Komatsu's work in the context of the March, 3, 2011, triple disaster, including an example of the use of "Japan sinks" as a catchphrase in post-3/11 media, see Gardner, "Narratives of Collapse and Generation."

35. Eighty thousand residents living within thirteen miles of the Fukushima Daiichi nuclear plant were ordered to evacuate on April 21, 2011, and the evacuation zone was extended to the north and west the following day. See Kingston, *Natural Disaster and Nuclear Crisis in Japan*, 1. On the issuing of thirty-four thousand portable dosimeters to school children, see Justin McCurry, "Fukushima Radiation Fears: Children Near Nuclear Plant to be Given Dosimeters," *Guardian*, June 28, 2011, https://www.theguardian.com/world/2011/jun/28/fukushima-radiation-fears-children-monitors.

36. See Allison, *Precarious Japan*, 43–55.

37. See Megumi Lim, "Seven Years after Tsunami, Japanese Live Uneasily with Seawalls," Reuters, March 8, 2018, https://www.reuters.com/article/us-japan-disaster-seawalls/seven-years-after-tsunami-japanese-live-uneasily-with-seawalls-idUSKCN1GL0DK.

38. See Ann Masui, "Once Aimed at Salarymen, Japan's New Capsule Hotels Reach Out to Tourists and Women," *Japan Times*, November 2, 2016, https://www.japantimes.co.jp/news/2016/11/02//business/aimed-salarymen-japans-new-capsule-hotels-reach-tourists-women/#.W235IthKjvw.

39. While an evaluation of the continuing influence of the Metabolists on global architectural discourse and practice is beyond the scope of this study, the recent surge in scholarly publications on this group, including many of the secondary works cited throughout the current study, suggest that the story of the Metabolists and their cultural influence is far from over. In one of these recent publications, Agnes Nyilas assesses the group's impact on architectural discourse as follows: "I would dare to suggest that their [the Metabolists'] notion of the city as a 'living system' has marked a turning point in the history of biological analogy in architecture, guiding the discussion towards two potential directions. One is the direction marked by the environment-conscious design approaches, which were taken up from the end of the last century as sustainable architecture or green architecture. The other is the direction marked by those design approaches which were based on the computer-aided form-generating process and led later to the concepts of 'evolutionary architecture' or 'cyber city.'" Nyilas, *Beyond Utopia*, 148.

Selected Filmography

Akira. Dir. Ōtomo Katsuhiro (1988). Flower Mound, Tex.: Funimation, 2013. Subtitled DVD.

Blade Runner. Dir. Ridley Scott (1982). Burbank, Calif.: Warner Home Video, 2007. DVD.

Fukkatsu no hi. (Day of resurrection, a.k.a. Virus). Dir. Fukasaku Kinji (1980). Tokyo: Kadokawa Films, 2011. DVD.

Godzilla. Dir. Honda Ishirō (1956). Irvington, N.Y.: Criterion Collection, 2012. Subtitled DVD.

Kōshiki chōhen kiroku eiga: nihon bankokuhaku. (Official feature-length documentary film: The Japan World Expo). Dir. Taniguchi Senkichi (1971). Tokyo: Geneon Entertainment, 2005. DVD.

Metropolis. Dir. Fritz Lang (1927). New York: Kino Classics, 2011. DVD with English intertitles.

Nihon chinbotsu. (Japan sinks). Dir. Moritani Shirō (1973). Tokyo: Tōhō, 2003. DVD.

Patlabor: The Movie. Dir. Oshii Mamoru (1989). Chatsworth, Calif.: Image Entertainment, 2006. Subtitled DVD.

Patlabor 2: The Movie. Dir. Oshii Mamoru (1993). Lincolnshire, Ill.: Manga Entertainment, 1995. Subtitled DVD.

Bibliography

Abe Kōbō. *Abe Kōbō zenshū 23* [Abe Kōbō collected works, vol. 23]. Tokyo: Shinchōsha, 1999.

Abe Kōbō. *The Box Man*. Translation of *Hako otoko* by E. Dale Saunders. New York: Knopf, 1974.

Abe Kōbō. *Inter Ice Age 4*. Translation of *Daiyon kanpyōki* by E. Dale Saunders. New York: Knopf, 1970.

Agamben, Giorgio. *The Open: Man and Animal*. Stanford, Calif.: Stanford University Press, 2004.

Akhavan-Majid, Roya. "Telecommunications Policymaking in Japan, 1970–1993: A Case Study in Elite Conflict" (1995). *Mass Communication Faculty Publications*. Paper 11. http://repository.stcloudstate.edu/comm_facpubs/11. Accessed February 11, 2016.

Aldiss, Brian W. *The Twinkling of an Eye: My Life as an Englishman*. New York: St. Martin's Press, 1998.

Allison, Anne. *Precarious Japan*. Durham, N.C.: Duke University Press, 2013.

Appadurai, Arjun. *Modernity at Large: Cultural Dimensions of Globalization*. Minneapolis: University of Minnesota Press, 1996.

Apter, David E., and Nagayo Sawa. *Against the State: Politics and Social Protest in Japan*. Cambridge, Mass.: Harvard University Press, 1984.

Asada Akira and Isozaki Arata. "From Molar Metabolism to Molecular Metabolism." In *Anyhow*, edited by Cynthia C. Davidson, 64–73. Cambridge, Mass.: MIT Press, 1998.

Avenell, Simon Andrew. *Making Japanese Citizens: Civil Society and the Mythology of the Shimin in Postwar Japan*. Berkeley: University of California Press, 2010.

Azuma Hiroki. *Otaku: Japan's Database Animals*. Minneapolis: University of Minnesota Press, 2009.

Bakhtin, M. M. *The Dialogic Imagination*. Edited by Michael Holquist. Translated by Caryl Emerson and Michael Holquist. Austin: University of Texas Press, 1981.

Banham, Reyner. *Megastructure: Urban Futures of the Recent Past*. New York: Harper & Row, 1976.

Banham, Reyner. *Theory and Design in the First Machine Age*. New York: Praeger, 1960.

Batty, Michael. "Fractals: Geometry between Dimensions." *New Scientist*, April 4, 1985, 31–35.

Baudrillard, Jean. *Simulacra and Simulation.* Translated by Sheila Faria Glaser. Ann Arbor: University of Michigan Press, 1994.

Befu, Harumi. *Hegemony of Homogeneity: An Anthropological Analysis of "Nihonjinron."* Melbourne: Trans Pacific Press, 2001.

Bell, Wendell. *Foundations of Futures Studies: Human Science for a New Era.* New Brunswick, N.J.: Transaction Publishers, 1997.

Bird, Lawrence. "States of Emergency: Urban Space and the Robotic Body in the *Metropolis* Tales." *Mechademia* 3 (2008): 127–48.

Black, Brian, and Gary J. Weisel. *Global Warming.* Santa Barbara, Calif.: Greenwood, 2010.

Bognár, Botand. *Tokyo.* New York: Academy Editions, 1997.

Bolton, Christopher. "From Ground Zero to Degree Zero: *Akira* from Origin to Oblivion." *Mechademia* 9 (2014): 295–315.

Bolton, Christopher. "The Mecha's Blind Spot: *Patlabor* 2 and the Phenomenology of Anime." *Science Fiction Studies* 29, no. 3 (November 2002): 453–74.

Bolton, Christopher. *Sublime Voices: The Fictional Science and Science Fiction of Abe Kōbō.* Cambridge, Mass.: Harvard University Asia Center, 2009.

Borggreen, Gunhild. "Ruins of the Future: Yanobe Kenji Revisits Expo '70." *Performance Paradigm Journal* no. 2 (March 2006): 119–31, http://www.performanceparadigm.net/wp-content/uploads/2007/06/10borggreen.pdf.

Bruno, Giuliana. "Ramble City: Postmodernism and *Blade Runner.*" In *Alien Zone: Cultural Theory and Contemporary Science Fiction Cinema,* edited by Annette Kuhn, 183–95. New York: Verso, 1990.

Bukatman, Scott. *Blade Runner.* 2nd ed. London: British Film Institute and Palgrave Macmillan, 2012.

Bukatman, Scott. *Terminal Identity: The Virtual Subject in Postmodern Science Fiction.* Durham, N.C.: Duke University Press, 1993.

Castells, Manuel, and Peter Hall. *Technopoles of the World: The Making of Twenty-First-Century Industrial Complexes.* New York: Routledge, 1994.

Chaplin, Sarah. "Cyberspace: Lingering on the Threshold; Architecture, Postmodernism and Difference." *Architectural Design* 65, no. 11/12 (November–December 1995): 32–35.

Cheung, Tobias. "Kurokawa's Metabolic Space." In *Images of the Body in Architecture: Anthropology and Built Space.* Edited by Kirsten Wagner and Jasper Cepl. Berlin: Wasmuth, 2014.

Cho, Hyunjung. "Expo '70: The Model City of an Information Society." In "Expo '70 and Japanese Art: Dissonant Voices." Special issue. *Review of Japanese Culture and Society* 23 (December 2011): 57–71.

Chun, Wendy Hui Kyong. *Control and Freedom: Power and Paranoia in the Age of Fiber Optics.* Cambridge, Mass.: MIT Press, 2006.

Claremont, Yasuko. "A Yakeato Poet." In *Legacies of the Asia-Pacific War: The Yakeato Generation,* edited by Roman Rosenbaum and Yasuko Claremont, 92–109. New York: Routledge, 2011.

Colligan-Taylor, Karen. *The Emergence of Environmental Literature in Japan.* New York: Garland, 1990.

Colomina, Beatriz. *Domesticity at War.* Cambridge, Mass.: MIT Press, 2007.

Colomina, Beatriz. "Enclosed by Images: Architecture in the Post-Sputnik Age." In *CTRL [SPACE]: Rhetorics of Surveillance from Bentham to Big Brother,* edited by Thomas Y. Levin, Ursula Frohne, and Peter Weibel, 322–37. Karlsruhe, Germany, Cambridge, Mass., and London: ZKM Center for Art and Media and MIT Press, 2002.

Colomina, Beatriz. "Unbreathed Air 1956." *Grey Room* 15 (Spring 2004): 28–59.

Conrads, Ulrich, and Hans-Günther Sperlich. *The Architecture of Fantasy: Utopian Building and Planning in Modern Times.* Translated and edited by Christiane Crasemann Collins and George R. Collins. New York: Frederick A. Praeger, 1962.

Csicsery-Ronay, Istvan, Jr. *The Seven Beauties of Science Fiction.* Middletown, Conn.: Wesleyan University Press, 2008.

Daniell, Thomas. "The Fugitive." In *Tarzans in the Media Forest,* by Itō Toyoo, 3–18. London: Architectural Association, 2011.

De Cauter, Lieven. *The Capsular Civilization: On the City in the Age of Fear.* Rotterdam, Netherlands: NAi Publishers, 2004.

De Cauter, Lieven. "The Capsule and the Network: Notes Toward a General Theory." In *The Cybercities Reader,* edited by Stephen Graham, 94–97. New York: Routledge, 2004.

Deleuze, Gilles. "Postscript on Control Societies." In *CTRL [SPACE]: Rhetorics of Surveillance from Bentham to Big Brother,* edited by Thomas Y. Levin, Ursula Frohne, and Peter Weibel, 316–21. Karlsruhe, Germany, Cambridge, Mass., and London: ZKM Center for Art and Media and MIT Press, 2002.

Dower, John W. *Embracing Defeat: Japan in the Wake of World War II.* New York: W. W. Norton and Company, 1999.

Doxiadis, C. A., and J. G. Papaioannou. *Ecumenopolis: The Inevitable City of the Future.* New York: W. W. Norton & Company, 1974.

Elias, Amy J., and Christian Moraru, eds. *The Planetary Turn: Relationality and Geoaesthetics in the Twenty-First Century.* Evanston, Ill.: Northwestern University Press, 2015.

Field, Norma. "Somehow: The Postmodern as Atmosphere." In *Postmodernism and Japan,* edited by Masao Miyoshi and H. D. Harootunian, 169–88. Durham, N.C.: Duke University Press, 1989.

Fishman, Robert. *Urban Utopias of the Twentieth Century: Ebenezer Howard, Frank Lloyd Wright, and Le Corbusier.* New York: Basic Books, 1977.

Fortin, David T. *Architecture and Science-Fiction Film: Philip K. Dick and the Spectacle of Home.* Burlington, Vt.: Ashgate, 2011.

Funakoshi Mikio. "Nihon bankoku hakurankai: 'Seiji no kisetsu' to 'keizai no kisetsu' no hazama de" [The Japan World Exposition: Between the "age of politics" and the "age of the economy"]. In *Banpaku kaifū: taimu kapuseru*

Expo '70 to Ōsaka banpaku [Opening the seal on the expo: The Osaka Expo and the Expo '70 time capsule], edited by Ōsaka Shiritsu Hakubutsukan, 12–15. Osaka: Ōsaka Shiritsu Hakubutsukan, 2000.

Furuhata, Yuriko. "Architecture as Atmospheric Media: Tange Lab and Cybernetics." *Media Theory in Japan*, edited by Marc Steinberg and Alexander Zahlten, 52–79. Durham, N.C.: Duke University Press, 2017.

Furuhata, Yuriko. "Multimedia Environments and Security Operations: Expo '70 as a Laboratory of Governance." *Grey Room* 54 (Winter 2014): 56–79.

Galantay, Ervin. "Osaka Expo: Designing the Environment." *The Nation*, August 31, 1970.

Galbraith, Patrick W. "Akihabara: Conditioning a Public 'Otaku' Image." *Mechademia* 5 (2010): 210–30.

Gardner, William O. "Narratives of Collapse and Generation: Komatsu Sakyō's Disaster Novels and the Metabolist Movement." In "Beyond Fukushima: Culture, Media, and Meaning from Catastrophe," special issue. *Japan Forum* 26, no. 3 (2014): 306–24.

Gibson, William. *Neuromancer*. New York: Ace Books, 1984.

Giddens, Anthony. *The Consequences of Modernity*. Cambridge: Polity Press, 1990.

GK. "Kono tenimuhō na kotai no sahō" [The making of this flawless individual]. *SD (Space Design)* 52 (March 1969): 54–55.

Gleik, James. *Chaos: Making a New Science*. New York: Penguin Books, 2008.

Gleiniger, Andrea, and Georg Vrachliotis. *Simulation: Presentation Technique and Cognitive Method*. Boston: Birkhäuser, 2008.

Gottmann, Jean. "Megalopolis or the Urbanization of the Northeastern Seaboard." *Economic Geography* 33, no. 3 (July 1957): 189–200.

Graham, Stephen, ed. *The Cybercities Reader*. New York: Routledge, 2004.

Greenhalgh, Paul. *Fair World: A History of Worlds Fairs and Exhibitions; From London to Shanghai, 1851–2010*. Winterbourne, U.K.: Papadakis, 2011.

Gregory, Sinda, and Larry McCaffery. "Not Just a Gibson Clone: An Interview with Goro Masaki." *Review of Contemporary Fiction* 22, no. 2 (Summer 2002): 75–81.

Hanes, Jeffrey E. "From Megalopolis to Megaroporisu." *Journal of Urban History* 19, no. 2 (February 1993): 56–94.

Harada, Kazue. *Japanese Women's Science Fiction: Posthuman Bodies and the Representation of Gender*. PhD diss., Washington University in St. Louis, 2015.

Harris, Chauncy D. "The Urban and Industrial Transformation of Japan." *Geographical Review* 72, no. 1 (January 1982): 50–89.

Haryū Ichirō. "Expo '70 as the Ruins of Culture (1970)." Translation of "Bunka no haikyo to shite no banpaku" by Ignacio Adriasola. In "Expo '70 and Japanese Art: Dissonant Voices," special issue. *Review of Japanese Culture and Society* 23 (December 2011): 44–56.

Hautajärvi, Harri. "Plastic Bubbles and Capsule Homes: Architectural Utopias of the Space Age." In *Futuro: Tomorrow's House from Yesterday*, edited by Marko Home and Mika Taanila, 56–79. Helsinki: Desura Oy Ltd., 2002.

Havens, Thomas R. H. *Architects of Affluence: The Tsutsumi Family and the Seibu-Seison Enterprises in Twentieth-Century Japan*. Cambridge, Mass.: Harvard University Council on East Asian Studies, 1994.

Hayamizu Kenrō. *Tōkyō bēta: Appudēto sare tsuzukeru toshi no monogatari* [Tokyo beta: A tale of the city continually updated]. Tokyo: Chikuma shobō, 2016.

Hayashi Yūjirō. "Futures Research in Japan." In *Handbook of Futures Research*, edited by J. Fowles, 31–38. Westport, Conn.: Greenwood, 1978.

Hayashi Yūjirō. *Nijūnengo no Nihon: yutaka na kokumin seikatsu e no hitotsu no bijon* [Japan twenty years hence: One vision of a prosperous life for the citizens]. Tokyo: Nihon Seisansei Honbu, 1966.

Hein, Laura E. "Growth versus Success: Japan's Economic Policy in Historical Perspective." In *Postwar Japan as History*, edited by Andrew Gordon, 99–122. Berkeley: University of California Press, 1993.

Heise, Ursula K. *Sense of Place and Sense of Planet: The Environmental Imagination of the Global*. New York: Oxford University Press, 2008.

Heuser, Sabine. *Virtual Geographies: Cyberpunk at the Intersection of the Postmodern and Science Fiction*. New York: Rodopi, 2003.

Hidaka Rokurō and Satō Tsuyoshi. *Nippon shindan* [Japan diagnosis]. Tokyo: San'ichi shobō, 1964.

Home, Marko. "Alternative Futures." In *Futuro: Tomorrow's House from Yesterday*, edited by Marko Home and Mika Taanila, 80–99. Helsinki: Desura Oy Ltd., 2002.

Hosoya Hiromi and Markus Schaefer. "Tokyo Metabolism: The Japanese Convenience Store." In *The Harvard Design School Guide to Shopping*, edited by Chuihua Judy Chung, Jeffrey Inaba, Rem Koolhaas, and Sze Tsung Leong, 748–64. Köln, Germany, and Cambridge, Mass.: Taschen and Harvard Design School, 2001.

Ichikawa Hiroo. "Reconstructing Tokyo: The Attempt to Transform a Metropolis." In *Rebuilding Urban Japan after 1945*, edited by Carola Hein, Jeffry M. Diefendorf, and Ishida Yorifusa, 50–67. New York: Palgrave MacMillan, 2003.

Igarashi Tarō. "Kishō Kurokawa: Buddhism and Metabolism." In *Kisho Kurokawa: Metabolism and Symbiosis*, edited by Peter Cachola Schmal, Ingeborg Flagge, and Jochen Visscher, 143–55. Berlin: Jovis Verlag, 2005.

Igarashi Tarō. "The Post-Bubble City and Japan's New International Design." *Discuss Japan: Japan Foreign Policy Forum* 5 (March 30, 2011): http://www.japanpolicyforum.jp/archives/culture/pt20110330183646.html.

Igarashi Tarō and Iso Tatsuo. *Bokura ga yume mita mirai toshi* [The future city we dreamed of]. Tokyo: PHP kenkyūsho, 2010.

Igarashi, Yoshikuni. *Bodies of Memory: Narratives of War in Postwar Japanese Culture, 1945–1970*. Princeton, N.J.: Princeton University Press, 2000.

Ishida Yorifusa. "Japanese Cities and Planning in the Reconstruction Period: 1945–55." In *Rebuilding Urban Japan after 1945*, edited by Carola Hein, Jeffry M. Diefendorf, and Ishida Yorifusa, 17–49. New York: Palgrave MacMillan, 2003.

Ishikawa Takashi. "Komatsu Sakyō—haikyō kara no toikake" [Komatsu Sakyō—questioning from the ruins]. In *Komatsu Sakyō zenshū kanzenban* [Komatsu Sakyō collected works complete edition], 407–29. Vol. 1. Tokyo: Jōsai kokusai daigaku shuppankai, 2006.

Isozaki Arata. "City Demolition Industry, Inc." Translation of "Toshi hakaigyō, KK." *South Atlantic Quarterly* 106, no. 4 (Fall 2007): 853–58.

Isozaki Arata. "Invisible City." Translation of "Mienai toshi." In *Architecture Culture 1943–1968: A Documentary Anthology*, edited by Joan Ockman, 402–7. New York: Rizzoli, 1993.

Isozaki Arata. *The Island Nation Aesthetic*. London: Academy Group, 1996.

Isozaki Arata. *Japan-ness in Architecture*. Translated by Sabu Kohso. Cambridge, Mass.: MIT Press, 2006.

Isozaki Arata. *Kūkan e* [Toward space]. Tokyo: Kajima shuppankai, 1997.

Isozaki Arata. "Ruins." Translation of "Haikyoron" by John D. Lamb. In *Kenchiku no mokujiroku*, edited by Miyamoto Ryūji, 11–19. Tokyo: Heibonsha, 1988.

Isozaki Arata. "Rumor City." Translation of "Ryūgen toshi" by Baryon Tensor Posadas and Kyoko Sato. *South Atlantic Quarterly* 106, no. 4 (Fall 2007): 859–69.

Itō, Mizuko, ed. *Personal, Portable, Pedestrian: Mobile Phones in Japanese Life*. Cambridge, Mass: MIT Press, 2005.

Itō Toyoo. *Kaze no henyōtai: kenchiku kuronikuru* [The wind's shape-changer: Architecture chronicles]. Tokyo: Seidosha, 2000.

Itō Toyoo. "The Lessones [sic] of Sendai Médiathèque." *Japan Architect* 41 (Spring 2001): 6–8.

Itō Toyoo. "A New Architecture Is Possible Only in the Sea of Consumption." Translation of "Shōhi no umi ni hitarazu shite kenchiku wa nai" by Maiko Behr. In *From Postwar to Postmodern: Art in Japan 1945–1989*, edited by Doryun Chong et al., 357–62. New York: The Museum of Modern Art, 2012.

Itō Toyoo. *Tarzans in the Media Forest*. Essays selected and translated by Thomas Daniell. London: Architectural Association, 2011.

Itō Toyoo. *Tōsō suru kenchiku* [Penetrating-layer architecture]. Tokyo: Seidosha, 2000.

Itō Toyoo. *Toyo Ito*. New York: Phaidon Press, 2009.

Itō Yasushi, ed. *Tsuitō: Komatsu Sakyō* [Memorial: Komatsu Sakyō]. Tokyo: Kawade shobō shinsha, 2011.

Itō Yōichi [as Ito Youichi]. "The Birth of Jōhō Shakai and Jōhōka Concepts in

Japan and Their Diffusion outside Japan." *Keio Communications Review* 13 (1991): 3–6.

Itō Yōichi [as Ito Youichi] and Yutaka Oishi. "Social Impacts of the New Utopias." In *Wired Cities: Shaping the Future of Communications*, edited by William H. Dutton, Jay G. Blumler, and Kenneth L. Kraemer, 201–20. Boston, Mass.: G. K. Hall and Co., 1987.

Ivy, Marilyn. "Formations of Mass Culture." In *Postwar Japan as History*, edited by Andrew Gordon, 239–58. Berkeley: University of California Press, 1993.

Jacobs, Jane. *The Death and Life of Great American Cities*. New York: Modern Library, 2011.

Jameson, Fredric. "Postmodernism, or the Cultural Logic of Late Capitalism." *New Left Review* 146 (July–August 1984): 59–92.

Japan Society of Futurology, eds. *Challenges from the Future: Proceedings of the International Future Research Conference*. Tokyo: Kodansha, 1970.

Josephson, Paul R. *Red Atom: Russia's Nuclear Power Program from Stalin to Today*. Pittsburgh: University of Pittsburgh Press, 2005.

Kapur, Nick. *Japan at the Crossroads: Conflict and Compromise after Anpo*. Cambridge, Mass.: Harvard University Press, 2018.

Karacas, Cary. "The Occupied City." In *Cartographic Japan: A History in Maps*, edited by Kären Wigen, Sugimoto Fumiko, and Cary Karacas, 194–98. Chicago: University of Chicago Press, 2016.

Karube Tadashi. *Abe Kōbō no toshi* [Abe Kōbō's City]. Tokyo: Kōdansha, 2012.

Kasahara Kazuto. "'Omatsuri hiroba' no tanjō" [The birth of the "festival plaza"]. In *Expo '70: Kyōgaku! Ōsaka bankoku hakurankai no subete* [Amazing!: All about the Osaka Expo], edited by Nakawada Minami, 48–49. Tokyo: Daiyamondosha, 2005.

Kasai Kiyoshi and Tatsumi Takayuki, eds. *3.11 no mirai: Nihon, SF, sōzōryoku* [The future of 3.11: Japan, SF, imagination]. Tokyo: Sakuhinsha, 2011.

Kawazoe Noboru. "Bankokuhaku no kenchiku" [The expo and architecture]. In *Nihon bankokuhaku: kenchiku, zōkei* [Japan Expo: Architecture, plastic arts], edited by Okamoto Tarō and Tange Kenzō, 209–12. Tokyo: Kōbunsha, 1971.

Kawazoe Noboru. "The City of the Future." *Zodiac: A Review of Contemporary Architecture* 9 (1961): 97–111.

Kawazoe Noboru. "Dai-Tōkyō saigo no hi: Tōkyō no metsubō—gaisetsu" [The last days of greater Tokyo: An outline of Tokyo's destruction]. *Kenchiku bunka* 171 (1961): 5–12.

Kawazoe Noboru. "Han-kachi to shite no kapuseru" [The capsule as anti-value]. *SD [Space Design]* 52 (March 1969): 37–45.

Kawazoe Noboru. *Kawazoe Noboru hyōronshū, vol. 2* [Collected critical writings of Kawazoe Noboru, vol. 2]. Tokyo: Sangyō Nōritsu Tanki Daigaku Shuppanbu, 1976.

Kawazoe Noboru, ed. *Metabolism 1960: The Proposals for New Urbanism.* Tokyo: Bijutsu shuppansha, 1960.

Kawazoe Noboru. "Tōkyō no henshin" [The transformation of Tokyo]. *Taiyō* 33 (March 1966): 45–52.

Kikutake Kiyonori. *Between Land and Sea.* Edited by Ken Tadashi Oshima. Zurich: Lars Müller Publishers and Harvard University Graduate School of Design, 2016.

Kikutake Kiyonori. "Ocean City." In *Metabolism 1960: The Proposals for New Urbanism,* edited by Kawazoe Noboru, 6–41. Tokyo: Bijutsu shuppansha, 1960.

Kingston, Jeffrey, ed. *Natural Disaster and Nuclear Crisis in Japan: Response and Recovery after Japan's 3/11.* New York: Routledge, 2012.

Kitazawa Masakuni. "Militarism in the Management Society." In *Authority and the Individual in Japan: Citizen Protest in Historical Perspective,* edited by J. Victor Koschmann, 200–6. Tokyo: University of Tokyo Press, 1978.

Kojève, Alexandre. *Introduction to the Reading of Hegel.* Edited by Allan Bloom. Translated by James H. Nichols Jr. Ithaca, N.Y.: Cornell University Press, 1969.

Komatsu Sakyō. *Adamu no sue* [Descendants of Adam]. Tokyo: Shinchōsha, 1973.

Komatsu Sakyō. "Banpaku kara kōgai e: Miraigaku no atarashii dankai" [From expo to pollution: A new stage for future studies]. *Jiyū* (December 1970): 42–51.

Komatsu Sakyō. *Fukkatsu no hi* [The day of resurrection]. Tokyo: Kadokawa Haruki, 1998.

Komatsu Sakyō. "Haikyo no kanata" [Beyond the ruins]. In *Komatsu Sakyō zenshū kanzenban* [Komatsu Sakyō collected works complete edition], vol. 28, 172–80. Tokyo: Jōsai kokusai daigaku shuppankai, 2006.

Komatsu Sakyō. "Haikyo no kūkan bunmei" [Civilization of the space of ruins]. In *Komatsu Sakyō zenshū kanzenban* [Komatsu Sakyō collected works complete edition], vol. 15, 173–85. Tokyo: Jōsai kokusai daigaku shuppankai, 2010.

Komatsu Sakyō. *Ijō kishō* [Abnormal weather]. Tokyo: Asahiya shuppan, 1974.

Komatsu Sakyō. *Japan Sinks.* Second abridged English edition. Translation of *Nihon chinbotsu* by Michael Gallagher. New York: Kodansha International, 1995.

Komatsu Sakyō. *Komatsu Sakyō zenshū kanzenban* [Komatsu Sakyō collected works complete edition]. Tokyo: Jōsai kokusai daigaku shuppankai, 2006–.

Komatsu Sakyō. *Kūchū toshi 008* [City in the air 008]. Tokyo: Kadokawa shoten, 1981.

Komatsu Sakyō. *Kyōdai purojectuo ugoku* [Moving a giant project]. Tokyo: Kōsaidō, 1994.

Komatsu Sakyō. *Nihon apacchi zoku* [The Japan Apache tribe]. Tokyo: Kadokawa shoten, 1971.

Komatsu Sakyō. *Nihon chinbotsu* [Japan sinks]. Two vols. Tokyo: Kōbunsha, 1995.

Komatsu Sakyō. "Nippon—70 nendai zenya" [Japan on the eve of the 1970s]. *Bungei shunjū* (February 1971): 220–70.

Komatsu Sakyō. *SF damashi* [SF soul]. Tokyo: Shinchōsha, 2006.

Komatsu Sakyō. *SF e no yuigon* [A last testament for SF]. Tokyo: Kōbunsha, 1997.

Komatsu Sakyō. *Shuto shōshitsu* [The capital vanishes]. Two vols. Tokyo: Kadokawa shunju, 1998.

Komatsu Sakyō. *Virus: The Day of Resurrection.* Translation of *Fukkatsu no hi* by Daniel Huddleston. San Francisco: Vis Media, 2012.

Komatsu Sakyō and Kurokawa Kishō. *Nihon taimu toraberu* [Japan time travel]. Tokyo: Yomiuri Shinbunsha, 1969.

Komatsu Sakyō and Tani Kōshū. *Nihon chinbotsu dainibu* [Japan sinks volume two]. Two vols. Tokyo: Shōgakukan, 2006.

Komatsuzaki Seisuke. "Telecommunications Policy in Japan." In *Wired Cities: Shaping the Future of Communications,* edited by William H. Dutton, Jay G. Blumler, and Kenneth L. Kraemer, 157–64. Boston: G. K. Hall and Co., 1987.

Koolhaus, Rem, and Hans Ulrich Obrist. *Project Japan: Metabolism Talks.* Cologne, Germany: Taschen, 2011.

Kotani Mari. "Alien Spaces and Alien Bodies in Japanese Women's Science Fiction." Translated by Miri Nakamura. In *Robot Ghosts and Wired Dreams: Japanese Science Fiction from Origins to Anime,* edited by Christopher Bolton et al., 47–74. Minneapolis: University of Minnesota Press, 2007.

Krige, John. "Techno-Utopian Dreams, Techno-Political Realities: The Education of Desire for the Peaceful Atom." In *Utopia/Dystopia,* edited by Michael D. Gordin et al., 151–75. Princeton, N.J.: Princeton University Press, 2010.

Krstic, Vladimir. "Liquid Constructions: Tokyo and the End of Space." In *Tokyo,* edited by Botond Bognar, 38–39. New York: Academy Editions, 1997.

Kuan, Seng. "Visions of Tokyo Bay." In *Kiyonori Kikutake: Between Land and Sea,* edited by Ken Tadashi Oshima, 27–45. Zurich, Switzerland: Lars Müller Publishers and Harvard University Graduate School of Design, 2016.

Kurihara Akira. *Kanri shakai to minshū risei: Nichijō ishiki no seiji shakaigaku* [The managed society and popular reason: The political sociology of everyday consciousness]. Tokyo: Shinyōsha, 1982.

KuroDalaiJee. "Performance Art and/as Activism: Expo '70 Destruction Joint-Struggle Group." "Expo '70 and Japanese Art: Dissonant Voices," special issue. *Review of Japanese Culture and Society* 23 (December 2011): 154–73.

Kurokawa Kishō. *Homo mobensu: toshi to ningen no mirai* [*Homo movens*: The future of cities and humans]. Tokyo: Chūō kōronsha, 1969.

Kurokawa Kishō. *Metabolism in Architecture*. Boulder, Colo.: Westview Press, 1977.

Kurokawa Kishō [Kurokawa Noriaki]. "Propositions d'urbanisme au Japon" [Propositions for urbanism in Japan]. *L'architecture d'aujourd'hui* 33, no. 101 (April–May 1962): 84–89.

Kurokawa Kishō. "Teijū tan'i keikaku no rinen to hōhō" [Concept and methodology of fixed units for planning]. *Kenchiku bunka* (June 1967): 93–128. (Translated as "Metapolis—The Hishino Plan" in Kurokawa, *Metabolism in Architecture*, 67–74.)

La Bare, Joshua. "The Future: 'Wrapped . . . in That Mysterious Japanese Way.'" *Science Fiction Studies* 27, no. 3 (November 1999): 22–47.

Langer, Jessica. *Postcolonialism and Science Fiction*. New York: Palgrave Macmillan, 2011.

Lem, Stanisław. *The Invincible*. Translation of the 1967 German edition of *Niezwyciężony*. New York: Seabury Press, 1973.

Leong, Sze Tsung. "Ulterior Spaces." In *The Harvard Design School Guide to Shopping*, edited by Chuihua Judy Chung, Jeffrey Inaba, Rem Koolhaas, and Sze Tsung Leong, 764–94. Köln, Germany, and Cambridge, Mass.: Taschen and Harvard Design School, 2001.

Lin, Zhongjie. *Kenzo Tange and the Metabolist Movement: Urban Utopias of Modern Japan*. New York: Routledge, 2010.

Lockyer, Angus. "The Logic of Spectacle, c. 1970." *Art History* 30, no. 4 (September 2007): 571–89.

Lynch, Kevin. *The Image of the City*. Cambridge, Mass.: MIT Press, 1960.

Macaulay, Rose. *The Pleasure of Ruins*. London: Weidenfeld and Nicolson, 1953.

Maeda Ai. *Toshi kūkan no naka no bungaku* [The literature of urban space]. Tokyo: Chikuma shobō, 1992.

Makabe Tomoharu. "Paruko no toshi senryaku" [Parco's urban strategy]. *Transonikku* 10 (June 1976): 31–57.

Maki Fumihiko. *Investigations in Collective Form*. St. Louis, Mo.: Washington University School of Architecture, 1964.

Maki Fumihiko. "Kapuseru de wa ōsama de aru" [In the capsule, one is king]. *SD [Space Design]* 52 (March 1969): 46.

Mandelbrot, Benoit B. *Fractals: Form, Chance, and Dimension*. San Francisco: W. H. Freeman and Company, 1977.

Masaki Gorō. *Viinasu shitei* [Venus city]. Tokyo: Hayakawa shobō, 1992.

Masuda Yoneji. *The Information Society as Post-Industrial Society*. Tokyo: Institute for the Information Society, 1980.

Masuda Yoneji. *Konpyūtopia: Konpyūta ga tsukuru shinjidai* [Computopia: The new age created by computers]. Tokyo: Daiyamondosha, 1967.

Matsushita Kiwa. "Depato: The Japanese Department Store." In *The Harvard*

Design School Guide to Shopping, edited by Chuihua Judy Chung, Jeffrey Inaba, Rem Koolhaas, and Sze Tsung Leong, 242–69. Köln, Germany, and Cambridge, Mass.: Taschen and Harvard Design School, 2001.

McCormack, Gavin. *The Emptiness of Japanese Affluence.* Armonk, N.Y.: M. E. Sharpe, 1996.

McQuire, Scott. *The Media City: Media, Architecture, and Urban Space.* London: Sage Publications, 2008.

Merril, Judith. "What Do You Mean: Science? Fiction?" *Extrapolation* 7, no. 2 (May 1966): 30–46.

Miyamoto Ryūji. *Kenchiku no mokujiroku* [Apocalypse of architecture]. Tokyo: Heibonsha, 1988.

Miyamoto Ryūji. *Kyūryū jōsai* (Kowloon walled city). Tokyo: Heibonsha, 1997.

Miyamoto Ryūji. "Temporary Ruins." In *Setting Sun: Writings by Japanese Photographers,* edited by Ivan Vartanian, Akihiro Hatanaka, and Yutaka Kambayashi, translated by Ivan Vartanian, 50–51. New York: Aperture, 2006.

Mori Bijutsukan, ed. *Metaborizumu no mirai toshi* [The future city of Metabolism]. Tokyo: Mori bijutsukan, 2011.

Morikawa Kaiichirō. "Denkiteki meikyū no foto koriāji" [The photo-collages of Electric Labyrinth]. In *10+1 bessatsu: 20 seiki kenchiku kenkyū* [10+1 supplement: Research in twentieth-century architecture], 14–15. Tokyo: INAX Shuppan, 1998.

Morikawa Kaiichirō. *Shuto no tanjō: Moeru toshi Akihabara* [The birth of a city of taste: The moe city Akihabara]. Tokyo: Gentōsha, 2003.

Morley, David, and Kevin Robins. *Spaces of Identity: Global Media, Electronic Landscapes, and Cultural Boundaries.* New York: Routledge, 1995.

Morris-Suzuki, Tessa. *Beyond Computopia: Information, Automation, and Democracy in Japan.* New York: Kegan Paul International, 1988.

Nagase Tadashi. "Fushoku suru kioku no Tōkyō: Oshii Mamoru no toshiron sekai" [The Tokyo of corroding memories: The world of Oshii Mamoru's urban theory]. *Yuriika* 28, no. 9 (August 1996): 198–207.

Nakamori, Yasufumi. "Criticism of Expo '70 in Print: Journals Ken, Bujitsu techō, and Dezain hihyō." "Expo '70 and Japanese Art: Dissonant Voices," special issue. *Review of Japanese Culture and Society* 23 (December 2011): 132–44.

Napier, Susan. "Panic Sites: The Imagination of Disaster from Godzilla to Akira." *Journal of Japanese Studies* 19, no. 2 (Summer 1993): 327–51.

National Building Museum. *Designing Tomorrow: America's Worlds Fairs of the 1930's.* New Haven, Conn.: Yale University Press, 2010.

Ndalianis, Angela. *Neo-Baroque Aesthetics and Contemporary Entertainment.* Cambridge, Mass.: MIT Press, 2004.

Neumann, Dietrich, ed. *Film Architecture: Set Designs from "Metropolis" to "Blade Runner."* New York: Prestel Verlag, 1999.

Nihon bankoku hakurankai kōshiki kiroku [Japan World Exposition official record]. Vol. 1. Osaka: Nihon Bankoku Hakurankai Kinen Kyôkai, 1972.

Nishiyama Uzō. "Bankokuhaku kaijō keikaku: chōsa kara kikaku e" [The expo site plan: From survey to project]. *Kenchiku zasshi* 85, no. 1021 (March 1970): 193–99.

Nosaka Akiyuki. "Yakeato yami-ichi ha no ben: Naokishō o jūshō shite" [The Burnt-Out Ruins and Black Market School speech: Receiving the Naoki Prize]. In *Nihon dojin no shisō* [The ideology of a Japanese native], 187–90. Tokyo: Chūō kōron, 1976.

Novak, Marcos. "Liquid Architectures in Cyberspace." In *Cyberspace: First Steps*, edited by Michael Benedikt. Cambridge, Mass.: MIT Press, 1991.

Nyilas, Agnes. *Beyond Utopia: Japanese Metabolism Architecture and the Birth of Mythopia*. New York: Routledge, 2018.

Ockman, Joan, ed. *Architecture Culture 1943–1968: A Documentary Anthology*. New York: Rizzoli, 1993.

Orbaugh, Sharalyn. "Future City Tokyo: 1909 and 2009." In *Science Fiction and the Prediction of the Future: Essays on Foresight and Fallacy*, edited by Gary Westfahl, Wong Kin Yuen, and Amy Kit-Sze Chan. Jefferson, N.C.: McFarland & Company, 2011.

Oshima, Ken Tadashi. "Introduction: Tectonic Visions between Land and Sea." In *Between Land and Sea*, by Kiyonori Kikutake, edited by Ken Tadashi Oshima, 11–26. Zurich, Switzerland: Lars Müller Publishers and Harvard University Graduate School of Design, 2016.

Ōtomo Katsuhiro. *Akira*. 6 vols. English edition. New York: Kodansha Comics, 2009–2011.

Packard, George R. *Protest in Tokyo: The Security Treaty Crisis of 1960*. Princeton, N.J.: Princeton University Press, 1966.

Papastergiadis, Nikos. *The Turbulence of Migration: Globalization, Deterritorialization, and Hybridity*. Malden, Mass.: Blackwell, 2000.

Park, Jane Chi Hyun. *Yellow Future: Oriental Style in Hollywood Cinema*. Minneapolis: University of Minnesota Press, 2010.

Park Yu-ha, "Kyōbō suru hyōgen: Kaiko Takeshi—Komatsu Sakyō—Yan Sogiru no 'apacchi' shōsetsu o megutte" [Conspiring expressions: Kaiko Takeshi—Komatsu Sakyō—Yang Sok Il]. *Nihon bungaku* 55, no. 11 (November 2006): 35–74.

Paulk, Charles. "Post-National Cool: William Gibson's Japan." *Science Fiction Studies* 38, no. 3 (November 2011): 478–500.

Pawley, Martin. "Architecture versus the Movies, or Form versus Content." *Architectural Design* 40, no. 482 (June 1970): 288–309.

Pawley, Martin. *Theory and Design in the Second Machine Age*. Cambridge, Mass.: Blackwell, 1990.

Perrow, Charles. *Normal Accidents: Living with High-Risk Technologies*. New York: Basic Books, 1984.

Posadas, Baryon Tensor. "Virtual Worlds and Identity Tourism in Japanese Cyberpunk." In *Dis-Orienting Planets: Racial Representations of Asia in Science Fiction*, edited by Isiah Lavender III, 144–59. Jackson: University Press of Mississippi, 2017.

Prichard, Franz K. *Ruined Maps: The Urban Revolution in Japanese Fiction, Documentary, and Photography of the 1960s and 1970s*. PhD diss., University of California Los Angeles, 2011.

Ramsden, Edmund, and Jon Adams. "Escaping the Laboratory: The Rodent Experiments of John B. Calhoun and Their Cultural Influence." *Journal of Social History* 42, no. 3 (Spring 2009): 761–97.

Reconstruction Design Council. "Towards Reconstruction: 'Hope beyond the Disaster': Report to the Prime Minister's Office in Response to the Great East Japan Earthquake." ReliefWeb, June 25, 2011. http://reliefweb.int/node/435471.

Reynolds, Jonathan M. *Allegories of Time and Space: Japanese Identity in Photography and Architecture*. Honolulu: University of Hawaii Press, 2015.

Roche, Maurice. *Mega-events and Modernity: Olympics and Expos in the Growth of Global Culture*. New York: Routledge, 2000.

Rosenbaum, Roman. "The 'Generation of the Burnt-out Ruins.'" *Japanese Studies* 27, no. 3 (2007): 281–93.

Rydell, Robert W. *World of Fairs: The Century-of-Progress Exhibitions*. Chicago: University of Chicago Press, 1993.

Sadler, Simon. *Archigram: Architecture without Architecture*. Cambridge, Mass.: MIT Press, 2005.

Sadler, Simon. "New Babylon versus Plug-In City." In *Exit Utopia: Architectural Provocations 1956–76*, edited by Martin van Schaik and Otakar Máčel, 57–67. New York: Prestel Verlag, 2005.

Sakaki, Atsuko. "'There's No Such Place as Home': Goto Meisei, or Identity as Alterity." In *Representing the Other in Modern Japanese Literature: A Critical Approach*, edited by Rachael Hutchinson and Mark Williams, 292–311. New York: Routledge, 2007.

Sammon, Paul M. *Future Noir: The Making of "Blade Runner."* New York: Harper Collins Publishers, 1996.

Sand, Jordan. *Tokyo Vernacular: Common Spaces, Local Histories, Found Objects*. Berkeley: University of California Press, 2013.

Sato, Kumiko. "How Information Technology Has (Not) Changed Feminism and Japanism: Cyberpunk and the Japanese Context." *Comparative Literature Studies* 41, no. 3 (2004): 335–55.

Sawaragi Noi. *Kuroi taiyō to akai kani: Okamoto Tarō no nihon* [Black sun and red crab: Okamoto Tarō's Japan]. Tokyo: Chūō Kōron Shinsha, 2003.

Sawaragi Noi. *Sensō to banpaku* [Wars and expos]. Tokyo: Bijutsu shuppansha, 2005.

Schaik, Martin van, and Otakar Máčel, eds. *Exit Utopia: Architectural Provocations 1956–1976*. New York: Prestel Verlag, 2005.

Schnellbächer, Thomas. "Has the Empire Sunk Yet?: The Pacific in Japanese Science Fiction." In *Robot Ghosts and Wired Dreams: Japanese Science Fiction from Origins to Anime*, edited by Christopher Bolton et al., 27–46. Minneapolis: University of Minnesota Press, 2007.

Schrijver, Lara. *Radical Games: Popping the Bubble of 1960's Architecture*. Rotterdam, Netherlands: NAi Publishers, 2009.

Simmel, Georg. "Two Essays." *Hudson Review* 11, no. 3 (Autumn 1958): 371–85.

Smithson, P[eter]. "Reflections on Kenzo Tange's Tokyo Bay Plan." *Architectural Design* (October 1964): 479–80.

Sorensen, André. *The Making of Urban Japan: Cities and Planning from Edo to the Twenty-First Century*. New York: Routledge, 2002.

Standish, Isolde. "*Akira*, Postmodernism, and Resistance." In *The Worlds of Japanese Popular Culture*, edited by D. P. Martinez, 56–74. Cambridge: Cambridge University Press, 1998.

Steinberg, Marc. *Anime's Media Mix: Franchising Toys and Characters in Japan*. Minneapolis: University of Minnesota Press, 2012.

Suvin, Darko. *Metamorphoses of Science Fiction: On the Poetics of a Literary Genre*. New Haven, Conn.: Yale University Press, 1979.

Tamai Mizuo. "Posutarization ni yoru Ōsaka banpaku: tēmakan no kūchū tenji" [The Osaka Expo created by posterization: The Theme Pavilion's aerial exhibit]. Tamai Mizuo intānetto shashinkan [Tamai Mizuo internet photography museum] part 36. http://www2.dokidoki.ne.jp/bellrose/museum/part36/part36.html. Accessed May 21, 2011.

Tanaka, Motoko. *Apocalypse in Contemporary Japanese Science Fiction*. New York: Palgrave Macmillan, 2014.

Tange Kenzō. "Bankokuhaku kaijō keikaku: kikaku kara keikaku e" [The expo site plan: From project to plan]. *Kenchiku zasshi* 85, no. 1021 (March 1970): 201–6.

Tange Kenzō. *Kenzo Tange 1946–1996: Architecture and Urban Design*, edited by Massimo Bettinotti. Milan: Electa, 1996.

Tange Kenzō. *Nihon rettō no shōraizō* [The future image of the Japanese archipelago]. Tokyo: Kōdansha, 1966.

Tange Kenzō. "A Plan for Tokyo, 1960: Toward a Structural Reorganization." Partial translation of "Tōkyō keikaku—1960: sono kōzō kaikaku no teian." In *Architecture Culture 1943–1968: A Documentary Anthology*, edited by Joan Ockman, 327–34. New York: Rizzoli, 1993.

Tange Kenzō. *Tōkyō keikaku—1960: sono kōzō kaikaku no teian* [A plan for Tokyo: Toward a spatial reorganization]. Tokyo: Tange Kenzō kenkyūshitsu, 1961.

Tange Kenzō with Kawazoe Noboru. "Nihon bankokuhakurankai no motarasu mono" [What the Japan World Exposition will bring]. *Taidan* dialogue between Tange Kenzō and Kawazoe Noboru. *Shinkenchiku* (May 1970): 145–51.

Tange Kenzō et al. "Mirai toshi Tōkyō" [Future city Tokyo]. *Taiyō* 33 (March 1966): 27–44.

Tatsumi Takayuki. *Full Metal Apache: Transactions between Cyberpunk Japan and Avant-Pop America*. Durham, N.C.: Duke University Press, 2006.

Tatsumi Takayuki. "The Japanese Reflection of Mirrorshades." In *Storming the Reality Studio: A Casebook of Cyberpunk and Postmodern Science Fiction*, edited by Larry McCaffery, 366–73. Durham, N.C.: Duke University Press, 1991.

Tatsumi Takayuki. "Transpacific Cyberpunk: Transgeneric Interactions between Prose, Cinema, and Manga." *Arts* 7, no. 9 (March 2018): 1–11.

Tatsuno, Sheridan. *The Technopolis Strategy: Japan, High Technology, and the Control of the Twenty-First Century*. New York: Prentice Hall Press, 1986.

Thompson, Fred. "Learning from Kikutake." In *Kiyonori Kikutake: Between Land and Sea*, edited by Ken Tadashi Oshima, 47–58. Zurich, Switzerland: Lars Müller Publishers and Harvard University Graduate School of Design, 2016.

Thornber, Karen Laura. *Ecoambiguity: Environmental Crises and East Asian Literatures*. Ann Arbor: University of Michigan Press, 2012.

Tillack, Peter. "Concrete Abstractions: Gōtō Meisei's Hapless Danchi Dwellers and the Japanese Economic Miracle." *Positions: East Asia Cultures Critique* 23, no. 2 (May 2015): 231–57.

Tomlinson, John. *Globalization and Culture*. Chicago: University of Chicago Press, 1999.

Tōno Yoshiaki. "Artists Participating in the World Expo, Speak Out!" Partial translation of "Hanron seyo!: 'Banpaku sanka' no geijutsuka tachi" by Christopher Stephens. In *From Postwar to Postmodern: Art in Japan 1945–1989*, edited by Doryun Chong et al., 247–52. New York: Museum of Modern Art, 2012.

Tōno Yoshiaki. "The Vertical Fair that Changed Shibuya: On Parco's Cultural Cachet." Partial translation of "Shibuya o kaetta rittai ennichi: Paruko no bunka rashisa ron" by Maiko Behr. In *From Postwar to Postmodern: Art in Japan 1945–1989*, edited by Doryun Chong et al., 316–19. New York: Museum of Modern Art, 2012.

Trexler, Adam. *Anthropocene Fictions: The Novel in a Time of Climate Change*. Charlottesville: University of Virginia Press, 2015.

Tsukio Yoshio. "Jōhō shisutemu" [Information systems]. "Expo '70," special issue. *Shinkenchiku* (May 1970): 282–83.

Tsutsui Yasutaka. *Tsutsui Yasutaka zenshū* [Tsutsui Yasutaka collected works]. Vol. 9. Tokyo: Shinchōsha, 1983.

Tsutsui, William M. "Oh No, There Goes Tokyo: Recreational Apocalypse and the City in Postwar Japanese Culture." In *Noir Urbanisms: Dystopic*

Images of the Modern City, edited by Gyan Prakash, 104–26. Princeton, N.J.: Princeton University Press, 2010.

Ueno Toshiya. "Japanimation and Techno-orientalism." In *The Uncanny: Experiments in Cyborg Culture*, edited by Bruce Grenville, 223–31. Vancouver, B.C., Canada: Vancouver Art Gallery and Arsenal Pulp Press, 2001.

Ueno Toshiya. *Kurenai no metaru sūtsu: anime to iu senjō* [Scarlet metalsuits: The battlefield called anime]. Tokyo: Kinokuniya shoten, 1998.

Umesao Tadao. "Jōhō sangyō ron" [Theory of the information industries]. *Chūō korōn* (March 1963): 45–58.

Urushima, Andrea Yuri Flores. "Genesis and Culmination of Uzō Nishiyama's Proposal of a 'Model Core of a Future City' for the Expo 70 Site (1960–73)." *Planning Perspectives* 22, no. 4 (2007): 391–416, http://dx.doi.org/10.1080/02665430701553399.

Waldo, Myra. *Japan Expo '70 Guide*. New York: Collier Books, 1970.

Weart, Spencer R. *The Discovery of Global Warming*. Rev. ed. Cambridge, Mass.: Harvard University Press, 2008.

Webb, Michael. "'Like Today, Only More So': The Credible Dystopia of *Blade Runner*." In *Film Architecture: Set Designs from "Metropolis" to "Blade Runner,"* edited by Dietrich Neumann, 44–47. New York: Prestel Verlag, 1999.

Wendelken, Cherie. "Putting Metabolism Back in Place: The Making of a Radically Decontextualized Architecture in Japan." *Anxious Modernisms: Experimentation in Postwar Architectural Culture*, edited by Sarah Wiliam Golhagen and Réjean Legault, 279–99. Montreal and Cambridge, Mass.: Canadian Centre for Architecture and Massachusetts Institute of Technology, 2000.

Wesemael, Pieter van. *Architecture of Instruction and Delight: A Socio-historical Analysis of World Exhibitions as a Didactic Phenomenon (1798–1851–1970)*. Rotterdam, Netherlands: Uitgeverij, 2001.

Winther-Tamaki, Bert. "To Put on a Big Face: The Globalist Stance of Okamoto Tarō's Tower of the Sun for the World Japan Exhibition." "Expo '70 and Japanese Art: Dissonant Voices," special issue. *Review of Japanese Culture and Society* 23 (December 2011): 81–101.

World Design Conference Organization, ed. *World Design Conference 1960 in Tokyo/Sekai dezain kaigi gijiroku*. Tokyo: Bijutsu shuppansha, 1960.

Yanobe Kenji. *Kenji Yanobe 1969–2005*. Kyoto: Seigensha Art Publishing, 2005.

Yatsuka Hajime. "An Architecture Floating on the Sea of Signs." In *The New Japanese Architecture*, by Botond Bognar, 38–41. New York: Rizzoli, 1990.

Yatsuka Hajime. "Gendai kenchiku ni okeru nōtēshon no bōken—mienai kenchiku e" [The adventure of notation in contemporary architecture—toward an invisible architecture]. *10+1* 3 (Spring 1995): 16–28.

Yatsuka Hajime. "Godzilla versus the Metabolist Mega-Monuments." In *Tokyo*, by Botand Bognar, 353–54. New York: Academy Editions, 1997.

Yatsuka Hajime. "'Metaborizumu nekusasu' to iu 'kindai no chōkoku'"

[The "overcoming modernity" known as the "Metabolism nexus"]. In *Metaborizumu no mirai toshi* [The future city of Metabolism], edited by Mori bijutsukan, 10–16. Tokyo: Mori bijutsukan, 2011.

Yiu, Angela. "A New Map of Hell: Sato Haruo's Dystopian Fiction." *Japan Forum* 21, no. 1 (March 2009): 53–73.

Yiu, Angela, ed. *Three Dimensional Reading: Stories of Time and Space in Japanese Modernist Fiction, 1911–1932*. Honolulu: University of Hawaii Press, 2013.

Yoshimi Shunya. *Banpaku gensō: sengo seiji no jubaku* [Expo fantasy: The spell of postwar politics]. Tokyo: Chikuma Shobō, 2005.

Yoshimi Shunya. *Hakurankai no seijigaku* [The political science of expos]. Tokyo: Chūō Kōronsha, 1992.

Yoshimi Shunya. *Toshi no doramatourugii: Tokyo—Sakariba no shakaishi* [Dramatology of the city: Tokyo—a social history of bustling places]. Tokyo: Kōbundō, 1987.

Yoshimoto, Midori. "From Space to Environment: The Origin of *Kankyō* and the Emergence of Intermedia Art in Japan." *Art Journal* 67, no. 3 (Fall 2008): 25–45.

Index

WILLIAM O. GARDNER is professor of Japanese language, literature, and film at Swarthmore College.